GENDER, AGE AND MUSICAL CREATIVITY

Gender, Age and Musical Creativity

Edited by

CATHERINE HAWORTH AND LISA COLTON
University of Huddersfield, UK

LONDON AND NEW YORK

First published 2015 by Ashgate Publishing

2 Park Square, Milton Park, Abingdon, Oxfordshire OX14 4RN
52 Vanderbilt Avenue, New York, NY 10017

Routledge is an imprint of the Taylor & Francis Group, an informa business

First issued in paperback 2020

Copyright © 2015 Catherine Haworth, Lisa Colton and the contributors

Catherine Haworth and Lisa Colton have asserted their right under the Copyright, Designs and Patents Act, 1988, to be identified as the editors of this work.

All rights reserved. No part of this book may be reprinted or reproduced or utilised in any form or by any electronic, mechanical, or other means, now known or hereafter invented, including photocopying and recording, or in any information storage or retrieval system, without permission in writing from the publishers.

Notice:
Product or corporate names may be trademarks or registered trademarks, and are used only for identification and explanation without intent to infringe.

British Library Cataloguing in Publication Data
A catalogue record for this book is available from the British Library

The Library of Congress has cataloged the printed edition as follows:
Gender, age and musical creativity / edited by Catherine Haworth and Lisa Colton.
    pages cm
  Includes bibliographical references and index.
  ISBN 978-1-4724-3085-4 (hardcover)
1. Sex in music. 2. Musical ability. 3. Creation
(Literary, artistic, etc.) I. Haworth, Catherine, editor. II. Colton, Lisa, editor.
  ML3838.G372 2015
  780.8–dc23

2014045778

ISBN 978-1-4724-3085-4 (hbk)
ISBN 978-0-367-59907-2 (pbk)

Contents

List of Figures and Tables		vii
List of Musical Examples		ix
Notes on Contributors		xi

Introduction: Gender, Age and Musical Creativity   1
Catherine Haworth and Lisa Colton

1   'Something revolting': Women, Creativity and Music after 50   7
   Sophie Fuller

PART I   PERFORMING IDENTITY IN EARLY EUROPEAN MUSICAL CULTURE

2   Noblewomen and Music in Italy, c. 1430–1520: Looking Past Isabella   27
   Tim Shephard

3   Age, Masculinity and Music in Early Modern England   41
   Kirsten Gibson

4   From Castrato to Bass: The Late Roles of Nicolò Grimaldi 'Nicolini'   61
   Anne Desler

PART II   GENDERED MUSICAL COMMUNITIES

5   Music as a Lifelong Pursuit for Bandsmen in the Southern Pennines, c. 1840–1914: Reflections on Working-Class Masculinity   83
   Stephen Etheridge

6   Intergenerational Relationships: The Case of the Society of Women Musicians   101
   Laura Seddon

7   Professionalism and Reception in the New York Composers'
    Forum: Intersections of Age and Gender   115
    Melissa J. de Graaf

**PART III   CONTEMPORARY CREATIVE PRACTICES AND
             IDENTITIES**

8   Urchins and Angels: Little Orphan Annie and Clichés of Child
    Singers   129
    Jacqueline Warwick

9   'Across the Evening Sky': The Late Voices of Sandy Denny,
    Judy Collins and Nina Simone   141
    Richard Elliott

10 Sanctuaries for Social Outsiders: A Queer Archive of Feelings in
    Songs by The Smiths   155
    Mimi Haddon

11 'New Music' as Patriarchal Category   171
    Lauren Redhead

12 *multiple/radical/forms/*comma*/traces/creativity/of/constraint:
    A piece for solo voice and various accompaniment*   185
    Caroline Lucas

Bibliography   203
Index   221

List of Figures and Tables

Figures

3.1	Thomas Sternhold, *Tenor of the Whole Psalmes in Foure Partes* (London: John Day, 1563), fol. Av. Reproduced by permission of the Huntington Library, San Marino, California	55
4.1	Nicolini (centre) during an opera rehearsal in London c. 1709; acting out his role in a musical rehearsal attests to the inseparability of musical and physical expression in his approach to operatic performance. Z13111, *The Rehearsal of an Opera* (Nicola (Nicolò) Francesco Leonardo Grimaldi ('Nicolini'); Francesca Margherita de L'Epine and twelve other sitters) by Marco Ricci, oil on canvas, c. 1708–1709. Photograph © National Portrait Gallery, London; unknown collection	64
4.2	Typical structure of *dramma per musica* cast	66
4.3	Nicolini as Idaspe in *Idaspe*, Venice 1730, with Francesca Cuzzoni as Berenice. Antonio Maria Zanetti the Elder, *Nicola Grimaldi detto Nicolini e Francesca Cuzzoni*. Venice, Fondazione Giorgio Cini, Gabinetto dei Disegni e delle Stampe (dall'album di caricature di Antonio Maria Zanetti, f. 12). Photograph: Venice, Fondazione Giorgio Cini, Matteo De Fina	76
5.1	Bacup Old Band, c. 1860	94
5.2	Helmshore Brass Band, c. 1909	98
12.1	Example of composer biography	188
12.2	Photograph of a section of the 'life-sized' score for *multiple/radical/forms...*	194
12.3	Examples of embroidery in graphic scores for *multiple/radical/forms...* and *[Unnamed Maps Series]*	200

Tables

4.1	Nicolini's late roles, 1724–31	78
11.1	Comparison of Saunders's and Walshe's works arising from discourse analysis	180

List of Musical Examples

4.1	'Il nocchier che si figura', *Ezio*, I.5, Venice 1728 (N. Porpora-P. Metastasio), bars 67–74	70
4.2	'Pallido il sole', *Artaserse*, II.15, Venice 1730 (J. A. Hasse-P. Metastasio), bars 13–24	71
4.3	'Stringi l'amata sposa', *Argeno*, I.12, Venice 1728 (Leonardo Leo-Domenico Lalli), bars 51–7	73
4.4	'Dovea svenarti allora', II.13, Venice 1729 (L. Leo-P. Metastasio), bars 62–72	74
10.1	Progression to the flattened-submediant at the lyrics 'let yourself lose yourself' in The Smiths, 'Stretch Out and Wait'	165

Notes on Contributors

Lisa Colton is Subject Leader for Music at the University of Huddersfield and director of the Centre for the Study of Music, Gender and Identity (MuGI). Her research focuses upon both medieval and twentieth-century topics and has appeared in *Plainsong and Medieval Music*, *Early Music*, *Journal of the Royal Musical Association*, *Contemporary Music Review* and *Music and Letters*. She has also contributed book chapters to projects including *St Edmund, King and Martyr: Changing Images of a Medieval Saint* (Boydell, 2009) and the forthcoming collections *Oxford Handbook of Music and Queerness* (Oxford University Press) and *Noise, Audition, Aurality: Histories of the Sonic Worlds of Europe c. 1500–1945* (Ashgate).

Anne Desler is Director of Performance at the Reid School of Music, University of Edinburgh. Her research on the *dramma per musica* is informed by her work as a professional singer as well as interdisciplinary studies in theatre history and Italian philology. Her current research projects include monographs on the artistic profile and impact of Carlo Broschi Farinelli and the aesthetics and practice of operatic acting c. 1680–1760. A study of canonisation in popular music arising from Anne's interest in meta-musicological issues was published in *Popular Music* in 2013.

Richard Elliott is Lecturer in Popular Music at the University of Sussex. He researches representations of loss, memory, nostalgia and space within popular music. He is the author of *Fado and the Place of Longing* (Ashgate, 2010) and *Nina Simone* (Equinox, 2013), and is currently writing a monograph on the representation of time, age and experience in popular music.

Stephen Etheridge is a graduate of Leeds College of Music and Leeds Metropolitan University. He is currently in the final stages of a PhD in social history and musicology at the University of Huddersfield, which examines the influence of brass bands on working-class and northern identities, c. 1840–1914. Stephen is a postgraduate member of the Royal Historical Society and was joint editor and contributor to *Class, Culture and Community: New Perspectives in Nineteenth and Twentieth Century Labour History* (Cambridge Scholars Publishing, 2012).

Sophie Fuller is Acting Head of Postgraduate Studies at Trinity Laban Conservatoire of Music and Dance. Her research interests include many different aspects of music, gender and sexuality, focusing in particular on musical life in late nineteenth- and twentieth-century Britain. Her published work includes the *Pandora Guide to Women Composers* (Pandora, 1994) and an edited collection, *Queer Episodes in Music and Modern Identity* (University of Illinois Press, 2002), winner of the Philip Brett Award. Her most recent work has been on the singer Clara Butt and music at the British seaside.

Kirsten Gibson is Lecturer in Music at Newcastle University. She completed her PhD on John Dowland's printed songs at Newcastle University in 2006 and has published articles on Dowland, early modern print culture and Elizabethan courtly lyrics in *Early Music History* (2007), *Journal of the Royal Musical Association* (2007), *Renaissance Studies* (2012) and *Early Music* (2013). She co-edited *Masculinity and Western Musical Practice* with Ian Biddle (Ashgate, 2009), to which she contributed a chapter on melancholy, masculinity and music in early modern England, and they are currently co-editing a collection, *Noise, Audition, Aurality: Histories of the Sonic Worlds of Europe, 1500–1918*, for Ashgate.

Melissa J. de Graaf is Assistant Professor of Musicology at the University of Miami, where she teaches courses in American Music, Twentieth-Century Music and Music and Gender. Her book *The New York Composers' Forum Concerts, 1935–1940* (University of Rochester Press, 2013) discusses issues of modernism, gender, race, politics and nationalism.

Mimi Haddon is an ABD doctoral student in musicology at McGill University. Her dissertation is a genre-study of post-punk music of the late 1970s and early 1980s. Her research interests include issues of genre, social identity, modernism and postmodernism, and processes of cultural legitimation. Her essay 'Paul Anka Sings "Smells Like Teen Spirit"' appears in the collection *This is the Sound of Irony*, edited by Katherine L. Turner (Ashgate).

Catherine Haworth is Lecturer in Music at the University of Huddersfield, where she is a member of the Centre for the Study of Music, Gender and Identity (MuGI). Her research focuses upon musical practices of representation and identity construction across various media, with a particular focus on music for film and television. Recent projects include articles on scoring the female detective in 1940s crime cinema, and music and medical discourse in the female gothic film, and guest editorship of the 2012 gender and sexuality special issue of *Music, Sound and the Moving Image*.

Caroline Lucas's practitioner-research explores music, identity and power. Alongside her creative practice she has published a number of articles about black metal identity construction, as well as research on whiteness and the politics of English folk music.

Lauren Redhead is Lecturer in Music at Canterbury Christ Church University. Her research examines the aesthetics and socio-semiotics of music, with a particular focus on recent contemporary music. She is also a practice-led researcher who examines themes in contemporary music through composition and experimental organ performance. Her compositions are published by Material Press.

Laura Seddon received her PhD from City University London in 2011 and continues to research in the area of gender and music. She is director of Contemporary Connections, an organisation that instigates musical projects combining historical research and contemporary compositional practice. She also teaches musicology and research/analytical skills. Her monograph *British Women Composers and Instrumental Chamber Music in the Early Twentieth Century* was published by Ashgate in 2013.

Tim Shephard is Lecturer in Musicology at the University of Sheffield and also holds a Visiting Research Fellowship at the Centre for Music, Gender and Identity, University of Huddersfield. His work concerns music, visual culture and identity in Renaissance Italy. He has contributed to several journals and is co-editor of the *Routledge Companion to Music and Visual Culture*. His book *Echoing Helicon: Music, Art and Identity in Renaissance Italy* was published by Oxford University Press in 2014.

Jacqueline Warwick is a musicologist at Dalhousie University, Canada and the author of *Girl Groups, Girl Culture: Popular Music and Identity in the 1960s* (Routledge, 2007). She is co-editor of *Musicological Identities: Essays in Honor of Susan McClary* (Ashgate, 2008) and a senior editor for the *Grove Dictionary of American Music, 2nd edition* (Oxford 2013).

Introduction
Gender, Age and Musical Creativity

Catherine Haworth and Lisa Colton

When Nicola LeFanu reflected on the impact of gender on composition and compositional success, she drew a distinction between the popular perception of the relationship between music and gender and her own appreciation of that relationship:

> Most people believe that music transcends gender, that you can't tell if music is written by a man or a woman. I know, however, that my music is written out of the wholeness of myself, and I happen to be a woman. I'm not bothered about whether or not I compose better or worse than a man, because I take both possibilities for granted; but I am interested in what I do that is different.[1]

The idea that the wholeness of an individual's experience informs his or her creative achievement – from informal jottings to deliberate, carefully crafted works of art – is one that has since come to be explored in a growing body of scholarship relating to music and gender. Much work in this area has examined the output of particular composers, typically focusing on either neglected women composers or, in more recent work, on the examination of issues of gender in the music of well-known composers such as Franz Schubert or Benjamin Britten.[2] Running in parallel to the scrutiny of particular works or composers has emerged equally focused work on performers and the gendered nature of performance itself. Scholarship relating to music and gender has become an established part of many standard music curricula, perhaps because of the flexibility of a theme that can relate to any composer by virtue of the fact that they experience life, to varying extents, through their gender. For example, Jeffrey Kallberg has argued that 'nearly every experience of music, including its creation, performance and perception, may incorporate assumptions about gender; and music itself can produce ideologies of gender'.[3]

---

[1] Nicola LeFanu, 'Master Musician: An Impregnable Taboo?', *Contact: A Journal of Contemporary Music* (1987), 4.

[2] For example, see Lawrence Kramer, *Franz Schubert: Sexuality, Subjectivity, Song* (Cambridge: Cambridge University Press, 1998); Clare Seymour, *The Operas of Benjamin Britten: Expression and Evasion* (Woodbridge: Boydell, 2007).

[3] Jeffrey Kallberg, 'Gender', *New Grove Dictionary of Music and Musicians*, 2nd Edition, ed. Stanley Sadie and John Tyrrell (London: Macmillan, 2001), vol. 8, 645.

Yet, if gender is still the most obvious way by which society is divided, conceptually speaking, there remain several further markers of 'difference' that have an equally significant impact on creativity and its reception. Some of these, such as ethnicity, class or religion, are convenient to organise into sub-categories: white/non-white, upper-/lower-class, gay/straight. Age, however, is not easily compartmentalised: when does 'young' become 'old'? How does one deal with a prodigious composer with a short lifespan, in comparison with a composer who lived into her nineties? What is the relationship between stylistic development and chronological age? In fact, the consideration of age functions to problematise categories of difference more broadly, reminding us that any lived experience embodies only shades of grey: there is no black and white, no standard barometer against which any marker of difference might be measured. In the chapters that follow, there are few that do not explore subtle distinctions between aspects of gender, musical creativity and age without also touching on other categorisations. This is because, as each author recognises, 'gender' and 'age' are flexible, culturally contingent aspects of lived experience; they do not exist in a vacuum, and so cannot be separated from other dominant forces.

This collection of essays was stimulated by a conference held in 2012 at the University of Huddersfield, where Sophie Fuller delivered a keynote lecture that focused on the careers of women musicians over the age of 50, with examples ranging from the classical operas of Elizabeth Maconchy and the songs of Maude Valérie White to popular musicians Patti Smith, Joan Armatrading and Joni Mitchell. What Fuller's initial lecture, now revised here as an extended chapter, shows is that within the life cycle, creative development and achievement do not take a standard path. Furthermore, for complex personal, economic and cultural reasons, women's creative careers, and the reception of their work, often bear little resemblance to those of men. A male composer's first major symphony in his sixties might be understood as a crowning achievement, a culmination of previous successes, whereas a woman in the same position might be dismissed or patronised as a 'late bloomer', or a retired amateur, even if the timing had more to do with the time-intensive work of raising a family than her personal creative development. There are exceptions, of course – Fuller notes the triumphant first performance of Minna Keal's Symphony op. 3 during the 1989 Proms season, when Keal was already 80 – but these remain few and far between, and such gendered double-standards apply across the 'classical' and 'popular' divide.

The older woman is defined by her age and her gender, and frequently described in pathological terms: a menopausal site of decay, ridicule, pity and striving for eternal youth. Fuller's discussion of Madonna's performance at the 2012 Super Bowl (and any glance at print or online 'celebrity news' coverage) reveals the extent to which the creative, cultural, professional lives of women, in particular, continue to be subsumed within discourse centred upon their appearance, physicality and perceived relationship to 'acceptable' models of feminine behaviour. But there are two sides to this story, here articulated through the reappropriation of Grace Williams's assertion that there was 'something revolting' in the idea of a symphony written by a woman over 50 – a maxim that she herself disproved with large-scale, successful works written later in life. Fuller celebrates Williams's creativity alongside a variety of past and present composing and performing women, reminding us that 'revolt' also signifies rebellion, change and challenge, and finding both inspiration and resonance in the refusal of these musicians to be silenced or marginalised.

Fuller's chapter exemplifies the broad coverage of this collection, which addresses a variety of musics and musicians from the early modern period through to the present day. The book is grouped into three sections underpinned by a chronological framework, since attitudes to, and understandings and experiences of, age and gender have shifted over the centuries. In Part I 'Performing Identity in Early European Musical Culture' each author deals with the central themes against further questions of patronage, agency and class. Kirsten Gibson and Tim Shephard remind us that even in the early modern period, there was no single or standard gender model against which women and girls, or men and boys, could be measured. Rather, gender was part of broader social frameworks, and understandings of it were additionally informed by an individual's family circumstances, education or career. In Tim Shephard's chapter, the ways in which female patrons and musicians at the early Italian court negotiated the constraints placed on them by age and gender are discussed with reference to women whose lives were more typical of their time than Isabella d'Este, whose activities have unfairly dominated the picture of female music-making and patronage in Renaissance Italy. Kirsten Gibson shows us that didactic texts, including those that pertained exclusively to music, functioned as a means to teach boys how to become men, and how men should reaffirm the appropriate markers of masculinity, depending on their maturity. Early modern texts show differentiated expectations for expressions of masculinity, dependent upon age, and music was an important part of that gendered performance. The performer is placed centre-stage in Anne Desler's consideration of castrato Nicolò Grimaldi, who negotiated his career against changing vocal capabilities in ways that capitalised on his strengths. A common theme in the first group of essays is the crucial place of music in shaping and reshaping the public identity of high profile men and women: whether professional or amateur, a demonstrable knowledge of music was essential for anyone considered of noble status, but for the professional musician, a positive reception into maturity required imagination and flexibility.

In Part II 'Gendered Musical Communities' each author tackles the role of institutions in fostering and sustaining creative identities at various stages of the life cycle or career. For Stephen Etheridge, the examination of musical career runs in parallel with brass players' employment in the industrial north of England. Focusing particularly on notions of masculinity in the brass band movement of the late nineteenth and early twentieth century, Etheridge finds a strong linkage between the construction of masculine ideals in Victorian society, in terms of the value placed on economic independence and moral behaviour, and the expression of those ideals in the homosocial space of the band room and in public performance. All three chapters in this section delve into little-known archival documents pertaining to localised groups and traditions. Melissa J. de Graaf and Laura Seddon explore the evidence relating to New York- and London-based collectives that promoted the early work of female composers. Local organisations provide a framework for creative activity, developing in a mutually beneficial relationship with the musicians they support, defining communities through gender and a shared sense of musical purpose.

Part III 'Contemporary Creative Practices and Identities' contains two main strands, both of which have strong ties to the case studies discussed by Fuller. Chapters by Richard Elliott, Jacqueline Warwick and Mimi Haddon consider gender and age in diverse popular music cultures, while Lauren Redhead and Caroline Lucas focus on issues of identity and its representation in contemporary art music. There is a dual focus on age throughout much of this section; authors consider not only issues of youth or ageing in the figure of the individual musician, but also the ways in which genres and scenes age over time.

Jacqueline Warwick's chapter investigates the cultural resonance of 'Little Orphan Annie' as a symbol of girlhood, mapping the character's journey from page to stage and screen over the course of nearly a century. Warwick examines Annie's development as both street urchin and urban angel against broader dichotomies of youth representation – and the musical stereotypes associated with them. As elsewhere in this volume, the voice is shown to have a special relationship with the ageing and gendered musical self, whether in the understanding and communication of our own subjectivities or in their (often problematic) representation by others. Annie's musical positioning can be traced through the voice-casting and vocal mannerisms of the various young actresses who have embodied the role as either brash 'belter' or soft-voiced ingénue – a dual vision of Annie, and girlhood itself, that reveals deep-seated societal anxieties around issues of youth, gender and class.

At the other end of the spectrum, Richard Elliott proposes an 'early sense of lateness' as a feature of songwriting and/or performance that connotes maturity, experience and reflection. Recordings of Sandy Denny's 'Who Knows Where the Time Goes', by Judy Collins, Nina Simone and Denny herself, demonstrate the links between early lateness and the cultural resonance of stardom in the often fickle world of popular performance. Denny's lyrics combine present and future tenses with explicit moments of remembrance; the song fosters a continuum of reflection and gathered experience that facilitates the performance of 'late voice' across diverse artists, recordings and musical styles. The always 'posthumous' nature of retrospective narration allows this sense of maturity to be communicated at any point in a career, creating a sense of poignant reflection that is only added to as 'Who Knows Where the Time Goes' itself ages and is re-recorded, re-voiced and re-heard.

The chapters by Lauren Redhead and Mimi Haddon also address broader ideas of ageing in relation to scenes, genres and cultural texts, arguing that our distance from, or nearness to, musical works and musicians affects their reception and the values ascribed to them. Haddon's discussion of Manchester-based indie band The Smiths adopts a queer historiographical methodology in its investigation of the intertextual references to pre-existing styles and material that abound in the group's work. She positions these references as opportunities for looking backwards, nostalgia, memory, haunting or regression: ageing sites of memory that often explicitly evoke the spectre of social exclusion and thereby offer poignant spaces for queer identification. This queer sensibility runs the gamut of The Smiths' output; Haddon describes a complex web of social and cultural references that archive texts as diverse as new wave cinema, folk music and Motown. In the work of both the band and lead singer Morrissey, musical and extra-musical signifiers create a 'multimedia scrapbook of failed connections from times past that codedly communicate the trauma of social exclusion', offering spaces of empathy for the queer outsider.

Lauren Redhead's focus is on the culture of 'New Music', which, despite its nature as a contemporary field that is at least partially defined by its rejection of prior boundaries, she reads as both a historical and a patriarchal category. Redhead uses feminist discourse analysis to investigate the reception of the solo bass clarinet piece *Caerulean* (2010) by Rebecca Saunders, and Jennifer Walshe's opera *XXX Live Nude Girls!!!* – both works that make a feature of experimental techniques and new sounds, but which are positioned very differently by their performers and reviewers. Arguing that the centrality of a particular, masculinised understanding of 'material' to New Music's critical, theoretical and musical existence underpins these differences in reception, Redhead demonstrates what can be understood as a contemporary continuation of the 'double-bind' identified in earlier writing about the 'female composer'. If their music does not fit the terms of New Music's discourse of material, women are denied access to a positioning as 'composer'; yet, if their work is acceptable under these terms it becomes a model of gendered difference within New Music, but one where that difference is also simultaneously effaced, given the patriarchal discourse surrounding the nature of musical material per se. Given the historicising – canonising – implications of this discourse, it is a question that has far-reaching consequences; not just for women, but for anyone who wishes to create music that sits outside traditional paradigms.

Through an explicitly autobiographical and self-reflexive account of her creative practice and its relationship to her subjectivity as composer and scholar, Caroline Lucas also poses challenging questions about identity within the academy and the contemporary music scene. The 2012 piece *multiple/radical/forms/*comma*/traces/creativity/of/constraint*, around which her chapter is structured, is both a reflection upon and a contribution to the practice-based research undertaken during her doctoral studies. In addition to her discussion of interlinked issues of gender and age in the figure of the developing 'female composer', Lucas's writing challenges the hegemony of communicative practices within academia and highlights the deeply engrained nature of our ways of writing about and understanding texts, authors and our own identities. This reveals perhaps uncomfortable truths about the continuing rigidity of our academic 'rules' and divisions – even in an era that claims to have embraced the philosophies of practice-as-research, interdisciplinary investigation and the subjectivity of both scholars and scholarship – and, in a fitting conclusion to a collection focused upon music and identity, encourages us to continue our efforts to document, question and challenge the politics of representation in and through all aspects of our communicative practices.

Together, these essays offer a look at the relationship between musical creativity, gender and age, through focused case studies from various chronological and cultural perspectives. In 1987, LeFanu asked 'Could there be a music which did not reflect its maker?'[4] This collection shows that although she was right to conclude that any music is an embodiment of elements of its author's life so far, the same could also be said of performance and other forms of musical expression, including that found in the practice of written scholarship. Furthermore, the relationship between an individual's age, gender and creative act can be emphasised or hidden away, made consciously or unconsciously, encouraged or suppressed, expressed at face value or subverted. Although there is, by extension, no simple or recoverable link between the various components that make up a creative personality, there is much to learn about music and its historical meaning by the examination of this subject.

---

[4] LeFanu, 'Master Musician', 4.

Chapter 1

'Something revolting': Women, Creativity and Music after 50

Sophie Fuller

In February 2012 a record-breaking 114 million viewers watched 53-year-old Madonna give the half-time performance at the Super Bowl, the annual championship game of the National Football League in the United States, in a jaw-dropping spectacle involving dancers, choirs, marching bands and younger singers (notably Nicki Minaj, M.I.A. and Cee Lo Green). A timely promotion for her forthcoming *MDNA* album, the show attracted the kind of mixed media attention, concentrating mainly on her age, that Madonna has come to expect. In the *Daily Telegraph*, Neil McCormick wrote that 'The past decade has seen a host of challengers arrive, young women like Beyoncé, Lady Gaga, Rihanna who are ready to take her crown but Madonna's pre-eminent status as the reigning Queen of Pop was emphasised by her majestic arrival, to the roar of the big guns of her mega hits',[1] while Jon Parales reported in the *New York Times* that although Madonna was 'still lithe, she measured her moves, letting her supporting cast offer distractions'.[2] MSN Entertainment headlined their report 'Super Bowl performance: has Madonna lost it?'[3] 49-year-old Sharon Osbourne tweeted: 'Madonna is back. She's the queen. Just sensational!' while 46-year-old Piers Morgan's reaction was to tweet: 'Yuk. Just put it away, Madonna. Seriously.'[4] Among the multitude of media reports after this performance was an insightful response from feminist commentator Naomi Wolf, writing for *The Guardian* under the title 'Madonna

---

[1] Neil McCormick, 'Madonna's Super Bowl Show Deconstructed', *Daily Telegraph*, 6 February 2012, accessed 17 April 2014, http://www.telegraph.co.uk/news/celebritynews/madonna/9063810/Madonnas-Super-Bowl-show-deconstructed.html.

[2] Quoted in 'Super Bowl: Madonna Gives "Shot of Brass"', *BBC News and Entertainment*, 6 February 2012, accessed 17 April 2014, http://www.bbc.co.uk/news/entertainment-arts-16904511.

[3] Felicity Thistlethwaite, 'Super Bowl Performance: Has Madonna Lost It?', *MSN Entertainment*, 6 February 2012, accessed 17 April 2014, http://music.uk.msn.com/features/super-bowl-performance-has-madonna-lost-it .

[4] Quoted in Sarah Fitzmaurice, 'Did Madonna Put on the Greatest Show on Earth?', *Mail Online*, 6 February 2012, accessed 17 April 2014, http://www.dailymail.co.uk/tvshowbiz/article-2097020/Madonna-Super-Bowl-halftime-2012-Singer-suffers-small-slip-up.html.

Acts Just Like a Serious Male Artist Would – and People Hate Her for It'.[5] I will return to the Material Girl (or should that now be Material Woman?) later.

In September of the same year, the UK Labour Party launched a Commission on Older Women, 'to ensure public policy properly considers the lives of women in their fifties and onwards, many of whom are balancing work with caring responsibilities across the generations within their families'.[6] At the launch the shadow home secretary, 43-year-old Yvette Cooper, drew attention to the generation of women born in the 1940s, 1950s and early 1960s, and the battles they had fought for many different kinds of equality – equal pay, improvements in childcare and maternity leave. But as she went on to explain: 'A toxic combination of sexism and ageism is causing problems for this generation.'[7]

The toxic combination of sexism and ageism is of course nothing new. It affects older women throughout the world in almost every aspect of their lives and has been explored and dissected by feminist thinkers and writers from Simone de Beauvoir to Germaine Greer and beyond. Any study of the older woman inevitably needs to take on board attitudes towards the menopause – the physical change that marks ageing so distinctly for most women. For both men and women, ageing is accompanied by numerous physical changes but society's negative view of menopause is key to understanding attitudes towards the ageing woman. Still something all too rarely discussed as anything other than a problem, a burden or source of humour, the menopause is more than just a physical reality – it is also a social construct.

Feminist scholars in the West have investigated factors such as the invisibility of the post-menopausal woman and highlighted the attitudes of a society that regards the older female body as inevitably diseased and deteriorating, in need of medical treatment, particularly in the form of hormone replacement therapy (HRT). In gynaecologist Robert Wilson's bestselling 1966 book promoting HRT, *Feminine Forever*, for example, he wrote of the menopause that 'no woman can be sure of escaping the horror of this living decay ... even the most valiant woman can no longer hide the fact that she is, in effect, no longer a woman'.[8] For men like Wilson, once a woman can no longer reproduce, she fails to fulfil her only truly valuable function in life and so is discarded and fades into invisibility. More

---

[5] Naomi Wolf, 'Madonna Acts Just Like A Serious Male Artist Would – and People Hate Her for It', *The Guardian*, 6 February 2012, accessed 17 April 2014, http://www.theguardian.com/commentisfree/cifamerica/2012/feb/06/madonna-hating-we-superbowl.

[6] 'Labour's Policy Review: Commission on Older Women', accessed 12 February 2014, http://www.yourbritain.org.uk/agenda-2015/policy-review/commission-on-older-women.

[7] Jane Martinson and Jo Adetunji, 'Generation of Women Hit by "Toxic Combination of Ageism and Sexism"', *The Guardian*, 29 September 2012, accessed 2 February 2014, http://www.theguardian.com/world/2012/sep/29/generation-women-toxic-ageism-sexism.

[8] Quoted in Jacqueline N. Zita, 'Heresy in the Female Body', in *The Other Within Us: Feminist Explorations of Women and Aging*, ed. Marilyn Pearsall (Boulder, CO: Westview Press, 1997), 98.

recently, in a 1992 article entitled 'Hormone Replacement Therapy: Protection against the Consequences of Menopause', P. B. Marshburn and P. R. Carr declared categorically: 'Anxiety, depression, irritability and fatigue increase after menopause.'[9]

Needless to say, many women, perhaps especially as we ourselves age, have raged against this view of the menopause and what it says about our place and value in society. While acknowledging the physical changes that can occur in our bodies, for many women the menopause can in fact be a time of freedom, renewed energy and exciting potential. In the 1990s a survey carried out in the United States found that only three per cent of the women questioned were regretful at the onset of menopause, while thirty-nine per cent were relieved.[10] Linda R. Gannon even argues that the menopausal woman can be regarded as in a state of wellness in comparison to the menstruating woman who is 'at heightened risk for disease, injury, and death'.[11]

Women who refuse to allow themselves to be medicalised or marginalised find not just a peaceful serenity and acceptance of ageing but often a new dynamic and power as they reach the pivotal age of 50. As feminist scholar Jacqueline Zita has written:

> To deconstruct the meanings of menopause in a male gerontocracy is to construct a social and cultural space for the empowerment of crones ... My hope is that more powerful and unruly women will emerge from this conceiving – old, wise, and furiously heretical.[12]

Germaine Greer, in her monograph *The Change*, has explained:

> There are positive aspects to being a frightening old woman. Though the old woman is both feared and reviled, she need not take the intolerance of others to heart, for women over fifty already form one of the largest groups in the population structure of the Western world. As long as they like themselves, they will not be an oppressed minority. In order to like themselves they must reject trivialisation by others of who and what they are.[13]

Elsewhere Greer has written:

---

[9] P. B. Marshburn and P. R. Carr quoted in Linda R. Gannon, *Women and Aging: Transcending the Myths* (London and New York: Routledge, 1999), 35.

[10] Study carried out by Judyth Reichenberg-Ullman, discussed in Zita, 'Heresy in the Female Body', 101.

[11] Gannon, *Women and Aging*, 86–7.

[12] Zita, 'Heresy in the Female Body', 110.

[13] Germaine Greer, *The Change: Women, Aging and the Menopause* (New York: Alfred A. Knopf, 1992), 4.

> Let the Masters in Menopause congregate in luxury hotels all over the world to deliver and to hearken to papers on the latest astonishing discoveries about the decline of grip strength in menopause or the number of stromal cells in the fifty-year-old ovary, the woman herself is too busy to listen. She is climbing her own mountain, in search of her own horizon, after years of being absorbed in the struggle of others. The way is hard, and she stumbles many times, but for once no one is scrambling after her, begging her to turn back ... The climacteric marks the end of apologizing. The chrysalis of conditioning has once and for all to break and the female woman finally to emerge.[14]

But climbing your own mountain can be difficult. Women are as bound by cultural stereotypes and beliefs as men and it can be hard to break out of the chrysalis, or even to acknowledge there is a chrysalis to be broken out of. The title of this chapter comes from a somewhat startling letter written by the Welsh composer Grace Williams (1906–77) to her friend Gerald Cockshutt in 1949, when she was in her early forties:

> Ten years ago I thought that no one could ever possibly want to hear music written by a woman in her forties. Well, the two Elizabeths [Maconchy and Lutyens] have proved me wrong. But I still feel the same way about women of 50+. There does seem something revolting – and perhaps a bit pathetic – in the thought of a symphony by a woman of 50.[15]

At this stage in her life, Williams was a successful freelance composer, writing music in a variety of genres, including several well-received orchestral works such as her *Fantasia on Welsh Nursery Themes* (1940) or her *Sea Sketches* for string orchestra (1944). What is particularly poignant about her remark is that she went on to complete her dynamic second symphony, a work still available on CD, in 1956, at the age of 50.[16] Was she merely expressing what she felt she was somehow expected to feel? 'Revolting' is such a strong word to use. Was she really so unsure of her own value that she felt there was something repellent about the public expression of complex musical creativity from an older woman? And why was the symphony singled out as a genre? Would a song or piano piece – traditionally women's genres – be more acceptable?

Williams certainly continued to express such feelings about herself as an older woman creating music. In 1966, she wrote to her friend and fellow composer Elizabeth Maconchy (1907–94) about a possible production of her opera

---

[14] Germaine Greer, 'Serenity and Power', in Pearsall, *The Other Within Us*, 272.
[15] Quoted in Malcolm Boyd, *Grace Williams* (Cardiff: University of Wales Press, 1996), 42.
[16] The CD is a remastering, made with the support of the Arts Council of Wales, of an EMI recording from 1974: *Grace Williams, Ballads, Fairest of Stars, Symphony No. 2*, CD, Lyrita, SRCD327 (1996).

The Parlour which she had completed five years earlier: 'A first opera by a woman of 60 - - - how would <u>we</u> react to it? – let alone the young!'[17] Williams is often distressingly self-deprecating and self-effacing, but these declarations of disgust at her age are particularly painful.

Ultimately, however, Williams does not seem to have listened to herself. She certainly did not feel enough revulsion at approaching old age to stop composing, as the catalogue of powerful, dynamic and beautiful music that she produced after the age of 50 bears witness. Indeed her biographer Malcolm Boyd, without drawing attention to her age, has noted that 'it is possible to recognise in the music she wrote after about 1954 a new sense of direction and an individuality not often apparent in the large-scale works she had written before that date', going on to talk of 'a new self-confidence and sense of identity'.[18]

Grace Williams was one of a number of British female composers – along with Elisabeth Lutyens (1906–83), Elizabeth Maconchy and others – whose music was first heard in the late 1920s and early 1930s, when it frequently confounded critics who were confused by music that was more modernist and challenging than anything they were expecting from young women.[19] In 1935, the critic for the *Evening News* reviewed a concert with new music by Lutyens (a song-cycle for tenor, four horns and strings), Maconchy (a ballet) and Williams (an orchestral suite) describing it as:

> an interesting study of the young female mind of today. This organ, when it takes up musical composition, works in mysterious ways. No lip-stick, silk stocking, or saucily tilted hat adorns the music evolved from its recesses.[20]

By the time these composers reached their fifties, their distinctive music – which they continued to write despite the struggle to get it heard – had been eclipsed as their male contemporaries – Benjamin Britten and Michael Tippett – became the grand old men of British music and a new generation of younger men – Harrison Birtwistle and Peter Maxwell Davies – took over the avant-garde. Nevertheless Lutyens, Maconchy and Williams, along with female contemporaries such as Priaulx Rainier (1903–86) or Phyllis Tate (1911–87), continued to compose for many more years, offering each other the support not found elsewhere. Shortly before Maconchy's 50th birthday, Williams wrote to her, saying:

> I've just heard your Strings Symphony & feel convinced that it is your best orchestral work – it's worth growing older if one can write mature music of such

---

[17] Grace Williams to Elizabeth Maconchy, 24 November 1966. Private collection.
[18] Boyd, *Grace Williams*, 36.
[19] For an introduction to the work of Lutyens, Maconchy and Williams, see Rhiannon Mathias, *Lutyens, Maconchy, Williams and Twentieth-Century British Music: A Blest Trio of Sirens* (Farnham: Ashgate, 2012).
[20] William McNaught, *Evening News*, 5 February 1935, Iris Lemare archive.

quality – deep & vital – & serious in a way that is more profoundly serious than one's early work can ever be. (So take heart as you approach the 19th! How much worse it would be if you were a singer!)[21]

Maconchy celebrated her fifties by turning to opera, producing a captivating trilogy of very different but equally compelling one-act works which are beginning to be heard again today. *The Sofa* (composed 1956–57, first performed 1959), to a libretto by Ursula Vaughan Williams after the play *Le Sofa* by Crébillon fils, and *The Departure* (composed 1961, first performed 1962), to a libretto by Anne Ridler, were both revived at London's Sadler's Wells by Independent Opera in 2007 to mark the centenary of Maconchy's birth, and issued by the company on CD two years later.[22] Completed in the year Maconchy turned 50, *The Sofa* is a lively, surreal and somewhat risqué work, in which a dissolute young man is turned into a sofa by his disapproving grandmother. The spell is only reversed when a couple make love on the sofa he has become. The work is a compelling demonstration of Maconchy's operatic skills, blending drama, lyrical beauty, humour and vocal acrobatics in a perfectly judged whole.

Sometimes a woman's advancing age can play in her favour. Some of the women of Maconchy's generation were still alive when Minna Keal's Symphony op. 3 received its premiere at the Promenade Concerts in 1989, played by the BBC Symphony Orchestra conducted by Oliver Knussen to widespread critical attention and acclaim.[23] One reviewer described her 1989 symphony as 'tightly argued, cast in a moderately modern though very accessible idiom, brimming with energy and invention'.[24]

Keal's story is perhaps now forgotten. Born in 1909 in the East End of London, she was a contemporary of Lutyens, Maconchy, Rainier, Tate and Williams. In 1928 she had studied composition for a year at the Royal Academy of Music with William Alwyn before her father died and she had to give up studying and the goal of a musical career in order to work in the family business. It was not until she retired at the age of 60, in 1969, that she took up composition again. Her teacher, Justin Conolly, was supportive and encouraging while the press were intrigued by this diminutive white-haired woman who was producing such rugged and

---

[21] Maconchy's birthday was on 19 March. Grace Williams to Elizabeth Maconchy, 10 March 1957, private collection.

[22] Elizabeth Maconchy, *The Sofa/The Departure*, CD, Chandos, CHAN 10508 (2009).

[23] On Minna Keal, see Tim Bullamore, 'Obituary: Minna Keal', *The Independent*, 16 November 1999, accessed 3 September 2012, http://www.independent.co.uk/arts-entertainment/obituary-minna-keal-1126413.html, and Alison Light, 'Minna Keal', *The Guardian*, 24 November 1999, accessed 3 September 2012, http://www.theguardian.com/news/1999/nov/24/guardianobituaries1.

[24] Hubert Culot, 'Review of LNT110: A *Life in Reverse: the Music of Minna Keal*', Lontano website, accessed 12 February 2014, http://www.lorelt.co.uk/review/life_in_reverse_keal/12.

complex music. Like her contemporaries as young female composers, Keal, as an 80-year-old grandmother, was confounding what was expected of a woman at her stage in life.

Inspiring though Keal's story and music are, it is instructive to compare her position at the end of the twentieth century with that of composers such as Maconchy who had no such *X-Factor* style 'back story' to attract this level of coverage or attention, despite a lifetime spent creating equally powerful music. Needless to say once Keal's 'story' had been told, she faded back into obscurity – although not before a couple of CDs and a television documentary had been made.[25] Like the child prodigy, the late starter is always fleetingly newsworthy.

The sixth decade seems to be a significant period of life for many women. Most are post-menopausal, relieved of the annoying pain of that monthly curse; many have seen their children grow and for those who have not chosen or not been able to have children, that possibility is no longer there to hover annoyingly at the edges of thought. Firmly ensconced in my own sixth decade, I continue to search for inspiration – people that awake my imagination, offer stimulation and encouragement. Increasingly my role models are older women who wear their life stories in their faces, who are still going strong after decades of everything that life has thrown at them, who have survived the 'toxic combination' of ageism and sexism and who continue to surprise, resist and not do what is expected. As always music is my constant companion, and in the music of women such as Joan Armatrading, Joni Mitchell, Patti Smith or Ethel Smyth, I hear determination, a defiance of expectation and a refusal to behave. Even in the music of Grace Williams, I hear a spirited contradiction of her own indoctrinated beliefs about the lack of any possible value in herself or her music. And their later work often shows these women to be becoming bolder in many different ways.

For the last couple of decades much of my own work, my musicological research, has involved uncovering the lives and music of women working in Britain in the last years of the nineteenth and the first years of the twentieth century. The ways in which this generation approached their sixth decade resonate strongly across the years. The woman I have been most drawn to is the now little-known songwriter Maude Valérie White (1855–1937). Educated at the Royal Academy of Music, White was one of Britain's leading songwriters in the 1880s and 1890s, supplementing a small private income with sales of her songs and the proceeds of concerts of her music. In her second volume of memoirs, *My Indian Summer*, published in 1932 when she was in her late seventies, White wrote of the period at the turn of the century when she was in her late forties:

> I had no home, no ties in England. My brothers and sisters were scattered all over the world, leading their own lives; I could go on with my own work wherever I

---

[25] *A Life in Reverse: The Music of Minna Keal*, CD, Lontano LNT110 (1996); Minna Keal, *Cello Concerto/Ballade*, CD, NMC, NMC DO48S (1997); *A Life in Reverse*, broadcast on BBC2, 18 August 1992.

went, and – I was middle-aged, and glorying in the fact! For middle-age – even now – is the most successful broom for sweeping tiresome complications out of a woman's life ... It ought to be welcomed with cheers – with the enthusiasm with which Mohammedans celebrate the end of Ramadan. As to the 'first grey hair', why, it's the outward and visible sign of liberty! – the liberty that refuses to be cramped and controlled by other people's opinions.[26]

In her early fifties, White moved her base from England to Taormina in Sicily, a new adventure in a place which had a reputation at that time as a place frequented by gay men.[27] A widely acknowledged freedom from Victorian propriety among the Northern European visitors together with the geographic remoteness and wildness of Sicily doubtless appealed to White as she gloried in her middle age. She loved the town and its music which she was to draw on in several of her songs.

Always a compulsive traveller, it was also at this time that White started visiting North Africa. Deeply attracted to and intrigued by the music of Algeria, she explained: 'Many people hate the music of the East. I love it. To me it seems like a savage, desperate cry for happiness and liberty.'[28] Echoes of this music also find their way into her songs, such as 'Song of the Sahara' written in 1904, her 49th year, to words from *The Garden of Allah*, a novel by her friend Robert Hichens (and later made into a film starring Marlene Dietrich).[29] Another song from that year is the hypnotically sensuous D'Annunzio setting 'Isaotta Blanzesmano', described by one of her publishers as like an opium dream.[30] The sultry, seductive quality of the song with its recurrent improvisatory piano accompaniment motif was a new musical departure for White, one that can also be heard in later songs such as her haunting setting of Verlaine's 'Le Foyer' (1924).[31]

---

[26] Maude Valérie White, *My Indian Summer* (London: Grayson & Grayson, 1932), 52.

[27] An 1899 diary entry by the bisexual Russian poet Zinaida Hippius refers to 'Taormina, white and blue town of the most humorous of all loves – homosexuality!' See Temira Pachmuss, ed. and trans., *Between Paris and St Petersburg: Selected Diaries of Zinaida Hippius* (Urbana: University of Illinois Press, 1975), 73–4. In her biography of Ethel Smyth, Louise Collis makes an unacknowledged reference to Smyth associating Sicily with 'colonies of Oscar-Wilde men'. See Louise Collis, *Impetuous Heart: The Story of Ethel Smyth* (London: William Kimber, 1984), 156.

[28] White, *My Indian Summer*, 33.

[29] 'A Song of the Sahara' was written in 1904 and published by Ricordi. Robert Hichens's novel *The Garden of Allah* was published by Methuen in the same year. At least two film versions have been made: a silent film, *The Crisis* (d. Colin Campbell, 1916), for which Hichens worked on the screenplay, and a later version directed by Richard Boleslawski and starring Marlene Dietrich, *The Garden of Allah* (1936).

[30] Tito Ricordi, quoted in White, *My Indian Summer*, 92. White first came across the poem in Hichens's novel *The Woman with the Fan* (1904) when 'it evoked a vision of beauty – and romance – that absolutely refused to leave me for days and days'. Maude Valérie White, *Friends and Memories* (London: Edward Arnold, 1914), 190.

[31] *Two Songs* ['Le Foyer' and 'La flûte invisible'] (London: Chappell, 1924).

One of the visitors to Casa Felice, White's cottage in Taormina, was her better known contemporary the composer Ethel Smyth (1958–44). Never a quiet or dutiful woman, Smyth was to mark the entry into her fifties by falling in love with Emmeline Pankhurst and deciding to devote two years of her life to the suffragette cause of votes for women. Like White, there are notable changes in Smyth's musical language at this time – a move away from a more solid Germanic approach to harmony and structure, towards a French-inspired lightness of touch. The year 1908, when Smyth turned 50, saw the first performances of her *Four Songs* to French texts for mezzo soprano and the somewhat unusual chamber ensemble of string trio, harp, flute and percussion. The resulting work provides a succinct example of Smyth's new musical language.

Smyth's published memoirs stop at the age of 50 – with the death of her only male lover – although there are plenty of letters and diaries that survive to continue her life story. An inspirational but difficult woman, she still awaits the biography she deserves. Smyth herself does not seem to have thought middle age worthy of discussion and I suspect she simply brushed it out of her way as she continued to play golf, fall in love and fight for hearings of her music.

A notable change in the musical language of both Smyth and White can be heard in their music after the age of 50. Moving into the late twentieth and early twenty-first century and to a different musical genre, are there any such discernible patterns for the women singer-songwriters I also admire, as they too enter middle age? Unlike the composers of White's or Williams's generations, these musicians are also performers, women who take to the stage and are therefore judged, like Madonna, on their appearance as well as on their musicianship and creativity.

Thinking about the careers and listening to the music of a fairly random selection of American, British and Canadian women, it has struck me that while inevitably continuing to create music in their own individual and distinctive languages, there are indeed certain similarities to their careers as they enter their fifties. Refusing to slow down or retire quietly into a lady-like silence, they also frequently strike out onto new musical paths. Faced with a world in which they are increasingly invisible and which so often overlooks their work, they often issue retrospective collections or re-workings of their previous successes. Many of them choose to branch out into paths beyond music and an ever sounding note is a freedom from caring what other people think, an embracing of, in Maude Valérie White's words, 'the liberty that refuses to be cramped and controlled by other people's opinions'.[32]

---

[32] Watson and Railton have outlined 'five principal "career options" available to mainstream women pop and rock performers as they age'. These are to die young, to disappear from public view, to 'replay past success in the present', to change career 'in order to remain in the public eye' and 'to maintain a career through ongoing chart success'. Paul Watson and Diane Railton, 'Rebel without a Pause: The Continuing Controversy in Madonna's Contemporary Music Videos', in *'Rock On': Women, Ageing and Popular Music*, ed. Ros Jennings and Abigail Gardner (Farnham: Ashgate, 2012), 139.

Many of these patterns can be seen in the music and career of singer-songwriter Joan Armatrading. Armatrading was born in St Kitts in 1943 and came to the UK to join her parents in Birmingham at the age of 7. She released her debut album *Whatever's For Us* in 1972. Much of this album was co-written with songwriter Pam Nestor but this collaborative partnership was not to last. Armatrading went on to critical acclaim with songs such as her first chart success 'Love and Affection' of 1976.

But the 1990s, when Armatrading was in her forties, was a difficult decade. She retained a devoted following but had little commercial success with a succession of albums. Undaunted, she started to turn her attention to other interests. After studying at the Open University, she graduated with a history degree in 2000, the year she turned 50. The following year she was awarded an MBE and in 2003, no longer attached to a major record label, released *Lovers Speak*, her first album in eight years.

In 2007 Armatrading released *Into the Blues* on the 429 record label, describing it as 'the CD I've been promising myself to write for a long time'.[33] This musical departure from a more pop-based sound was also a commercial and critical success, reaching no. 1 on the US Billboard Blues Chart and making Armatrading the first UK female musician nominated for a Grammy Blues award. A remarkably gutsy and raw album, *Into the Blues* was the first of a trilogy in which Armatrading explored blues, rock (*This Charming Life*, 2010) and jazz (*Starlight*, 2013) creating, producing and performing all songs – even playing almost all instruments – on all three albums.[34] *Into the Blues* was deservedly the best received of the trilogy, foregrounding her mesmeric guitar technique and powerful vocal range. Always a defiantly private person who refused to talk about her sexuality despite much media speculation, in 2011 Armatrading threw caution to the winds, embracing a 'liberty that refuses to be cramped and controlled by other people's opinions' and entered into a civil partnership with her long-term partner, visual artist Maggie Butler.[35]

The media is not often kind to famous women as they reach 50, especially if they dare to continue to perform in what is seen as a sexually provocative way – something Armatrading has never even begun to embrace. The woman

---

[33] 429 Record press release, *429 Records*, accessed 17 April 2014, http://www.429records.com/sites/429records/429details/d_joan3.asp.

[34] In Armatrading's own words: 'I thought it would be good to do one genre and stay with that and I hit on coming up with a trilogy, and the trilogy would be blues, rock, jazz.' Mike Ragogna, 'A Conversation with Joan Armatrading', *Huff Post Entertainment*, 27 February 2013, accessed 17 April 2014, http://www.huffingtonpost.com/mike-ragogna/-emstarlightem-a-conversa_b_2770475.html.

[35] See Diane Anderson-Minshall, 'Joan Armatrading Still Sings of Love and Affection', *advocate.com*, 26 February 2013, accessed 17 April 2014, http://www.advocate.com/arts-entertainment/music/2013/02/26/joan-armatrading-still-sings-love-and-affection?page=0,0.

who is probably the best known and most talked about female musician in her fifties – Madonna – reached the age of 50 in 2008 not long before her Super Bowl performance. The year 2008 was the one in which she divorced Guy Ritchie and the year after she left Warner Brothers and signed to Live Nation. Renowned for her constant musical and performative reinventions, and her continual control over all aspects of her career, Madonna also began to diversify her talents into other non-musical fields. Already notorious for her 'acting' in films such as the laughable *Swept Away* (2002) and as the author of a series of cloying children's books,[36] she has recently stepped up the pace. In 2008, at 50, she not only released her eleventh studio album, *Hard Candy*, and embarked on her Sweet and Sticky tour, but also directed her first feature film, *Filth and Wisdom* – a comedy set in London – as well as writing and producing a documentary, *I Am Because We Are*, about AIDS orphans in Malawi. In 2007, Lucy O'Brien, author of the pioneering history of women in popular music *She Bop*,[37] published a biography of Madonna, explaining: 'I wanted to look at her life and work as she was approaching fifty – what kind of issues would this bring up?'[38] O'Brien finds that Madonna 'seemed to relish the challenge of defying middle age ... "I'm not going to be defined by my age ... Why should any woman? I'm not going to slow down, get off this ride, stay home and get fat."'[39]

As she continued to defy middle age, or perhaps to diversify in ways we might in fact expect, in 2010 Madonna launched a clothing line, Material Girl, and Hard Candy Fitness, a chain of fitness centres. In 2011 she directed her second feature film *W.E.*, about Edward and Wallace Simpson, a work which prompted a mixed critical reaction. The following year, 2012, saw her Super Bowl performance and the release of *MDNA*, her twelfth studio album. As the media reaction to the Super Bowl performance has shown, Madonna is seldom allowed to forget her age or the fact that she is a mother, although now no longer a wife. In a BBC review of *MDNA*, available on Amazon, Nick Levine describes the opening song as 'a fairly charmless genero-banger called Girls Gone Wild[40] on which this 53-year-old mother-of-four trills: "You got me in the zone/DJ play my favourite song"'.[41]

---

[36] *Swept Away* was directed by Ritchie. Madonna's first children's book was *The English Roses* (London: Puffin, 2003). It was followed by several more in the series. For a typical review, see Kate Kellaway, 'Immaterial Girl', *The Observer*, 21 September 2003, accessed 17 April 2014, http://www.theguardian.com/books/2003/sep/21/booksforchildrenandteenagers.madonna.

[37] Lucy O'Brien, *She Bop: The Definitive History of Women in Rock, Pop and Soul* (London: Penguin, 1996). A revised and expanded edition was published as *She Bop II* in 2003 and a further expanded third edition as *She Bop: The Definitive History of Women in Popular Music* in 2012.

[38] Lucy O'Brien, *Madonna: Like An Icon* (London: Bantam, 2007), 15.

[39] O'Brien, *Madonna*, 474.

[40] The track is in fact called 'Girl Gone Wild'.

[41] Nick Levine, review of *MDNA*, amazon.co.uk, accessed 3 September 2012, http://www.amazon.co.uk/MDNA-Madonna/dp/product-description/B007FOV0QW/ref=dp_pro

Women are quick to join in. In March 2012, under the heading 'Oh, Madge! The Bottom Line is No Woman Over 50 Should Really be Wearing Fishnets', journalist Liz Jones, 54 herself, wrote in the *Daily Mail*:

> For a 53-year-old woman to play the fashionable sex kitten is a bit sad, to be honest. I'm embarrassed for Madonna — she is letting the side down. Memo to the postmenopausal: forget the fashion mantra of only exposing one erogenous zone at a time. After 50 you have no erogenous zones. Accept it. Move on. Cover up.[42]

Other women can be more generous. The considerably younger journalist Meghan Casserly, a staff writer for the online magazine *ForbesWoman*, sees Madonna as an inspiration. Referring to the video for 'Girl Gone Wild' Casserly writes:

> Madonna reclaimed her title as the best 'half naked exhibitionist diva in town,' making Gaga's reign seem a mere blip. (Let's revisit Gaga after she's married, mothered her soccer team-sized family and is facing or passing menopause.) But how, how, I ask, is a woman in midlife still making headlines for being the hottest thing in town? Is she the living, breathing embodiment of the Margaret Meade quote: 'There is no greater power in the world than the zest of a post-menopausal woman.'[43]

Madonna has long attracted much attention from academics as well as the popular print and online media. In an article on her later videos, but written before the video for 'Girl Gone Wild', Paul Watson and Diane Railton agree that in recent videos (such as 'Jump', '4 Seconds' or 'Give it 2 me') she 'appears eternally youthful, literally untouched by the so-called ravages of time' but they see this as something positive and argue that 'Madonna is re-authoring gendered scripts of ageing in a way that presents a challenge to discourses of attractive older femininity' and that by continuing to offer 'scandalous desire' her 'later videos might contain her most radical rebellion yet'.[44] In her essay 'Madonna: Like a Crone', Lucy O'Brien suggests that as an older artist, Madonna has the opportunity 'to reshape the music industry for years to come' but cannot yet offer evidence that she has started to do so.[45]

---

ddesc_0?ie=UTF8&n=229816&s=music.
[42] Liz Jones, 'Oh, Madge! The Bottom Line is No Woman Over 50 Should Really be Wearing Fishnets', *Mail Online*, 27 March 2012, accessed 3 September 2012, http://www.dailymail.co.uk/femail/article-2120876/Madonna-Bottom-line-woman-50-really-wearing-fishnets.html.
[43] Meghan Casserly, 'Madonna's Mighty Menopausal Comeback', *Forbes*, 27 March 2012, accessed 3 September 2012, http://www.forbes.com/sites/meghancasserly/2012/03/27/madonnas-mighty-menopausal-comeback-still-sexy-or-still-selling-sex/.
[44] Watson and Railton, 'Rebel without a Pause', 151.
[45] Lucy O'Brien, 'Madonna: Like a Crone', in Jennings and Gardner, *'Rock On'*, 31.

I cannot agree that Madonna's later videos offer the viewer a rebellious vision of ageing femininity. I have no problem with Madonna doing what she has always done – and elements of the video for 'Girl Gone Wild' are little more than insipid echoes of the far more audacious and innovative video for 'Justify my Love' (1990), itself a more inventive song. But it is disturbing to me that in the more than twenty years that divide the two songs and videos, Madonna does not appear to have aged at all. A combination of yoga, surgery, Botox and airbrushing have kept her looking unnaturally 'young'. Her face is as frozen as her music. To me it is a problem that a woman who is probably the most prominent older woman in the music industry does not wear her age on her face or continue to grow musically. In 2007, O'Brien wondered about Madonna: 'In her fifties will she still be trying to defeat the aging process? Or will she go within and explore something more artistically radical, as did her dance icon Martha Graham who at the age of fifty choreographed *Herodiade*, one of her most powerful pieces.'[46] Sadly, we are still waiting for Madonna's *Herodiade*.

Madonna is of course not alone in her refusal to age. Slightly younger pop performer Kylie Minogue (b. 1968) is approaching her fifties with a remarkably similar celebration of a lithe, adolescent-like body and little change to her bubble-gum pop sound, despite a new collaboration with singer-songwriter Sia Furley for her twelfth studio album, *Kiss Me Once* (2014), and a claim to be searching for something 'new': 'I felt like I needed a new landscape ... So far the support has been great, and it's just another part of this amalgamation of "new" that I had wished for and was struck by.'[47] The video for the song 'Sexercise' shows Kylie working out in a white leotard and high red stilettos, her singing voice as treated as her body.

Madonna and Kylie are both primarily performers and entertainers working within the field of pop music. A musician who, like Armatrading, works in a somewhat different musical field is Canadian singer-songwriter Joni Mitchell (b. 1943). Mitchell is a hugely influential and important musical force and a compelling performer, who retained her trademark long blonde hair into her fifties and sixties. Her debut album, *Song to a Seagull*, was released in 1968 and in the 1970s she moved through the starkly personal *Blue* (1971) to the beginnings of a jazz-fusion language on albums such as *Hejira* (1976) and *Mingus* (1979).[48] The 1980s, when Mitchell was in her forties, was a difficult decade. The albums

---

[46] O'Brien, *Madonna*, 480.
[47] Andrew Hampp, 'Kylie Minogue's Comeback "Kiss": Pop Star Finds New Life with Sia, Pharrell & Roc Nation', *Billboard*, 28 February 2014, accessed 17 April 2014, http://www.billboard.com/articles/columns/pop-shop/5922959/kylie-minogues-comeback-kiss-pop-star-finds-new-life-with-sia.
[48] On Mitchell, see Lloyd Whitesell, *The Music of Joni Mitchell* (New York: Oxford University Press, 2008); Karen O'Brien, *Joni Mitchell: Shadows and Light* (London: Virgin, 2001).

she released were more rock driven and not particularly well received. Facing ill health and litigation, she herself has described the decade as 'kind of hard on me'.[49]

In 1994, the year after she turned 50, Mitchell released what many regarded as a comeback album, *Turbulent Indigo*. This is certainly a collection that looks back to the style of her earlier work, with powerful, deftly told commentaries on modern life. Interviewed that year by Giles Smith for *The Independent*, she told him:

> I'm going into my fifties as a female songwriter, and there aren't a lot of role models for this. But I'm a pioneering spirit. I come from pioneering stock. I realise we were the generation who said all people over 30 should be shot, but I'm not going to put my hair in a bun and wear black. I need to create a vital middle age.[50]

In an illuminating interview with Jody Denburg a few years later Mitchell explained that she hadn't anticipated the higher profile and recognition that followed *Turbulent Indigo*, stating, 'I felt that I had been doing good work for 20 some years and that it was not being recognized at all', before going on to talk about the music business and being middle-aged:

> The business is sick. And ... the genuinely gifted, such as myself, and there aren't a lot in any generation, being shunned from the airwaves in favor of tits-and-ass bubble gum kind of junk food is a tragedy. And there is no other arena for me to make music in. So I feel constantly in a position of injustice. There's a civil liberties thing here. Is it my chronological age? That should never be held against an artist. We're all going to grow middle-aged. We need middle-aged songs. I'm an unusual thing. I'm a viable voice. For some reason, even though I want to quit all the time, you know, I still have a driving wheel to do this thing.[51]

Continuing to be unhappy with the state of the music industry, in 2002 Mitchell issued what she claimed would be her last album – *Travelogue*, a collection of re-workings of earlier songs with lush orchestral accompaniments. Nevertheless five years later, in 2007, she issued *Shine*, an album of new material. She was driven

---

[49] Wally Brees, 'Jody Denberg's Conversation with Joni Mitchell', *Joni Mitchell Official Site*, 8 September 1998, accessed 3 September 2012, http://jonimitchell.com/library/view.cfm?id=1362.

[50] Giles Smith, 'Interview with Joni Mitchell', *The Independent*, 29 October 1994, accessed 3 September 2012, http://www.independent.co.uk/arts-entertainment/arts-the-everpopular-tortured-artist-effect-they-said-there-was-a-problem-with-the-voice-they-said-she-preferred-to-paint-these-days-but-finally-after-all-the-rumours-heres-a-new-joni-mitchell-album-giles-smith-talked-to-her-1445570.html.

[51] Brees, 'Denberg's Conversation with Joni Mitchell'.

to create this work – as well as the associated ballet – by recent developments in international politics, specifically the Iraq war.

Another woman always keen to reflect the current state of the world in her musical work and who moved beyond the musical world in her middle age is the singer-songwriter Patti Smith (b. 1946). Hailed as one of the original punk icons, Smith came to critical attention with her debut album *Horses* in 1975. But after a successful and critically acclaimed early career, she spent most of the 1980s in early retirement, living in the country and bringing up her children. In 1994 her husband died of a heart attack, the first in a stream of losses that included her brother and her long-time keyboard player. Two years later, in 1996, the year she turned 50, Smith released the album *Gone Again* and *The Patti Smith Masters*, a box set of her past work.[52] Michael Bracewell, writing in *The Guardian* that year, summarised the importance of this renaissance for many of her fans:

> Patti Smith was the high priestess of punk, an outlaw with God on her mind, who re-invented the role of women in rock. That was 20 years ago. Now, a 50-year-old widow with two children, she's found her voice again.[53]

In 2002 Smith released *Land (1975–2002)*, another compilation album. The following years saw new albums as well as diversification into writing (*Just Kids*, a memoir of her friendship with Robert Mapplethorpe)[54] and photography.[55] In 2012, at the age of 66, she issued *Banga*, her first collection of new material since *Trampin'* (2004).

Smith is an important icon for many women. Sara Bran, who describes herself as 'copywriter, ghostwriter and social media thingy', wrote an article for the *Huffington Post* in 2011 entitled 'The Empress's Old Clothes: On Why Every Ageing Woman Needs Patti Smith'. She describes decluttering her attic and coming across a suitcase of her old clothes, which leads to a meditation on midlife in which she writes:

> If it had a soundtrack, midlife would be accompanied by the juddering strings of a suspense thriller or perhaps the ghostly crackle and bleep of one of those creepy satellite dishes listening for life on Mars. 'Is there life over 50?' The message is sent out across the universe and if you listen hard enough you can

---

[52] Smith has not been as well served as Mitchell in terms of monographs or biographies but see Nick Johnstone, *Patti Smith* (London: Omnibus, 1997, revised edn, 2012) or Patti Smith, *Just Kids* (London: Bloomsbury, 2010).
[53] Michael Bracewell, 'Woman as Warrior', *The Guardian* (weekend supplement), 22 June 1996.
[54] Patti Smith, *Just Kids* (London: Bloomsbury, 2010).
[55] Smith had been taking photographs since the 1960s but only started exhibiting and publishing her photographic work in the twenty-first century. See Susan Lubowsky Talbott and Erin Monroe, *Patti Smith – Camera Solo* (New Haven: Yale University Press, 2012).

hear the whispers of invisible older women answering, 'Yes, don't be scared.' But that's my point, I can't bloody hear them so I don't want to throw the old me into the Oxfam bags yet. Where have all my cultural icons gone? Where are the amazing sisters who will pull me through the next phase of my life? Where are the older women who have survived motherhood (yes, it is a question of survival) AND the menopausal storm without resorting to surgery and its demeaning ugly sisters Botox and Microdermabrasion?

As I reached the bottom of the Dreadful Suitcase of Hell, I realized that Patti Smith is the only woman I could think of who can guide me now. She found her voice again at 50 and released a violent warrior of an album in the wake of her midlife fury. And so, with Patti on the CD player I finally found myself able to bag up the past and send it to the charity shop.[56]

It is important to Bran, to me and to countless others that we can find creative role models who are older women. In his fascinating posthumous book *On Late Style* (2006), Edward Said discusses how artistic lateness, rather than the wisdom, harmony and acceptance it seems to bring for some writers and musicians can be instead a period of 'intransigence, difficult and unresolved contradiction'.[57] But all the examples Said gives are men; his musicians are Mozart, Beethoven, Richard Strauss, Benjamin Britten and Glenn Gould. There is obviously much to learn from men but to me this – like so much in our society and culture – becomes something only half told. From Smyth to Smith, most of the women I have discussed in this chapter can certainly be seen as intransigent and difficult as well as being, in Jacqueline Zita's words 'old, wise and furiously heretical'.[58]

There are, of course, many more women working or who have worked in various fields of music whose lives and work after or approaching the pivotal age of 50 are ripe for exploration: Tori Amos (b. 1963), Kate Bush (b. 1958), Diamanda Gallas (b. 1955), Kim Gordon (b. 1953), Chrissie Hynde (b. 1951), and many, many others. Certain musical genres, such as Country or Jazz and Blues, may seem to offer the older woman a degree of respect that is lacking in others. But most successful women in these genres stay firmly within the boundaries and stereotypes expected of them. Country music enthusiasts, for example, delight in the longevity of Dolly Parton (b. 1946), who reassuringly sings of 'my man' and in her sixties has a face, hair and body even more frozen in time than Madonna.[59] But these fans were quick to recoil from the sexual and gender ambiguity of k.d. lang (b. 1961). Lang, now in her sixth decade, continues to perform, record

---

[56] Sara Bran, 'The Empress's Old Clothes: On Why Every Ageing Woman Needs Patti Smith', *The Huffington Post*, 10 August 2011, accessed 3 September 2012, http://www.huffingtonpost.co.uk/sara-bran/the-empresss-old-clothes-_b_922973.html.

[57] Edward Said, *On Late Style* (London: Bloomsbury, 2006), 7.

[58] Zita, 'Heresy in the Female Body', 110.

[59] See Dolly Parton's website: http://www.dollyparton.com.

and refuse to conform. In early 2014 she branched out by making her Broadway debut, wearing a beautifully tailored suit, in the musical *After Midnight*.[60]

There is so much to relish in the work of older women who have shown us their different ways of ageing. I hear the bold voice of Joni Mitchell at her 70th birthday tribute concert and see the defiantly long grey hair of Patti Smith as she sings 'This is the girl', her tribute to Amy Winehouse – a talented woman who will never have the chance to age.[61] Maybe what Grace Williams had somewhere in the back of her mind with her strange use of the word 'revolting' to describe a 50-year old woman creating a symphony was the other meaning of that word – someone in the act of leading a revolt, of rebelling – of indeed being fiercely, ferociously and unapologetically heretical.

---

[60] Elisabeth Vincentelli, 'Sassy, Gender-bending Twist to "After Midnight" from k.d. lang', *New York Post*, 14 February 2014, accessed 22 April 2014, http://nypost.com/2014/02/14/k-d-lang-adds-saucy-gender-bending-twist-to-after-midnight/.

[61] Both performances available on YouTube, accessed 22 April 2013: 'Joni Mitchell sings at Massey Hall – 70th Birthday concert June 18, 2013', http://www.youtube.com/watch?v=XdpTGFZSgfA; 'Patti Smith debuts "This Is The Girl" Winehouse tribute, NYC, 5/13/1', http://www.youtube.com/watch?v=OOrhXVJ7JoA.

PART I
Performing Identity in Early European Musical Culture

PART I

Chapter 2

Noblewomen and Music in Italy, c. 1430–1520: Looking Past Isabella

Tim Shephard

The scholarly discussion of musical women at the courts of Renaissance Italy in the period c. 1430–1520 has thus far been dominated by the figure of Isabella d'Este, the eldest daughter of the Duke and Duchess of Ferrara who, at the age of 16, married the ruler of the neighbouring state of Mantua. From the 1490s on, Isabella kept at her court professional musicians proficient in setting Italian amatory verse to music, and she corresponded extensively with noble poets from across Italy who hoped she would distinguish their Petrarch-inspired literary efforts by singing them herself.[1] Isabella's case, however, is counter-exemplary: there is no other Italian noblewoman of the fifteenth or early sixteenth centuries who made so much noise about her passion for music, or is known to have patronised it on a comparable scale. In this chapter I will attempt very briefly to sketch out what might be a more normative view of noblewomen's musicianship in Italy, using sources from the period c. 1430–1520.[2]

Commentators on Italian song c. 1500 often identified women not as performers of music, but as its ideal listeners – specifically, as the characteristic audience for performances of love songs given by men. Writing just before 1500, the literato Calmeta (Vincenzo Colli) – who had served as secretary to Isabella's sister Beatrice, the Duchess of Milan – noted in a treatise on vernacular poetics that

---

[1] See in particular William Prizer, 'Isabella d'Este and Lucrezia Borgia as Patrons of Music: The Frottola at Mantua and Ferrara', *Journal of the American Musicological Society* 38 (1985); and Prizer, 'Una "Virtù Molto Conveniente a Madonne": Isabella d'Este as a Musician', *Journal of Musicology* 17 (1999).

[2] Four important studies have already 'looked beyond Isabella', all with a different focus to this chapter: Howard Mayer Brown, 'Women Singers and Women's Songs in Fifteenth-Century Italy', in *Women Making Music: the Western Art Tradition, 1150-1950*, ed. Jane Bowers and Judith Tick (Urbana: University of Illinois Press, 1986); Stefano Lorenzetti, '"Quel celeste cantar che mi disface": Immagine della donna ed educazione alla musica nell'ideale pedagogico del rinascimento italiano', *Studi musicali* 23 (1994); Judith Bryce, 'Performing for Strangers: Women, Dance, and Music in Quattrocento Florence', *Renaissance Quarterly* 54 (2001); and Bonnie J. Blackburn, 'Anna Inglese and Other Women Singers in the Fifteenth Century: Gleanings from the Sforza Archives', in *Sleuthing the Muse: Essays in Honour of William Prizer*, ed. Kristine K. Forney and Jeremy L. Smith (Hillsdale, NY: Pendragon, 2012).

some, 'taking delight in the art of song, will desire with greatly ornamented song to gratify their women, and in this music will insert amorous words'.[3] Similarly, a few years later the Mantuan nobleman Baldassare Castiglione commented in his famous treatise on the courtier that music was of great value as recreation, especially at court, where 'many things are done to please the ladies, whose tender and gentle souls are very susceptible to harmony and sweetness'.[4]

Calmeta's comment appears in the course of explaining a threefold hierarchy of poetry: melismatic love song for the enjoyment of women occupies the lowest rank; more elegant verse sung in a restrained style takes the middle ground, pleasing both lovers and the erudite; and the top rung is occupied by 'more elevated' (*più elevato*) verse in a 'grandiloquent style' (*stile grandiloquo*) exemplified by Dante – presumably, therefore, epic verse treating heroic topics, which in Renaissance Italy was recited musically rather than sung as such.[5] This hierarchy embodies a gendering of music that can be found very commonly in Renaissance Italy, and also in some of the most popular and widely read ancient texts. Quintilian, working to justify his decision to give music a place in the education of the orator, explained that he eschewed the lascivious music of the theatres, which he felt was effeminising his contemporaries, but approved of 'the music of old which was employed to sing the praises of brave men and was sung by the brave themselves'.[6] Pier Paolo Vergerio, in one of the foundational treatises on education for fifteenth-century Italy, echoed exactly these points to justify his own treatment of music: 'it was once a celebrated fact among the archaic heroes that Homer depicted Achilles withdrawing from battle and resting this way – singing praises of mighty men, to be sure, not love songs.'[7] A century later, Castiglione elaborated this distinction at length in his book on the courtier. One of his disputants, Gaspare, rejects music on

---

[3] 'Saranno alcuni altri i quali, dilettandosi d'arte di canto, disiderano col cantar, massimamente diminuito, gratificar la sua donna, e in quella musica parole amorose inferire.' Calmeta, *Qual stile tra' volgari poeti sia da imitare*, in Calmeta, *Prose e lettere edite e inedite*, ed. Cecil Grayson (Bologna: Commissione per i testi di lingua, 1959), 21. Translations are mine if not otherwise credited.

[4] 'molte cose si fanno per satisfar alle donne, gli animi delle quali, teneri e molli, facilmente sono dall'armonia penetrati e di dolcezza ripieni.' Baldassare Castiglione, *Il cortegiano, con una scelta delle opere minore*, ed. Bruno Maier (Torino: UTET, 1955), 168; Castiglione, *The Book of the Courtier*, trans. George Bull (London: Penguin, 1967), 94.

[5] Calmeta, *Prose e lettere*, ed. Grayson, 21–3. On the practice of reciting epic verse, see Elena Abramov-van Rijk, *Parlar Cantando: The Practice of Reciting Verses in Italy from 1300 to 1600* (Bern: Peter Lang, 2009).

[6] *Institutio oratoria* I.x.31. H. E. Butler, trans., *The Institutio Oratoria of Quintilian* (London: Heinemann, 1920), 175.

[7] 'et fuit quondam prescis heroibus celebre, ut Achillem Homerus inducit a pugna redeuntem in hac re solitum acquiescere, non quidem amatorias cantiones, sed virorum fortium laudes modulantem.' Vergerio, *De ingenuis moribus et liberalibus adulescentiae studiis liber*, in Craig W. Kallendorf, ed. and trans., *Humanist Educational Treatises* (Cambridge, MA: Harvard University Press, 2002), 84–7.

the grounds that it is effeminate, 'certainly very suited to women ... but not to real men'.[8] In response, Count Lodovico Canossa reels off a list of the ancient heroes and commanders who were known to have enjoyed music. Here and elsewhere in Renaissance Italy, love song is paradigmatically associated with effeminacy and women, while 'heroic' song is associated with military virtue and men.

While this distinction helped to clarify the case for the virtuous masculine exercise of musical interests, it left women in a more conflicted position. Musical commentators throughout the fifteenth century claimed repeatedly that 'lascivious' song served to break down the barricades of women's chastity and facilitate seduction. The Florentine scholar Poggio Bracciolini told a story, in his book of *Facetiae*, about a man whose beautiful wife attracted a following of local men. The 'lascivious crowd' (*lascivientium turba*) of suitors 'serenaded' (*serenatas*) her at night from the street beneath the conjugal bedroom window, until one night, the man being awakened by 'the sound of their trumpets' (*tubarum cantu* – a phallic *double entendre* is probably intended), he discouraged them by displaying his impressively large penis at the window.[9] A few decades later, in a treatise dedicated to Beatrice d'Aragona, daughter of his employer the King of Naples, the musician and music theorist Johannes Tinctoris noted that music has the effect of 'attracting love' (*amorem allicere*), and quoted Ovid's *Ars Amatoria* in support of the claim: '"Song is seductive: girls should learn to sing (her voice,/And not her face, has many a girl's procuress been).'"[10] A few decades on again Calmeta, in his *vita* of the nobleman-*improvisatore* Serafino de' Cimminelli (Aquilano) published in 1504, noted that while at the court of Lodovico Sforza and Beatrice d'Este in Milan Serafino used his music to pursue another man's wife – a 'woman of questionable virtue' (*donna di mediocre onestà*) who was, incidentally, 'a very sweet singer' (*molto soave cantatrice*).[11] Later in the *vita* he ascribed Serafino's interest in sonnets partly to the same motive: 'Seeing that amorous sonnets were prized, and thinking either that his facility would well enable him to follow that style or that he could with it better enflame the breasts of beautiful young women,

---

[8] 'La musica penso ... che insieme con molte altre vanità sia alle donne conveniente sí, e forse ancor ad alcuni che hanno similitudine d'omini, ma non a quelli che veramente sono; i quali non deono con delizie effeminare gli animi.' Castiglione, *Il Cortegiano*, ed. Maier, 168–9; Castiglione, *Book of the Courtier*, trans. Bull, 94.

[9] Poggius Bracciolini, *Opera Omnia*, 4 vols (Turin: Bottega d'Erasmo, 1964), 1: 483.

[10] 'Unde Ovidius puellis amorem virorum allicere cupientibus praecipit ut cantare discant. Enimvero in tertio libro *De arte amandi* sic inquit: *Res est blanda canor: discant cantare puellae/(Pro facie multis vox sua lena fuit).*' Tinctoris, *Complexus effectuum musices*, in J. Donald Cullington, ed. and trans., with Reinhard Strohm, *'That liberal and virtuous art': Three Humanist Treatises on Music* (Newtownabbey: University of Ulster, 2001), 81 and 64.

[11] Calmeta, *Vita del facondo poeta vulgare Serafino Aquilano*, in Calmeta, *Prose e lettere*, ed. Grayson, 63.

Serafino decided to try his hand at some such sonnets.'[12] These represent but a tiny sample of the available examples.[13]

The idea that women were the most receptive audience for 'effeminate' love songs, and that at the same time such 'lascivious' songs were capable of prompting illicit liaisons, was obviously in tension with the requirement that women remain chaste both before and during marriage. The importance of chastity to the noblewomen of Renaissance Italy cannot be overstated, and the responsibility for upholding it fell squarely on women's shoulders. Castiglione noted with regret that 'we ourselves, as men, have made it a rule that a dissolute way of life is not to be thought evil or blameworthy or disgraceful, whereas in women it leads to such complete opprobrium and shame that once a woman has been spoken ill of, whether the accusation be true or false, she is utterly disgraced for ever'.[14] In recognition of this dissonance, Quintilian asserted that lascivious music, although 'effeminate', was inappropriate 'for the use of a modest girl'.[15] His view was commonplace in Renaissance Italy. For example, in 1505 or shortly after, the Duchess of Ferrara, Lucrezia Borgia, had a portrait medal made, the reverse of which shows Cupid blindfolded and bound to a tree, his bow and arrows and a collection of musical instruments discarded behind him, all encircled by the motto 'Modesty evident in virtue and beauty is most precious'.[16] Here music is numbered among the tools of Cupid, who has been overcome by the noblewoman's exemplary modesty.

---

[12] 'vedendo lui li amorosi sonetti allora essere in pregio, di essercitarsi alquanto in quelli prese deliberazione e tutto ad emulare al Tebaldeo, ingenioso poeta, se dispose, o fusse che meglio quello stile per la facilità li paresse de potere conseguire, o vero parendoli che ad incendere li teneri petti de leggiadre giovenette più fusse accomodato.' Calmeta, *Prose e lettere*, ed. Grayson, 69; trans. Gary Tomlinson in Oliver Strunk and Leo Treitler, eds, *Source Readings in Music History*, rev. edn (New York: Norton, 1998), 324.

[13] For further examples, see Flora Dennis, 'Unlocking the Gates of Chastity: Music and the Erotic in the Domestic Sphere in Fifteenth and Sixteenth-century Italy', in *Erotic Cultures of Renaissance Italy*, ed. Sara F. Matthews-Grieco (Farnham: Ashgate, 2010).

[14] 'noi stessi avemo fatta una legge, che in noi non sia vicio né mancamento né infamia alcuna la vita dissoluta e nelle donne sia tanto estremo obbrobrio e vergogna, che quella di chi una volta si parla male, o falsa o vera che sia la calunnia che se le dà, sia per sempre vituperata.' Castiglione, *Il Cortegiano*, ed. Maier, 322; Castiglione, *Book of the Courtier*, trans. Bull, 195.

[15] *Institutio oratoria* I.x.31. Butler, trans., *Institutio Oratoria*, 175.

[16] VIRTUTI AC FORMAE PVDICITIA PRAECIOSISSIMVM. On this medal, see George Francis Hill, *A Corpus of Italian Medals of the Renaissance Before Cellini*, 2 vols (Florence: Studio per edizioni scelte, 1984; orig. London: British Museum, 1930), 1: 58–9; and Kari Lawe, 'La medaglia dell'Amorino bendato: uno studio su una delle medaglie di Lucrezia Borgia', in *The Court of Ferrara and its Patronage, 1441–1598*, ed. Marianne Pade, Lene Wange Petersen and Daniela Quarta (Copenhagen: Copenhagen University, 1990). On Lucrezia's musical activities, see Prizer, 'Isabella d'Este and Lucrezia Borgia', 2–13.

Nonetheless, noblewomen certainly did make music at the Italian courts, and they did both sing and listen to love song. To do so without inviting censure, their musicianship had to be wrapped up in packaging that asserted their modesty (and thus their chastity). Partly this was a question of the manner of performance: Castiglione advised women to engage in music 'very circumspectly', and if they must perform to wait to be 'coaxed a little, [beginning] with a certain shyness, suggesting the dignified modesty that brazen women cannot understand'.[17] He went on to note that a woman performing music or dance should 'wear clothes that do not make her seem vain and frivolous'.[18] I have argued at length elsewhere that another element of the packaging could be the visual environment in which women's musical performances took place – carefully chosen decorations could assert a noblewoman's virtue in general terms, or even suggest virtuous readings for her musicianship specifically.[19]

A critically important aspect of the virtuous presentation of women's musicianship – and one that required the cooperation of the audience – consisted in its description after the event in correspondence, treatises and poems. Here several overlapping strategies were common: a writer could assert a female musician's virtue, honour or innocence outright; he could establish her virtue indirectly by noting her superior beauty, drawing on the common contemporary understanding of beauty as the exterior manifestation of virtue;[20] or he could sacralise her musicianship by configuring it as angelic. Reporting to the Marchesa of Mantua, Barbara of Brandenburg, on musical performances given by a daughter of the leading house of Florence, Bianca de' Medici, for the entertainment of Pope Pius II in 1460, Teodoro da Montefeltro noted that Bianca and her companions were 'as lovely an angels in paradise' (*como anzeli di paradisso*), that Bianca herself was 'well-formed' (*ben formata*) and was known locally as 'the beautiful Bianca' (*la bella Biancha*), and he described the song she played on the organ as 'angelic' (*un canto angelico*).[21] Recommending Anna Inglese – the only professional female

---

[17] 'faccia con riguardo, e con quella molle delicatura che avemo detto convenirsele ... quando ella viene a danzar o far musica di che sorte si sia, deve indurvisi con lassarene alquanto pregare, e con una certa timidità, che mostri quella nobile vergogna che è contraria della imprudenzia.' Castiglione, *Il Cortegiano*, ed. Maier, 347–8; Castiglione, *Book of the Courtier*, trans. Bull, 215.

[18] 'Deve ... vestirsi di sorte, che non paia vana e leggier.' Castiglione, *Il Cortegiano*, ed. Maier, 348; Castiglione, *Book of the Courtier*, trans. Bull, 215.

[19] Tim Shephard, 'Constructing Isabella d'Este's Musical Decorum in the Visual Sphere', *Renaissance Studies* 25 (2011).

[20] See, for example, Luke Syson and Dora Thornton, *Objects of Virtue: Art in Renaissance Italy* (London: British Museum Press, 2001), 51–6; and Kirsten Kennedy, 'Protecting the Body, Portraying the Soul', in *Medieval and Renaissance Art: People and Possessions*, ed. Glyn Davies and Kirsten Kennedy (London: V&A Publishing, 2009), 246–50.

[21] Translation and transcription of this letter published in William Prizer, 'Games of Venus: Secular Music in the Late Quattrocento and Early Cinquecento', *Journal of*

musician known to have worked in Italy in the fifteenth century – Marchese Guglielmo Paleologo VIII of Monferrato assured the Duke of Milan in 1468 that she was 'a very honourable person' (*persona honorevole*).[22] Reporting to the Duchess of Milan on her daughter Ippolita Sforza's activities in Naples, the dancing master Ambrosio noted in 1470 that Ippolita's new father-in-law, the King of Naples, found listening to her sing to be 'like Paradise'.[23] In the prologue to his volume of *Triumphi* commemorating his recently deceased employer Beatrice d'Este, Calmeta noted that 'She was a lady of letters, music, sound [probably instrumental performance], and of all the other best-loved virtuous exercises', and then recalled that in transacting matters of state she rose above her sex to display almost masculine virtue.[24]

Alongside assertions of the innocent and virtuous nature of noblewomen's musical activities, efforts were made to reconfigure the topic of love itself as not licentious but virtuous and even divine. In offering first to Beatrice d'Este and then to Bianca Maria Sforza the same book of amorous verse, the Sforza court poet Gasparo Visconti found it necessary to devote the entire dedication to a defence of Love, which he acknowledged to be under attack on religious, philosophical and moral grounds. His first point in Love's defence was that amorous song could be found in the Old Testament, in the form of the *Song of Songs*, in which context licentious content is understood not literally, but tropologically – the implication is that his own amorous verse should similarly be understood as expressing virtuous sentiments indirectly.[25] Further on in the dedication he argued that Love (*Amor*) is to be identified with the Christian virtue Charity (*Carità*).

Musicology 9 (1991): 3–4 and 53–4.

[22] Translation and transcription of this letter published in Blackburn, 'Anna Inglese and Other Women Singers', 238 and 250.

[23] 'La Maesta de Re non ave altro piacere nei altro paradiso non parel che trove se non quando la vede danzare e anche canthare.' Eileen Southern, 'A Prima Ballerina of the Fifteenth Century', in *Music and Context: Essays for John M. Ward*, ed. Anne Dhu Shapiro (Cambridge, MA: Department of Music, Harvard University, 1985), 192.

[24] 'Fu donna de littere, musica, sòno e d'ogni altro exercizio virtuoso amantissima, e ne le cose de lo stato sopra el sexo e l'età, de toleranzia virile.' Calmeta, *Triumphi*, ed. Rossella Guberti (Bologna: Commissione per i Testi di Lingua, 2004), 3. On Beatrice's musical activities, see William F. Prizer, 'Music at the Court of the Sforza: The Birth and Death of a Musical Centre', *Musica Disciplina* 43 (1989): 173–4 and 182; and Paul A. Merkley and Lora L. M. Merkley, *Music and Patronage in the Sforza Court* (Turnhout: Brepols, 1999), 414–18 and 421–3.

[25] 'E primamente se per teologia si vol questo concepto mantenere, dico che una de le non inferior parte che in la prefata teologia si contene, qual è tutto il Vechi Testamento, seria di necessità gettar da canto, ove non solamente è tractato de amoroso stile, come si vede ne la *Cantica dei cantici*, ma di sentenzie poco oneste, a chi litteralmente, obmesso il tropologico senso, la volesse interpretare.' Gasparo Visconti, *I Canzonieri per Beatrice d'Este e per Bianca Maria Sforza*, ed. Paolo Bongrani (Milan: Il saggiatore, 1979), 4.

These strategies of reception are brought together and elaborated in a poem dating to shortly before 1500 by Pietro Bembo, later printed in a revised version in 1535, in which he describes seeing 'his' lady singing with friends in a meadow.[26] She is a 'lovely and innocent little angel' (*leggiadra e candida angioletta*) and her friends are 'honest and praiseworthy' (*onestade e pregio amiche*); on hearing them sing Bembo thinks he has been transported up to heaven (*mi parea pur su nel cielo*), until he realises that they are beautiful maidens. However, Bembo also plays with the moral ambivalence of the women's position, comparing their singing to that of the Sirens and acknowledging that in hearing the women's song he has been struck by Love's dart. A few years later, in his famous dialogue *Gli Asolani*, published in 1505, he would make a case for the divine virtue of love itself, much greater in its dimensions and much more sophisticated in its arguments than Visconti's.

As Bembo's poem implies, however, even when carefully and correctly packaged, women's musicianship remained morally ambiguous. The concerns were serious enough that some commentators preferred women to avoid secular music altogether. In a 1433 treatise on education, the Vatican administrator Maffeo Vegio admonished mothers to keep their daughters indoors, teaching them the habit of piety, and not to let them associate

> with unknown girls, above all with those who sport unusual hairstyles, who go out without a veil, who sprinkle themselves with rare perfumes, who adorn themselves with vanity, who are always in search of greater refinement and elegance, who embellish their hair and face with the rarest ointments ... who indulge in singing love songs with passion, so that your daughters do not follow their example, as the poet's license will become the girl's: A seductive thing is the song that girls learn to sing.[27]

Vegio's views in general betray the strong influence of the popular religious authority Bernardino da Siena, and Vegio's negative reading of music specifically is familiar from the Church Fathers. Among the letters of St Jerome are two addressing the education of girls in which advice is given on musical pastimes. In the letter to Laeta, Jerome calls for the soul of her daughter Paula to be denied 'knowledge of worldly songs' and to be nourished instead on 'sweet psalms'; Paula is to be kept innocent of all knowledge of musical instruments, and to learn

---

[26] Pietro Bembo, *Prose e rime*, ed. Carlo Dionisotti, 2nd edn (Turin: Unione Tipografico-Editrice, 1966), 518–19 (no. 16).

[27] 'ne extranearum puellarum habeant commercium, earum praecipuae quae calamistratae, quae dispalliatae incedunt, quae peregrinos olent odores, quae ambitiosius se ornantatque induunt, quae cultioris formae suae curiosiores videntur, quae exquisitoribus medicamentis fucant capillos et faciem ... quae amatoris cantibus cupidè indulgent, ne earum exemplo observare incipiant, quod a lascivo poeta lascivis puellis praecipitur: Res est blanda canor, discant cantare puellae.' Vegio, *De liberorum educatione*, in Lorenzetti, '"Quel celeste cantar che mi disface"', 245.

the Psalter for her entertainment.[28] In a letter advising Gaudentius on his daughter Pacatula, Jerome repeated the requirement that the girl 'learn the Psalter by heart', and warned that she must 'never look upon young men, never those with curled hair who with sweetness of voice wound the spirit through the ears'.[29]

It can hardly be doubted that noblewomen were aware of and sometimes shared these views, because these were exactly the texts they were brought up to read and trust. In a treatise on women's literary studies addressed to Battista da Montefeltro (whose husband was the Malatesta lord of Pesaro), the Florentine statesman Leonardo Bruni wrote that 'the Christian woman' should first and foremost 'yearn to acquire a knowledge of sacred letters', naming Augustine, Lactantius, Jerome, Ambrose and Cyprian as the best authors.[30] His advice tallies with surviving inventories of women's libraries: for example, as Duchess of Ferrara, Eleonora d'Aragona owned Augustine's *De immortalitate animae* and two volumes of Jerome, one of them in the vernacular, as well as many other types of religious text.[31] The association of noblewomen with piety and devotion in Renaissance Italy was paradigmatic, and evidence of female religiosity was received with unanimous praise. For ruling women in particular, it was partly through pious and charitable works that they lived out the public role expected of them by their subjects and their peers. Ruling women furnished their rooms with devotional objects, filled their libraries with religious books, personally oversaw the religious instruction of their children, regularly gave alms to the poor, visited holy women and founded and sponsored convents.[32] It is very likely that this religious dimension of noblewomen's lives shaped their engagement with music more than we have thus far realised. Eleonora d'Aragona, for example, features hardly at all in Lewis Lockwood's magisterial account of music at her husband's court;[33] but from the inventory of her library we learn that she owned three copies

---

[28] James McKinnon, ed., *Music in Early Christian Literature* (Cambridge: Cambridge University Press, 1987), 142.

[29] McKinnon, *Music in Early Christian Literature*, 144.

[30] 'Primum igitur sacrarum litterarum cognitionem sibi acquirere studeat christiana mulier.' Bruni, *De studiis et litteris liber ad Baptistam de Malatestis*, in Kallendorf, ed. and trans., *Humanist Educational Treatises*, 92–125, at 107.

[31] See the inventory of Eleonora's library published in Giulio Bertoni, *La Biblioteca Estense e la coltura Ferrarese ai tempi del duca Ercole primo (1471–1505)* (Turin: Loescher, 1903), 229–33, items 14, 32 and 37.

[32] See, for example, Werner L. Gundersheimer, 'Women, Learning and Power: Eleonora of Aragon and the Court of Ferrara', in *Beyond their Sex: Learned Women of the European Past*, ed. Patricia Labalme (New York: New York University Press, 1984); Evelyn Welch, 'The Art of Expenditure: The Court of Paola Malatesta Gonzaga in Fifteenth-century Mantua', *Renaissance Studies* 16 (2002); and Diane Yvonne Ghirardo, 'Lucrezia Borgia's Palace in Renaissance Ferrara', *Journal of the Society of Architectural Historians* 64 (2005).

[33] Lewis Lockwood, *Music in Renaissance Ferrara 1400–1505: The Creation of a Musical Centre in the Fifteenth Century* (Oxford: Oxford University Press, 1984).

of the Psalms (one of them an abridged vernacular translation),[34] which following Jerome's advice she may have sung often, and two books of Marian laude which she very likely also sang.[35] Upon her death in 1493, a Ferrarese chronicler described her recent mode of life with great approval: 'she stayed in the monastery of the nuns [the Franciscan convent of Corpus Domini, which she sponsored], and eschewed dances and songs and festivities.'[36]

If music was sometimes rejected from the education of girls, it was usually accepted into the education of boys – albeit often with the stipulation that they steer clear of love songs. Here the rationale draws on a very ancient association of music with moral training. Castiglione noted that

> Plato and Aristotle insist that a well-educated man should also be a musician; and with innumerable arguments they show that music exerts a powerful influence on us, and, for many reasons that would take too long to explain, they say that it has to be learned in childhood, not so much for the sake of its audible melodies but because of its capacity to breed good new habits and a virtuous disposition.[37]

He had in mind Book 3 of Plato's *Republic* and Book 8 of Aristotle's *Politics*, both of which treat music's role in education in considerable detail; and Castiglione had no doubt also encountered the same ideas repeated more briefly by Cicero and Quintilian, whose purchase among the literati in Renaissance Italy was immense. Plato and Aristotle built on the Pythagorean idea that musical harmony can be described in terms of proportion, and that the same proportional mathematical system underlies the organisation of both the heavens and the human soul. The relationship of similarity thus established between music and the soul could be used to explain its capacity to stir the emotions. Thus, Plato sought to establish which

---

[34] Bertoni, *La Biblioteca Estense*, 229–33, items 30, 33 and 34.

[35] Bertoni, *La Biblioteca Estense*, 229–33, items 71 and 72. On the cultivation and performance of laude by women, particularly in the context of Franciscan convents, see Patrick Macey, '"Infiamma il mio cor": Savonarolan *Laude* by and for Dominican Nuns in Tuscany', in *The Crannied Wall: Women, Religion, and the Arts in Early Modern Europe*, ed. Craig A. Monson (Ann Arbor: University of Michigan Press, 1992); and Macey, 'Filippo Salviati, Caterina de' Ricci, and Serafino Razzi: Patronage Practices for the Lauda and Madrigal at the Convent of S. Vincenzo in Prato', in *Cappelle musicali fra corte, stato e chiesa nell'Italia del Rinascimento*, ed. Franco Piperno, Gabriella Biagi Ravenni and Andrea Chegai (Florence: Leo S. Olschki, 2007).

[36] 'stava in li monasteri de Suore, et gli spiaceva li bali et canti et feste.' Luciano Chiappini, *Eleonora d'Aragona, prima duchessa di Ferrara* (Rovigo: S.T.E.R., 1956), 95.

[37] 'Platone ed Aristotele vogliono che l'om bene instituito sia ancor musico, e con infinite ragioni mostrano la forza della musica in noi essere grandissima, e per molte cause, che or saria lungo a dir, doversi necessariamente imparar da pueritia; non tanto per quella superficial melodia che si sente, ma per esser sufficiente ad indur in noi un novo abito bono ed un costume tendente alla virtù.' Castiglione, *Il Cortegiano*, ed. Maier, 169; Castiglione, *Book of the Courtier*, trans. Bull, 95.

musical modes stirred which emotions, and to reject from his system of education those modes whose effects upon the human soul he considered deleterious.

Music's role in education, according to this view, is through its ethical potency to shape the student's soul into the image and habit of virtue. In effect, then, expertise in music is the same as expertise in morality. For Plato, this expertise consists in soundness of judgement, the ability to tell the good from the bad: 'one who was properly educated in music ... would praise beautiful things and take delight in them and receive them into his soul to foster its growth and become himself beautiful and good. The ugly he would rightly disapprove of and hate.'[38] According to Quintilian, this happy outcome is, however, not the result of listening to 'psalteries and viols' but rather of 'knowledge of the principles of music, which have power to excite or assuage the emotions of mankind'.[39] These points exactly were taken up the Vatican administrator Paolo Cortese, writing on the musical diversions appropriate to the ideal cardinal:

> many agree to resort to it [music] as to a certain discipline that is engaged in the knowledge of concordance and modes ... it must be said that music must be sought after for the sake of morals, inasmuch as the habit of passing judgement on what is similar to morals in its rational basis cannot be considered to be different from the habit of passing judgement on the rational basis of morals themselves, and of becoming expert in this latter judgement through imitation.[40]

Although these arguments concerning music's role in education related to boys rather than girls, they provided another avenue through which women's musicianship could seek validation. If a woman could be said to have studied 'the principles of the art' – that is, to have acquired sufficient 'knowledge of concordance and mode' to exhibit sound musical 'judgement' – then her musicianship would amount to nothing less than expertise in morality, which could certainly be called a 'virtuous exercise'. This strategy is nowhere more in evidence than in Tinctoris' writings on the musicianship of Beatrice d'Aragona, the Neapolitan princess to whom he acted as music tutor. In the dedication of his dictionary of musical terms, compiled by 1475, he praised her for 'making judgement upon its [music's] every species, not merely through others, like the Kings of the Medes and the Persians,

---

[38] *The Republic* III.xii. Plato, *The Republic*, trans. Paul Shorey (London: Heinemann, 1930), 259.

[39] *Institutio oratoria* I.x.31. Butler, trans., *Institutio Oratoria*, 175.

[40] 'multi eam cantanque disciplinam quandam adhibendam esse volunt, que in symphonie modorumque cognitione versetur ... eodemque modo dicendum est, eam morum causa esse expetendam, siquidem consuescere de eo iudicare, quod simile morum rationi sit, nihil aliud videri potest quam consuescere de morum ratione iudicare, in eoque exerceri imitando.' Cortese, *De cardinalatu*, in Nino Pirrotta, 'Music and Cultural Tendencies in 15th-Century Italy', *Journal of the American Musicological Society* 19 (1966): 148 and 152 (Pirrotta's translation).

but also by yourself'.[41] In the first chapter of his treatise on mode completed in the following year, Tinctoris went further, incorporating praise of Beatrice's musicianship into an evaluation of the nature of mode. He begins by describing the system of mode then in use for plainchant, and contrasting it with Aristotle's discussion of mode in terms of ethos (or 'individual quality', in Tinctoris' terms). The question of ethos allows him to mention the influence of music on the soul, which appropriately he substantiates by quoting Augustine. This brings him on to note, along Aristotelian lines, the importance of musical expertise for the correct judgement of music – he lampoons contemporaries who cannot tell the difference between 'calflike bellowings' (*vitulinos mugitus*) and music that is 'rational' (*moderatis rationabilibus*) and 'angelic' (*angelicis cantibus*).[42] He then introduces Beatrice into the discussion. She has devoted herself 'most fervently to the study of this science [*scientiae*]', with the result that 'she delights more strongly not only by her song, but also by her judgement' (*non modo cantu et pronunciatione vehementius gaudeat*). Tinctoris encapsulates his compliment in a dual classicising comparison: Beatrice excels other women in majesty just as Diana (the famously chaste goddess) excels her nymphs, and she excels other women in music just as Calliope (the muse associated with epic – that is, heroic – poetry) excels the other muses.

Tellingly, Tinctoris introduced this celebration of Beatrice's musical judgement by quoting from Book 8 of Aristotle's *Politics*: '"The young should give themselves to the practice of the art of music so that, as old men, they can judge and enjoy it correctly."'[43] It was, he claimed, following 'the council of this philosopher of first authority' that Beatrice set out to study music. As Aristotle implies in the passage quoted by Tinctoris, the actual practice of music was acceptable in the young to breed good judgement, but should ideally be abandoned in adulthood. This precept – which, of course, concerns class more than it does gender – appears to have been widely accepted at the Italian courts, at least as far as public musical performance was concerned. A majority of references to women's amateur musical performance in public, at least until the 1520s, concern 'girls' (*fanciulle*) and 'damsels' (*donzelle* – meaning unmarried, chaste young women); often the reporter seems at pains to establish the performer's youth. When Duke René of Anjou visited the court of the Duke and Duchess of Milan in 1453, a 9-year-

---

[41] 'deductionem in omni suo genere per alios more principum Persarum atque medorum, sed etiam per teipsam assumens.' Johannes Tinctoris, *Dictionary of Musical Terms*, ed. and trans. Carl Parrish (London: Free Press of Glencoe, 1963), 2–3.

[42] *De natura et proprietate tonorum*, in Johannes Tinctoris, *Opera Theoretica*, ed. Albert Seay, 2 vols (Rome: American Institute of Musicology, 1975), 1: 65–104, at 69; Tinctoris, *Concerning the Nature and Propriety of Tones*, trans. Albert Seay, 2nd edn (Colorado Springs: Colorado College Music Press, 1976), 5.

[43] '"Iuvenes arti musicae operam dare ut senes effecti recte de ea iudicare gaudereque possint."' Tinctoris, *Opera Theoretica*, ed. Seay, 69; Tinctoris, *Concerning the Nature and Propriety of Tones*, trans. Seay, 5.

old Ippolita Sforza entertained him with singing.[44] Teodoro da Montefeltro, in his account of Bianca de' Medici's performance mentioned above, refers to her as 'damsel', reporting her age accurately to be 14 years, and refers to another woman who performed as a 'zovene' (youngster). In 1460 a young Galeazzo Maria Sforza reported to his mother on the singing of a 'damisella' in Bologna to entertain Pope Pius II, no doubt a daughter of a leading local family.[45]

Far from graduating into the public sphere, upon reaching adulthood – marked in most cases by marriage and motherhood – noblewomen took on a new range of responsibilities and ideals of conduct that kept them largely within the overlapping spheres of palace and church. Even ruling women who took an active role in the life of their state were generally visible to the local chroniclers only when getting married, giving birth, performing noteworthy acts of piety and dying; their husbands, meanwhile, appeared on almost every page.[46] A noblewoman's adulthood would be shaped to a very large extent by her marriage, and the significance of this fact for women's musicianship has yet to be fully understood. The role of the wife was the subject of a large and surprisingly coherent body of theory and comment.[47] Francesco Barbaro, a Venetian aristocrat whose popular treatise on wifely conduct was certainly read at the courts, named as the primary quality of a wife 'the faculty of obedience, which is her master and companion, because nothing more important, nothing greater can be demanded of a wife than this'.[48] According to Barbaro and others, a man had a right to exercise control over every aspect of his wife's person, including her manner, speech, apparel, diet, possessions and domestic arrangements. While such conservative attitudes might seem to sit better in the republican contexts of Venice and Florence, in fact they were repeated in marriage treatises written by and for courtly nobles.[49]

---

[44] Southern, 'A Prima Ballerina of the Fifteenth Century', 184–5.

[45] Blackburn, 'Anna Inglese and Other Women Singers', 245 and 251.

[46] This is the case, for example, for the Duchess of Ferrara, Lucrezia Borgia, in the chronicle that covers her reign: Giovanni Maria Zerbinati, *Croniche di Ferrara: quali comenzano del anno 1500 sino al 1527*, ed. Maria Giuseppina Muzzarelli (Ferrara: Deputazione Provinciale Ferrarese di Storia Patria, 1989).

[47] An excellent survey is Catherine E. King, *Renaissance Women Patrons: Wives and Widows in Italy c. 1300–1550* (Manchester: Manchester University Press, 1998), 22–9.

[48] 'de obsequendi facilitate, quae illius dux et comes est, nonnulla dixerimus, qua nihil gratius est, nihil magis expetitur.' Francesco Barbaro, *De re uxoria*, ed. Attilio Gnesotto (Padua: Tipografia Giov. Batt. Randi, 1915), 63; translation in Benjamin G. Kohl and Ronald G. Witt, eds and trans., *The Earthly Republic: Italian Humanists on Government and Society* (Philadelphia: University of Pennsylvania Press, 1978), 189–230, at 193. Barbaro's treatise was, for instance, in the library of the Este court in Ferrara – see Bertoni, *La Biblioteca Estense*, 239, no. 115.

[49] See, for example, Agostino Strozzi, *Defensio mulierum*, in Francesco Zambrini, *La Defensione delle Donne d'Autore Anonimo* (Bologna: Commissione per i testi di lingua, 1876), 121–53 (for the identification of the author see Conor Fahy, 'Three Early Renaissance Treatises on Women', *Italian Studies* 2 (1956): 40–44).

Their potential effects on women's musical activities are suggested by a letter of 1505 in which we learn that the lutenist-singer Bartolomeo Tromboncino will join the household of the Duchess of Ferrara, Lucrezia Borgia. Far from reflecting Lucrezia's own initiative, the letter makes it clear that Tromboncino was assigned to her staff at 'the wish of our lord the duke' as part of sweeping and unwelcome revisions to her household.[50]

For all that, it is undeniably the case that noblewomen did make music with pleasure and enjoyment in Renaissance Italy, and not only as girls. My purpose in this chapter has not been to argue that musical activities were impossible for Italian noblewomen, but to provide a counterbalance to the classic accounts of Isabella d'Este's enthusiastic and highly visible cultivation of vernacular love song. In practice, women's relationship with music was more ambivalent than the case of the celebrated marchesa would seem to imply – in fact, I have argued elsewhere that it was ambivalent even for Isabella herself.[51] Widely held, deeply ingrained ideas about music on the one hand, and about feminine conduct on the other, rendered women's involvement in music – and especially love song – at one and the same time both inevitable and profoundly problematic. This circumstance shaped the ways in which women performed music and also the ways in which their musicianship was described and understood. Meanwhile, noblewomen's almost unanimous investment in the religious sphere very likely brought with it musical experiences that scholars have yet to consider seriously.[52]

I would like to conclude by discussing a text in which many of the attitudes and mechanisms surrounding music that I have mentioned are put into play together with great subtlety and finesse: Bembo's dialogue on love, *Gli Asolani*, published in 1505 with a dedication to Lucrezia Borgia.[53] The scene is set in the castle of the Queen of Cyprus at Asolo in the Veneto, during the period of festivity following the marriage of one of the queen's ladies-in-waiting to a local nobleman. The story opens after dinner one day, as two 'charming girls' (*vaghe fanciulle*), after seeking the queen's blessing, entertain the company by singing to the lute: the first sings of the pains of love, the second of its joys. The queen then summons one of her own ladies-in-waiting (*sua damigiella* – her damsel) to respond with a song of her own. This third musician is evidently older than the two 'girls', and Bembo informs us that she is 'of exceptional beauty and indeed, in the opinion of all beholders, more beautiful than any other at the celebrations' – a quality which in itself establishes

---

[50] 'El pare, che la volunta del signore nostro duca siá, che.' The document is published in part in Prizer, 'Isabella d'Este and Lucrezia Borgia', 31, where this feature is not remarked upon.

[51] Shephard, 'Isabella d'Este's Musical Decorum'.

[52] For an exception, albeit one concerned with Isabella, see William Prizer, 'Laude di popolo, laude di corte: Some Thoughts on the Style and Function of the Renaissance Lauda', in *La Musica a Firenze al Tempo di Lorenzo il Magnifico*, ed. Piero Gargiulo (Florence: Leo S. Olschki, 1993).

[53] Bembo, *Prose e rime*, ed. Dionisotti, 313–504.

her superior virtue.[54] Of course, she cannot refuse the command of her queen, but, in proper fashion, she blushes at the idea of performing in public – something to which, Bembo assures us, she was unused. In her song, which is judged to be by far the best of the three, she reveals love to be a form of 'pure reason' (*raggio puro*) and 'virtue' (*virtute*), a 'straight and secure road' (*camin dritto e securo*) which would lead people from their present unfortunate state to 'the original beauty' (*la prima beltade*).[55] In this scenario, all three women are clearly identified as young and unmarried – the first two as children, the third as a young woman, designations that are maintained later in the text when their performances are mentioned by one of the protagonists. While the two girls are presented as equals, the third singer is established as in every respect their superior: she is older (but still young), more beautiful, more modest, a better musician and a wiser poet of love, able to explain through her song why her amorous subject matter is not only decorous, but virtuous. The queen, meanwhile, does not sing at all – as befits her age and her station – but rather exercises her judgement, clearly signalled by her decision to contrast the girls' performances with that of her own servant; therefore her position is highest of all.

---

[54] 'bellissima sopra modo e per giudicio d'ogniun che la vide più d'assai che altra che in quelle nozze v'avesse.' Bembo, *Prose e rime*, ed. Dionisotti, 319; Bembo, *Gli Asolani*, trans. Gottfried, 11.

[55] Bembo, *Prose e rime*, ed. Dionisotti, 320; Bembo, *Gli Asolani*, trans. Gottfried, 11.

Chapter 3
Age, Masculinity and Music in Early Modern England

Kirsten Gibson

Over the last two decades early modern English masculinity has come under scrutiny. Despite the range of this research, a unifying feature has been to expose the underlying workings of the sixteenth- and seventeenth-century patriarchal order, which was fractured with inconsistencies, anxieties and instabilities, and to interrogate the relationships between this order, on the one hand, and lived experiences and constructions of masculinity, on the other.[1] The superiority of Man – over Woman – within this order was primarily based on scriptural precedent and understandings of biological sex and the humoral regime that were still extensively influenced by the writings of Aristotle and Galen. Yet, as these studies have also shown, there was not a single, unified early modern English masculinity. In such a deeply ordered society as that of early modern England masculine identities were not constituted simply on the basis of differences between the sexes, but also on hierarchically-ordered differences between men. Constructions, representations and experiences of masculinity were, therefore, determined by factors including men's social position, marital status, wealth, education, profession and age. Indeed, age, along with marital status was, as Alexandra Shepard has shown, a central 'determinant of early modern hierarchies of masculinity'.[2] At the pinnacle of these hierarchies was 'manhood', which figured not only as a life stage, but also as the status against which 'other' masculine identities were defined, and through which many early modern men were excluded 'from the full patriarchal dividend'.[3]

---

[1] See, for instance, Alan Bray, 'To be a Man in Early Modern Society: The Case of Michael Wigglesworth', *History Workshop Journal* 41 (1996); Mark Breitenberg, *Anxious Masculinity in Early Modern England* (Cambridge: Cambridge University Press, 1996); Anthony Fletcher, 'Manhood, the Male Body, Courtship and the Household in Early Modern England', *History* 84 (1999); Elizabeth Foyster, *Manhood in Early Modern England: Honour, Sex and Marriage* (New York: Longman, 1999); Bruce R. Smith, *Shakespeare and Masculinity* (Oxford: Oxford University Press, 2000); Alexandra Shepard, *Meanings of Manhood in Early Modern England* (Oxford: Oxford University Press, 2003); Will Fisher, *Materializing Gender in Early Modern English Literature and Culture* (Cambridge: Cambridge University Press, 2006).

[2] Shepard, *Meanings*, 23.

[3] Shepard, *Meanings*, 23. See also Foyster, *Manhood*.

Much of this scholarship is rooted in literary and historical studies, but musicological studies have also turned their attention to early modern men, specifically socially elite, literate men. These studies have considered the auditory effects of music on men, dual constructions of women and music as 'effeminising' agents, and the ways in which music figured as both cause and cure for male suffers of love-sickness and other melancholy disorders.[4] Age also figured in debates about music and masculinity, though it has received less systematic attention.[5] Alongside gender, nevertheless, it played a significant role in determining prescribed norms about appropriate musical practice, especially for the socially elite men to whom the vast majority of advice literature, medical writings and related discourses – including many collections of printed music – were generically addressed. The issue of age is rehearsed in perhaps the most widely disseminated of all renaissance conduct books, Baldassare Castiglione's *The Courtyer*. In answer to Gaspare's request to 'gladly learne whiche is the best [sort of music], and at what time the Courtyer ought to practise it', Federico answers that there is a 'time and season' when different 'sortes of musike are to be practised' and that in making appropriate musical choices, 'the seasoning of the whole muste bee discreation'; the ideal courtier, among other things, 'shall knowe his age'.[6]

Federico's comments are, as we shall see, primarily directed at deterring old men from singing love songs, especially in the company of women, but the notion that there was a 'time and season' – including that designated by life stage – for noble and gentlemen to employ music, or that certain types of music were considered more, or less, suited to a particular life stage, is scattered across a whole range of literature. This chapter traces the culturally predominant ideals about masculinity, age and music as they were articulated in prescriptive writings directed at socially elite Englishmen and, where possible, considers suggestive

---

[4] This is exemplified in the work of Linda Phyllis Austern, and includes her '"Alluring the Auditorie to Effeminacie": Music and the Idea of the Feminine in Early Modern England', *Music and Letters* 74 (1993); '"For, Love's a Good Musician": Performance, Audition and Erotic Disorders in Early Modern Europe', *Musical Quarterly* 82 (1998); and 'Music and Manly Wit in Seventeenth-Century England: The Case of the Catch', in *Concepts of Creativity in Seventeenth-Century England*, ed. Rebecca Herissone and Alan Howard (Woodbridge: The Boydell Press, 2013). See also Kirsten Gibson, 'Music, Melancholy and Masculinity in Early Modern England', in *Masculinity and Western Musical Practice*, ed. Ian Biddle and Kirsten Gibson (Farnham: Ashgate, 2009).

[5] Two pieces by Austern touch on aspects of age in relation to male musical practice in early modern England. They are 'Domestic Song and the Circulation of Masculine Social Energy in Early Modern England', in *Gender and Song in Early Modern England*, ed. Leslie Dunn and Katherine Larson (Farnham: Ashgate, 2114) and '"Lo Here I Burn": Musical Figurations and Fantasies of Male Desire in Early Modern England', in *Eroticism in Early Modern Music*, ed. Bonnie Blackburn and Laurie Stras (Farnham: Ashgate, forthcoming). I thank Professor Austern for allowing me to view advance copies of these chapters.

[6] Baldassare Castiglione, *The Courtyer of Count Baldessar Castilio*, trans. Thomas Hoby (London, 1561), Sig. Miiiiv.

evidence that points to the ways in which, in practice, such men – as amateur, recreational musicians – adopted or contravened these ideals in the articulation of their masculine identities.

The Ages of Man

Life was commonly understood by early modern thinkers as a series of distinct stages, and they were almost always understood in masculine terms. In his *Differences of the Ages of Mans Life*, Henry Cuffe explains, '*An age is a period and tearme of mans life, wherein his naturall complexion and temperature naturally and of its owne accord is euidently changed.*'[7] Such changes were grounded on Galenic humoral theory, which conceptualised the body's consitution and health in terms of the ever-shifting balance between the four principal humours contained within it. In their 'optimum' or normative states men were thought to be of a hot and dry constitution whereas women were considered to be cold and moist. Humoral constitution also changed, however, as the body aged. In the Galenic paradigm, the life cycle was divided into four stages, each of which was aligned with a humour, element, season and constitution: childhood (blood, air, spring, hot and moist), youth (choler, fire, summer, hot and dry), manhood or maturity (melancholy, earth, autumn, cold and dry) and old age (phlegm, water, winter, cold and moist).[8]

The division of life into four stages was only one model that was in currency in sixteenth- and seventeenth-century England. Drawing on classical precepts alongside Christian theology, early moderns variously divided life into three, four, six or seven stages, and in some cases developed systems with up to twelve stages.[9] The simplest tripartite model, derived from Aristotle, defined the stages as, in Cuffe's words, '*child-hood, floursshing man-age,* and *old-age*', Galenic and Pythagorean systems proposed four stages, while the seven-stage model, influenced by Ptolemaic astrology, linked the seven ages with the seven planets.[10] Combining humoral theory with the seven ages, Sir Walter Ralegh, for instance, considers the ways in which 'the little World of man' is 'compared, and made more like the Vniuersall' since 'the foure Complexions resemble the foure Elements, and the seuen Ages of man the seuen Planets': infancy, he writes, is aligned with the moon; the second age with Mercury, 'wherein we are taught and instructed'; the third age is associated with Venus, 'the dayes of loue, desire, and vanitie'; the fourth with the Sun, which is 'the strong, flourishing, and beautifull age of mans life'; the fifth is presided over by Mars, 'in which we seeke honor and victorie';

---

[7] Henry Cuffe, *The Differences of the Ages of Mans Life* (London, 1607), 113–14. Italics appear as in the original and I continue this in subsequent primary source quotations.
[8] Smith, *Shakespeare*, 72.
[9] Shepard, *Meanings*, 54.
[10] Cuffe, *Differences*, 116 and Smith, *Shakespeare*, 71.

the sixth is 'ascribed to *Iupiter*, in which we begin to take accompt of our times, iudge of our selues, and grow to the perfection of our vnderstanding'; and, finally, the seventh is assigned to Saturn, 'wherein our dayes are sad and ouer-cast'.[11]

Not only did the number of stages differ in early modern thinking about age; the duration and ages of each stage also varied. Cuffe, for instance, combines various models to produce an overarching tripartite scheme consisting of childhood, middle age and old age, in which each age is subdivided into stages. Childhood, divided into four phases, lasts up to the age of 25, the '*flourishing* and *middle age*', divided into two phases, lasts to around the age of 50 and, finally, old age is divided into two stages.[12] Cuffe's positioning of middle age as between 25 and 50 years was similar to the ages and durations proposed by many of his contemporaries: Levinus Lemnius and Jehan Goeurot, for instance, also regard 'youth' as between ages 25 and 35 and 'man's age' or 'middle age' as between 35 and 50.[13] Others perceived the onset of old age at a much earlier point. In Thomas Elyot's four-stage scheme, for instance, youth (ages 25 to 40) is directly followed by old age (ages 40 to 60).[14] There was, however, commonality in the treatment of the main phases of life. 'Manhood', sometimes with the final stages of youth, was invariably defined as the peak of man's life cycle, and was characterised – in humoral, social and moral terms – as the period of greatest stability. This was the stage in which the body reached its most balanced state, and, in contrast to youthful excess and 'the deprivations of old age', it was commonly 'characterized by the ability to control youthful energies' without yet being threatened by the 'debilitating decline' of old age.[15]

Age was a significant marker through which masculine status was understood, but while ageing is a bodily experience, the making and maintenance of masculine identity was primarily dependent on social and cultural, rather than biological, factors. In an age still deeply influenced by Aristotelian biology, in which the female generative organs were considered to be inverted versions of those of the male, there was a disjuncture between the single biological sex, on the one hand, and the two social sexes – 'with radically different rights and obligations' – on the other.[16] In this context, 'strict sumptuary laws of the body attempted to stabilize gender',[17] but gender identity needed also to be continually re-asserted through

---

[11] Walter Ralegh, *The History of the World* (London, 1617), 31.

[12] Cuffe, *Differences*, 117–20.

[13] See Shepard, *Meanings*, 55 for a full set of comparisons. The works here referred to are Levinus Lemnius, *The Touchstone of Complexions* (London, 1633) and Jehan Goeurot, *The Regiment of Life*, trans. Thomas Phayer (London, 1546).

[14] Shepard, *Meanings*, 55; Thomas Elyot, *The Castel of Helth* (London, 1561).

[15] Shepard, *Meanings*, 23.

[16] See Thomas Laqueur, *Making Sex: Body and Gender from the Greeks to Freud* (Cambridge, MA: Harvard University Press, 1990), 134.

[17] Laqueur, *Making Sex*, 125.

a whole range of expected social conventions and outward cultural markers dependent on a man's social station, age, education, profession and marital status.

Music was one such marker. Yet, its place in discourses concerned with masculine status was contested; it was a practice through which such status – if not seasoned with 'discreation' – could be denied. Based on a tangled web of classical writings and scripture, and mediated through medieval interpretations, the writings of the early church fathers and Protestant ideology, music occupied a dualistic position in early modern culture. As one of the liberal sciences and a biblically endorsed mode of devotion, which was also considered to have medicinal and civilising qualities, music was regarded as a necessary skill for the refined gentleman. Yet its sensuality, alongside the time required to become a skilful practitioner, also placed music as a force that threatened normative masculinity. It is no coincidence that music was frequently figured in feminine terms, and was often personified as a woman, since according to early modern patriarchal discourse they exhibited the same dualistic qualities; both, in their most negative manifestations, threatened the maintenance of masculine status, reason, strength, moderation and self-control through inciting excessive lust, sensuality and idleness.[18] Prescriptive texts wrestled with the role and place of music in the fashioning of masculine identity. Although there were overarching ideals regarding the proper use and consumption of music for gentlemen, the 'time and season' was one of the most significant factors that informed such judgements.

Childhood: The Making of the Man, Education, Music

Childhood was, in Cuffe's scheme, subdivided into infancy (to age 3 or 4), boyhood (to around 9), the '*budding* and *blossoming age*' (to 18) and finally youth (to 25).[19] William Vaughan posits childhood, the second of the seven ages, as between ages 7 and 14; under the influence of Mercury, 'children are vnconstant, tractable, and soone enclined to learne'.[20] Likewise, in one of the most well-known descriptions of the seven ages, Shakespeare's 'whining school-boy' is depicted with his 'shining morning face, creeping like a snail/Unwillingly to school'.[21] Childhood was invariably understood as the age of learning. 'AS the Spring is the onely fitting seede time for graine, setting and planting', writes Henry Peacham, 'So youth, the *Aprill* of mans life, is the most naturall and conuenient season to scatter the Seeds of knowledge vpon the ground of the mind ... For, *in the foundation of youth, well ordered and taught consists* (saith *Plato* ...) *the flourishing of the*

---

[18] Austern, '"Alluring the Auditorie"', 347.
[19] Cuffe, *Differences*, 118.
[20] William Vaughan, *Approved Directions for Health* (London, 1612), 112.
[21] William Shakespeare, *As You Like It*, II, vii, 145–7, in W. J. Craig, ed., *William Shakespeare The Complete Works* (London: Magpie Books, 1993), 227.

Common-wealth.'[22] Yet, although '*A Childe*' might have been considered 'a Man in a small Letter',[23] the male child's assurance of achieving the status of manhood in the one-sex regime, assuming he survived childhood, was far from assured: 'The baby's penis merely indicated a potential for the attainment of a masculinity which needed to be socially inculcated.'[24] Education played a significant role in this inculcation; it was designed to instil in boys the qualities and skills needed to attain fully fledged patriarchal manhood in order that they would play their part well in the '*flourishing of the Common-wealth*'.

The educational schemes on which these foundations were to be laid were based on Classical writings, mediated through the humanist agenda. In his 1581 *Positions*, London schoolmaster Richard Mulcaster set out his pedagogical scheme in which children were 'to be trained vp ... for the helping forward of the abilities of the minde, in these fower things ... *Reading* ... *VVriting* ... *Drawing* ... [and] *Musick*'.[25] As Elyot had asserted in the 1530s, drawing on ancient precepts, 'the perfecte vnderstandynge of musyke' provided a means of 'better attaining the knowlege of a publyke weale' because it is 'made of an ordre of astates and degrees, and by reason therof conteyneth in it a perfect harmony'.[26] Although theoretical knowledge of music could encourage 'knowlege of a publyke weale', Mulcaster, like his contemporaries, and following classical precedent, also included in his scheme music 'by the instrument ... [and] by the voice'.[27] Such education would equip boys destined to operate in the upper ranks of society with necessary cultural capital, since practical musicianship was increasingly viewed as a desirable social skill.

The fictional dialogue that opens Thomas Morley's *A Plaine and Easie Introduction to Practicall Musicke* in 1597 illustrates the desirability of musical skill for an Elizabethan gentleman making his way in the world:

> *Phi.* ... But supper being ended, and Musicke bookes, according to the custome being brought to the table: the mistresse of the house presented mee with a part, earnestly requesting mee to sing. But when after manie excuses, I protested vnfainedly that I could not: euerie one began to wonder. Yea, some whispered to others, demaunding how I was brought vp.[28]

---

[22] Henry Peacham, *The Compleat Gentleman* (London, 1622), 21.
[23] John Earle, *Micro-cosmographie* (London, 1628), Sig. Br.
[24] Fletcher, 'Manhood', 421.
[25] Richard Mulcaster, *Positions ... which are Necessarie for the Training vp of Children* (London, 1581), 36 and 39–40.
[26] Thomas Elyot, *The Boke Named the Gouernour* (London, 1537), fol. 23r.
[27] Mulcaster, *Positions*, 39–40.
[28] Thomas Morley, *A Plaine and Easie Introduction to Practicall Musicke* (London, 1597), Sig. B2r.

This episode, playing on anxieties of social inadequacy, was, perhaps, a ploy to encourage potential buyers to purchase the book, but we might also surmise that it played on anxieties that were grounded in reality. Musical skill was consistently included in conduct literature from at least the Count's assertion at the beginning of the sixteenth century that 'I am not pleased with the Courtyer if he be not also a musitien.'[29] Humphrey Braham advises in 1555 that 'sume knowledge in Musike, or to know the vse of musicall Instrumentes is muche commendable', while in 1622 Peacham counsels his gentleman reader that 'I desire no more in you then to sing your part sure, and at the first sight, withall, to play the same vpon your Violl, or the exercise of the Lute, priuately to your selfe.'[30] Writing almost a hundred years after Hoby's translation of Castiglione, William Higford likewise observes that 'in all Ages Musick hath been esteemed a quality becoming a noble personage'.[31]

In his autobiography, the self-styled gentleman music tutor Thomas Whythorne specifically points to the influence of such books, the 'counsel' of which 'the nobility and the worshipful do much follow in these days. For many of those estates have schoolmasters in their houses to teach their children both to sing pricksong, and also to play on musical instruments.'[32] A wealth of surviving archival evidence, of course, substantiates Whythorne's observation.[33] There was agreement across a range of literature that childhood was the time most apt for musical learning, both for its civilising qualities and for the physical benefits suited to young bodies. Music, as the Count advises, 'ought necessarilye to be learned from a mans childhoode, not onely for the superficial melodie that is hard', but also 'to bring into vs a newe habite that is good, and a custome enclyning to vertue'.[34] Mulcaster asserts it 'is best learned in childehood, when it can do least harme, and may best be had'.[35] Instrumental music, he continues, will 'get the vse of our small ioyntes, before they be knitte, to haue them the nimbler', while vocal music, 'by the waye of *Phisick*', will 'sprede the voice instrumentes within the bodie, while they be yet but young'.[36]

Singing was, in particular, regarded as a useful practice for children (and adults) both in its capacity as a mild form of exercise and as a preparative for oratorical skill. '[B]y the waie of exercise', writes Mulcaster, singing does 'stretche, and

---

[29] Castiglione, *Courtyer*, Sig. Iiir.
[30] Humphrey Braham, *The Institucion of a Gentleman* (London, 1568; first printed 1555), Sigs Aiiiv and Bir; Peacham, *Compleat*, 100.
[31] William Higford, *Institution of a Gentleman* (London, 1660), 77.
[32] Thomas Whythorne, *The Autobiography of Thomas Whythorne*, Modern-Spelling Edition, ed. James M. Osborn (London: Oxford University Press, 1962), 205.
[33] See Christopher Marsh, *Music and Society in Early Modern England* (Cambridge: Cambridge University Press, 2010), 198–214.
[34] Castiglione, *Courtyer*, Sig. Iiiv.
[35] Mulcaster, *Positions*, 37.
[36] Mulcaster, *Positions*, 39–40.

kepe open the hollow passages, and inward pipes',[37] while Peacham agrees it 'openeth the breast and pipes' and 'is a most ready helpe for a bad pronunciation, and distinct speaking'.[38] In his *Psalmes, Sonets, & Songs* William Byrd sets out eight reasons 'to perswade euery one to learne to sing'. Ultimately, it should be 'imployed' to 'honour & serue God', but among his other reasons are its health benefits and its application as the 'best meanes to procure a perfect pronunciation, and to make a good Orator'.[39] It is an argument that had been rehearsed forty years earlier in Roger Ascham's *Toxophilus the Schole of Shootinge*: 'I wysshe from the bottome of my heart', asserts Philologus, 'that the laudable custome of Englande to teache chyldren their plainesong and priksong, were not so decayed … as it is' since 'how fit youth is made, by learning to sing, for grammar and other sciences'. Learning to sing, he continues, is of particular use to two 'degrees of me[n]ne, which haue the highest offices vnder the king in all this realme', that is lawyers and preachers, 'For all voices … may be holpen and brought to a good poynt, by learnyng to synge.' So useful to such men is singing, he argues, that some who had 'learned not to sing, whan they were boyes, were fayne to take peyne in it, whan they were men'.[40] Vocal training, perhaps above other forms of musical education, provided boys with not only a desirable social ornament, but also the grounds for effective oratorical skills, required of boys who would, as adults, enter public life.

The place of music in education was considered to help boys attain a better knowledge of the 'publyke weale', to train and develop their voices for oratory and to furnish them with cultural capital. Learning to use music well and in moderation during childhood, to harness its most positive attributes while resisting its most negative, was also significant in preparing boys for the next phase of life, in which the sensual delights of music combined with the lustiness associated with this age were perceived to pose a particular threat to the safe attainment of manhood.

Youth: Effeminacy, Love, Music

The stages and ages of 'youth' varied between writers, and were not clear cut.[41] The third phase of childhood in Cuffe's scheme, 'our *budding* and *blossoming age*', lasted from age 8 or 9 to 18, and was followed by 'youth' between 18 and 25. There followed a second 'youth' or 'prime', which was the first stage of 'our *flourishing* and *middle age*', from age 25 to 35 or 40.[42] Indeed, most writers whose

---

[37] Mulcaster, *Positions*, 37.

[38] Peacham, *Compleat*, 98.

[39] William Byrd, *Psalmes, Sonets, & Songs of Sadnes and Pietie* (London, 1588), fol. 1v.

[40] Roger Ascham, *Toxophilus the Schole of Shootinge* (London, 1545), Sigs Ciiir–v.

[41] Ilana Krausman Ben-Amos, *Adolescence and Youth in Early Modern England* (New Haven and London: Yale University Press, 1994), 10–38.

[42] Cuffe, *Differences*, 118.

schemes included more than four stages distinguished between the earliest phase of youth, what Vaughan terms 'the stripling age', and the 'prime' of youth.[43] Lemnius, outlining the humoral underpinnings, distinguishes between 'wylfull and slypperye Adolescencie', which lasts to age 25, and 'Youth or flourishing Age', to the age of 35, 'durynge which Age ... this temperamente in continuaunce and processe of time, beginneth to bee taken for Hoate and Drye, whereas Adolescencye is aboundantlye stoared both of moysture, and heate'.[44]

Adolescent youth was considered an especially unstable and dangerous period. While this age could exhibit vitality, vigour, spiritedness and courageous action, it was also an age ubiquitously characterised by excess, sensuality and intemperance. 'Youth', according to Nicholas Ling, 'is an indiscreete heate, outragious, blind, heady, violent, and vaine.'[45] In one courtship manual, addressed to 'the youthful gentry', 'Youth' is defined as 'loose, wild, unbrideled, giddy, amorous ... wanton ... untemperate, dissolute ... voluptuous ... indiscreet, riotous, tender, soft, lascivious ... inconstant'.[46] As such, youth was particularly prone 'to prodigality, gluttonie, drunkennes, lechery, & sundry kinds of vices', but while all vices were of concern, one, above all others, provided the greatest source of anxiety.[47] The third of the seven ages was governed by Venus and was, therefore, especially prone to lust and lasciviousness; this was the age of the 'lover,/Sighing like furnace, with a woeful ballad/Made to his mistress' eyebrow'.[48] According to Earle the young man 'pursues all vanities for happinesse' and 'conceiues his Youth as the season of his Lust'.[49] Excessive lust and obsessive desire was also considered a strain of melancholy, which, according to Robert Burton was 'most euident amongst such as are young and lusty, in the flower of their yeres, nobly descended, high fedde, and such as liue idle and at ease'.[50]

The childishness, inconstancy, fickleness, superficiality, indiscretion and sensuality of young lovers, alongside the designation of excessive lust as a melancholy disorder, marked them as 'effeminate'.[51] While normative masculinity was defined against effeminacy, it was also, in humoral terms, the natural state of adolescent boys, whose constitutions were, like women's, abundantly moist. Rosalind, in *As You Like It*, defines the effeminacy that characterises both women and boys in describing the figure of the young lover, 'a moonish youth', as

---

[43] Vaughan, *Directions*, 113.
[44] Levinus Lemnius, *The Touchstone of Complexions ... Englished by Thomas Newton* (London, 1576), fol. 29v.
[45] Cuffe, *Differences*, p. 116 and N. L. [Nicholas Ling], *Politeuphuia VVits common wealth* ([London], 1598), fols 224v–225r.
[46] Edward Phillips, *The Mysteries of Love and Eloquence* (London, 1685), 48.
[47] Vaughan, *Directions*, 113.
[48] Shakespeare, *As You Like It*, II, vii, 147–9, p. 227.
[49] Earle, *Micro-cosmographie*, Sigs F7r and F7v.
[50] Robert Burton, *The Anatomy of Melancholy* (Oxford, 1621), III, i, 542.
[51] See Breitenberg, *Anxious Masculinity*, 35–68.

'effeminate,/changeable, longing and liking; proud,/fantastical, apish, shallow, inconstant .../... as boys and/women are, for the most part, cattle of this/colour'.[52] Music was closely associated with love, sexual enticement and the frippery of youth, and over indulgence in its pleasures – as well as immodest lust, and its fulfilment – was a sure way to effeminacy. Nicholas Breton's caricature of '*An Effeminate Foole*' includes musical indulgence as a marker of his effeminacy: the 'figure of a Baby', he 'loues nothing but ... to keepe among Wenches, and, to play with trifles ... to play on a Fiddle, and sing a Loue-song'; he is 'a man-Childe, and a Womans man'.[53] Lemnius, likewise, describes 'yong Striplings' whose behaviour includes 'mowing with their mouthes, in voice, gesture ... clapping of hands, light songs, [and] vaine joyfulnesse',[54] and Burton gives the example of those whose melancholy disorder has been instigated or exacerbated by excessive indulgence in music, and for whom music cannot provide a cure: 'some light *inamorato*, some idle phantasticke, who capers in conceit all day long, and thinks of nothing else, but how to make Gigges, Sonnets, Madrigals in commendation of his Mistresse'.[55] The music most commonly associated with such young lovers – and deemed most dangerous – was '*meretricious scurrilous Songs* ... [and] *effeminate musicke*'.[56]

The idea that there were civilising and effeminising musics – with corresponding effects – was based on ancient Greek writings about musics now lost to early modern ears. The music of the Lydians, as writers recount time and again, had been considered 'verie ill for yong men ... for a ... softe, and smoth swetnesse', whereas the music of the Dorians was praised 'because of a manlye, rough and stoute sounde' that could 'encourage yong stomakes, to attempte manlye matters'.[57] Yet how these ideas translated onto modern music – 'whether these balades & roundes, these galiardes, pauanes and daunces ... be lyker the Musike of the Lydians or the Dorians', as Toxophilus asks – was culturally contingent.[58] Nevertheless, there were certain characteristics that were generally regarded as corrupting and effeminate: chromaticism (the semitone), fast, elaborate passagework, 'sweet' harmony (thirds and sixths), the use of certain instruments and the setting of amorous lyrics. Morley, for instance, begins his discussion of 'light musicke' with the madrigal – the music of Burton's 'light *inamorato*' – which is defined both through amorous lyrics and the music needed to appropriately set them. 'If therefore you will compose in this kind', advises Morley, 'you must possesse your selfe with an amorus humor ... so that you must in your mnsicke [sic] be wauering like the wind, sometime wanton,

---

[52] Shakespeare, *As You Like It*, III, ii, 436–42, p. 231.
[53] Nicholas Breton, *The Good and the Badde, or Descriptions of the Worthies, and Vnworthies of this Age* (London, 1616), 30–31.
[54] Lemnius, *Touchstone* (1633), 156.
[55] Burton, *Anatomy*, II, ii, 374–5.
[56] William Prynne, *Histrio-mastix* (London, 1633), 243.
[57] Ascham, *Toxophilus*, Sig. Cv.
[58] Ascham, *Toxophilus*, Sig. Cv.

somtime drooping, sometime graue and staide, otherwhile effeminate.'[59] It was the combination of sensual sound with lust-provoking words that was considered particularly corrupting: 'Ribaldrous amorous Songs ... *contaminate the soules, effeminate the minds ... of these that heare or sing them, exciting, enticeing them to lust; to whoredome, adultery, prophanes, wantonnesse ... excesse.*'[60]

The immoderate sex such songs were presumed to lead to was not only effeminising, but also considered dangerous to man's health since it 'weakeneth strength ... extinguisheth radicall moisture, and hastneth on old age and death'. Yet, in moderation, it was also a necessary 'expedient for preseruation of health'.[61] Sexual initiation, despite moral strictures, was likewise necessary in the assertion of masculinity: 'adult manhood was defined in terms of sexual assertiveness and performance, learnt, practiced and displayed', writes Anthony Fletcher, and 'Young men had to prepare themselves for this world.'[62] Historical evidence suggests that pre-marital sexual activity was not uncommon; the London bachelor's 'social round' of alehouse, brothel and playhouse, for instance, 'provided the experience through which male honour was sought and manhood attained'.[63] In this context, such '*scurrilous Songs*' – and especially into the seventeenth century bawdy catches – provided a channel, in homosocial singing, through which male sexual exploits, fantasies and bravado could be imaginatively explored, enacted and performed in the assertion of manhood among men.[64]

Music, moreover, was not wholly to be avoided by youth. The divine and medicinal qualities of music meant that writers also recommended it as an antidote to melancholy disorders and disappointments in love (when not already perpetuated by it): ''Tis Musick, Wine, and Voice; that remove,/The pangs and tortures of a fruitless love'.[65] Certainly, Philip Sidney was keen to encourage his younger brother, Robert (then 16), to continue his musical activities while he was travelling the continent in 1580: 'sweete brother take a delight to keepe and increase your musick, you will not beleive what a want I finde of it in my melancholie times'.[66] Music was also encouraged in youth as a wholesome recreation to allay idleness, the avoidance of which was a common theme in advice to young men. Ling's *Politeuphuia* advises that 'Youth ought to exercise themselues in musicke, and to employ theyr time in those harmonies which stirre vp to commendable operations

[59] Morley, *Plaine and Easie*, 180.
[60] Prynne, *Histrio-Mastix*, 265–7.
[61] Vaughan, *Directions*, 69–70.
[62] Fletcher, 'Manhood', 426.
[63] Fletcher, 'Manhood', 425; Ben-Amos, *Adolescence*, 201.
[64] Austern, '"Lo Here I Burn"', 17.
[65] Anon, *The Art of Courtship* (London, 1686), Sig. A5v.
[66] Katherine Duncan-Jones, '"Melancholie Times": Musical Recollections of Sidney by William Byrd and Thomas Watson', in *The Well Enchanting Skill: Music, Poetry, and Drama in the Culture of the Renaissance: Essays in Honour of F. Sternfield*, ed. John Caldwell, E. Olleson and S. Wollenburg (Oxford: Clarendon Press, 1990), 171.

& morrall vertues.'[67] The music such commentators had in mind was the '*singing of Psalmes and pious Ditties;* [and] *playing upon musicall Instruments*'.[68] Used either openly 'to y[e] prasie and glory of God' or else 'priuatly in a mans secret Chamber or house for his owne solace ... to driue away the fantasies of idle thoughts', music was 'commendable and tollerable'.[69] It was such music Higford had in mind in his advice to his grandson in the mid-seventeenth century. After expounding the value of music, he continues, 'I have sent you a book of the Psalmes composed in four parts ... whereby you may be invited to proceed farther in this divine faculty.' In addition, he goes on, when 'oppressed with serious and weighty business to take your viol and sing to it, will be a singular ease and refreshment'.[70]

Nor were all associations between music, youth, love and desire negative or counter to dominant moral codes. Both music and love in their highest forms, following the Platonic tradition, could incite virtue: 'Loue maketh a man that is naturally addicted to vice, to bee endued vvith virtue.'[71] As young men entered the later stages of their youth, the pursuit of courtship became a necessity if they were to enter into marriage. Music, as one of the '*the joyes of love*',[72] was commonly associated with wooing and could play an instrumental role in its pursuit: 'an amorous fellowe' as Burton writes, 'must learne to sing and dance; [and] play vpon some Instrument or other'.[73] When Whythorne 'hoped to become a married man, with the rest of that holy estate', he tells his reader, rather than deliver to his beloved his verses in writing, 'for fear of afterclaps', he would 'sing them oftentimes unto her on the virginals or lute' to make his 'first entrance' in his 'suit unto her'.[74] Song, in this context, provided a 'safe' means of broaching the topic of courtship, and printed songbooks – packed with amorous songs – might, as Austern speculates, have served a 'similar function' to printed courtship manuals, helping 'the tongue-tied metamorphose into a suave seducer'.[75] 'Without question', Burton observes, 'so many gentlemen and gentlewomen would not be so well qualified' in music and dancing 'if loue did not incite them'.[76] Amorous songs that were, by some commentators, viewed as dangerous, effeminising agents, simultaneously provided a channel through which to perform sexuality, necessary to young men in the assertion of their masculinity, while, at the same time, they could be applied in the pursuit of marriage and entry into 'man's estate'.

---

[67] Ling, *Politeuphuia*, fol. 197r.
[68] Prynne, *Histrio-Mastix*, 966.
[69] Philip Stubbes, *The Anatomie of Abuses* (London, 1583), Sig. O4v.
[70] Higford, *Institution*, 79–80.
[71] Ling, *Politeuphuia*, fol. 19r.
[72] Phillips, *Mysteries*, 182.
[73] Burton, *Anatomy*, III, ii, 619.
[74] Whythorne, *Autobiography*, 63–4.
[75] Austern, '"Lo Here I Burn"', 14.
[76] Burton, *Anatomy*, III, ii, 619.

Manhood: Responsibility, Refreshment and Recreation

The age described by Cuffe as *'flourishing man-age'*, was deemed the pinnacle of patriarchal masculinity; it was, in humoral terms, the most temperate stage, and the age in which man – informed by the experiences of youth, but beyond its excessive impulses – was most able to exercise moderation, self-control and self-mastery.[77] Cuffe divided the *'flourishing* and *middle age'* into two parts: *'youth'*, as we have seen, from 25 to 35 or 40, and *'Manhood'* lasting up to 50.[78] 'Mans Age', according to Lemnius, also lasts to the 'fiftyeth yeare or somewhat further' and is the time in which 'man is in his full rypenes, and leauing former pleasures and delightes, his mynde aduysedlye, carefullye, and wysely dealeth in euery thinge that he enterpryseth'.[79] Although 'manhood' was a stage that could be defined by age, it was also a status to be achieved. The most significant rite of passage through which it could be attained was marriage, which 'symbolized the transition from a dependent minority to social and political maturity'.[80] This was the age and status that was marked by temperance, moderation, judgement and responsibility on various levels – state, civic, social and familial.

Music figured for socially elite men who had attained the status of manhood – when used moderately and with good judgement – as an appropriate and refined form of recreation that could relieve the mind of the stresses of worldly responsibility: 'RECREATION', as Richard Brathwaite characterises it, is 'a refresher of the minde, and an enabler of the bodie to any office wherein it shall be imployed'.[81] Over half a century earlier, Braham also set out the parameters of recreation for those 'borne to more waightye matters, to more graue studyes, offices and uocations'.[82] Warning against 'excessyue and unmeasureable' indulgence in pastimes that take men away from their responsibilities, he also acknowledges 'that honest pastymes are allowable, so that they be measurably vsed'.[83] Music, as one of the 'soft and effeminate *Recreations*', had to be approached with care. Elyot advises that 'It were ... better, that no musike were taught to a noble man' than through 'inordinate delyte' he be elicited 'to wantonnes, abandonynge grauitie and the necessary cure and office in the publike weale to hym commytted', yet when used with moderation and judgement, it 'serueth for recreation, after tedious or laborious affaires'.[84] Such use of music was emphasised in dedications of music

---

[77] Cuffe, *Differences*, 116.
[78] Cuffe, *Differences*, 119.
[79] Lemnius, *Touchstone* (1576), fol. 30r.
[80] Shepard, *Meanings*, 74–5; see Ira Clark, *Comedy, Youth, Manhood in Early Modern England* (Newark and London: University of Delaware Press and Associated University Presses, 2003), 16–18.
[81] Richard Brathwaite, *The English Gentleman* (London, 1630), 165.
[82] Braham, *Institucion*, Sig. Evir.
[83] Braham, *Institucion*, Sig. Evir.
[84] Elyot, *Gouernour*, fols 22v–23r.

books to noble patrons concerned with the affairs of state. In the dedication of his *Psalmes, Sonets, & Songs* to Sir Christopher Hatton, Elizabeth I's Lord Chancellor, Byrd writes that he hopes 'these poore songs of mine might happily yield some sweetness, repose and recreation vnto your Lordships minde, after your dayly paynes & cares taken in the high affaires of the Common wealth'.[85]

The use of music as refreshment from the pressures of state affairs is reflected – at least in idealised form – in the posthumously commissioned portrait of Sir Henry Unton (c. 1596).[86] The portrait shows scenes from his life including his studies at Oxford, his youthful travels to Italy, his service as a soldier in the Netherlands and his diplomatic mission to France. Alongside depictions of his 'public' life are a series of images depicting him at home. Here, he is shown – as head of the household – presiding over a banquet at which a masque is performed, sitting alone in his closet, discoursing with divines and playing viol consort music in his chamber with a group of men. The act of music-making for refreshment – either solitarily or in company – was one aspect of the idealised use of music for early modern gentlemen, but equally important was the sociability of homosocial music-making, as exemplified in Unton's portrait, providing opportunities for the display of manhood, status and refinement among peers, alongside acting as a means of reinforcing social ties of various kinds.

While viol consort music provided one means of musical sociability, possibly more widespread was the singing of part-songs. It is this kind of sociable singing that is represented in the dialogue opening Morley's *Plaine and Easie Introduction*, and it had also been drawn on some years earlier in Claudius Hollybande's *The French Schoolmaister*.[87] This tutor includes a series of conversations, taken from 'everyday' situations, which are given in English on the left-hand page and in French on the right. One such situation is a family meal with guests, at the end of which the host asks 'shall we haue a song?' The company agreeing, the host gives his wife the key to his closet and instructs her to fetch his 'bookes of musick'. He then proceeds to share out the singing parts among the company: 'David/ shall make the base: Jhon, [sic] the tenor:/and James the treble./Begine: James, take your tune.'[88] In this episode we see some of the hallmarks of 'manhood' enacted through sociable singing: by requesting his wife fetch the books, and giving her access to his locked closet, the host emphasises his position as head, demonstrating his governance of the household; his music books, containing 'faire songes', represent his good judgement, knowledge and skill which he shares for the pleasure of his company; and it is he that directs the singing, designating who will sing which part. In so doing, Austern writes, 'the host solidifies his position

---

[85] Byrd, *Psalmes*, Sig. Aiir.
[86] This image can be accessed at The National Portrait Gallery online: http://www.npg.org.uk/collections/search/portrait/mw06456/Sir-Henry-Unton#description (accessed 18 December 2013).
[87] Claudius Hollybande, *The French Schoolmaister* (London, 1573).
[88] Hollybande, *Schoolmaister*, 126–8.

Figure 3.1   Thomas Sternhold, *Tenor of the Whole Psalmes in Foure Partes* (London: John Day, 1563), fol. Av. Reproduced by permission of the Huntington Library, San Marino, California

as both governor of his household and member of the wider patriarchy', while such music-making stood at 'the interface between self, family, and community'.[89] At the bawdiest end of the spectrum, as we have seen, catches likewise provided opportunities to perform and assert sexuality among peers.

It was not only through all-male music-making that gentlemen could assert their patriarchal positions within their families, household and the wider community, as the woodcut included at the beginning of the Tenor part book of John Day's 1563 edition of *The Whole Psalmes in Foure Partes* suggests (see Figure 3.1).[90] The image, suffused with tropes of Protestant patriarchal manhood, presents an idealised scene of domestic life, at least for upper-ranking families to which a book of four-part psalm settings would be aimed. Here, the father – stern, solid

---

[89]   Austern, 'Domestic Song', 10 and 13. See also Richard Wistreich, 'Music Books and Sociability', *Il saggiatore musicale* 18 (2011). I thank Professor Wistreich for allowing me to view an advance copy of this article.

[90]   John Day, *Tenor of the Whole Psalmes in Foure Partes* (London, 1563).

and upright – teaches the mother, submissive and obedient, and their children the hexachord in order to channel musical knowledge into Godly devotion. In so doing, he asserts his position as family head, while exercising his patriarchal responsibility to govern and instil in those under his rule Godly behaviour, mirroring the intention of the songbook, 'set forth for the encrease of vertue: and abolishyng of other vayne and trifling ballades'.[91] The household was, after all, 'the arena ... in which a man displayed his masculinity', and in so doing he 'had to show control, over his children and servants as well as over his wife'.[92] Music in this context, as in the sociability of homosocial music-making or solitary recreation, provided opportunities for the assertion of manhood through patriarchal power and responsibility, on the one hand, and the exercise of moderation and good judgement, on the other.

Old Age: Judgement, Discretion and Devotion

The final phase of man's life, according to Cuffe, began – for those who reached it – around the fiftieth year, from which point 'our heats and moistures decay'. Cuffe divides old age into two stages, the first lasting to 65, in which 'our strength and heat are euidently impaired' though 'there remaineth a will and readinesse to bee doing' and the second, 'decrepit old age', in which 'our strength and heat is so farre decaied', that 'all abilitie' and 'willingnesse' is 'taken away'.[93] Writers following the astrological scheme made similar distinctions. The sixth age, under the influence of Jupiter, is associated with 'equity, temperance and religion'; the seventh age, influenced by Saturn, 'causeth man to be drooping, decrepit, froward, cold, and melancholick'.[94] Explaining old age as a possible cause of melancholy, Burton tells his reader that it is 'colde and dry ... the same quality as melancholy is'. Those in the latter stages of old age are, according to Burton, 'not able to manage their estates ... ful of ache, sorrow and griefe, children againe'; they are 'angry, waspish, displeased with euery thing, *suspitious of all, wayward, covetous*'.[95]

One recurring trope of old age is the unseemliness of lust or love matters: 'Youth may loue, and yongmen may admire', goes one verse, 'If old age cannot, yet it will desire'.[96] In his discussion of love-melancholy, Burton notes that it is 'more tollerable in youth, and such as are yet in their hote blood; but for an old foole to dote ... what more odious ... and yet what so common?'

---

[91] Day, *Whole Psalmes*, title page.
[92] Fletcher, 'Manhood', 432.
[93] Cuffe, *Differences*, 120.
[94] Vaughan, *Directions*, 113–14.
[95] Burton, *Anatomy*, I, v, 78–9.
[96] Robert Allott, *Englands Parnassus* (London, 1600), 323.

How many decrepit, hoarie, harsh, writhen, burstenbellied and crooked, toothlesse, bald, bleare-eyed, impotent, rotten old men shall you see flickering still in euery place. One gets him a young wife, another a Curtisan, and when he can scarce lift his legge ouer a sil ... what can be more vnseemely?[97]

It was this same trope, over a century earlier, that had prompted Federico to advise that the courtier, in making musical judgements, 'shall knowe his age'. For, he goes on, 'it were no meete matter, but an yll sight to see a man of eny estimation being olde, horeheaded and toothlesse, full of wrinkles with a lute in his armes playing vpon it & singing in the middes of a company of women' since 'suche songes conteine in them woordes of loue, and in olde men loue is a thing to bee iested at'.[98] Although love songs and performance in front of women were deemed inappropriate, musical practice was acceptable for the aged in solitude: 'let them doe it secretly, and onely to ridde their mindes of those troublesome cares and greuous disquietinges that oure life is full of'.[99]

The music most apt in age, and most representative of idealised old age, was that which was contemplative and turned the mind towards God. In the astrological scheme, the sixth age was considered one of 'equity, temperance and religion', and the seventh the time when 'we ... prepare for our eternall habitation'.[100] The positive attributes of age included experience and judgement, wisdom, moderation and contemplation. While young men's 'access to patriarchal manhood was contingent on their adherence to its tenets', old men's continued claims to it, grounded 'in terms of wisdom and authority, temperance and piety', were, as Shepard observes, 'dependent upon their appropriate behaviour'.[101] When Sir Henry Lee retired as the Queen's Champion at the accession-day Tilts of 1590, the verse he likely wrote – or at least commissioned – to be sung before the queen, drew on courtly chivalric tradition and common tropes of old age: the speaker's 'Golden lockes' are now 'Siluer turn'd'; 'from Court to Cottage he [will] depart' where he will 'saddest' sit 'in homely Cell'; the courtier who was once 'A man at Armes must now serue on his knees/And feede on praiers'; the 'Louers Sonets' of his youth are now to be 'turn'd to holy Psalmes'.[102] The figure cut by Lee is reflective of the vision of old age presented in Peacham's emblem book, *Minerua Britanna* of 1612, in which he advises among other things to 'Desire of God but this, when thou art old/To haue a home, and somewhat of thine owne ... where thou maiest in quiet sing alone.'[103] The theme is continued in another lyric by, or about, Lee, which was set as three interconnected songs in John Dowland's

---

[97] Burton, *Anatomy*, III, i, 541.
[98] Castiglione, *Courtyer*, Sig. Miiiiv.
[99] Castiglione, *Courtyer*, Sig. Nir.
[100] Vaughan, *Directions*, 113; Ralegh, *History*, 31.
[101] Shepard, *Meanings*, 42.
[102] George Peele, *Polyhymnia* (London, 1590), Sig. B4v.
[103] Henry Peacham, *Minerua Britanna* (London, 1612), 179.

Second Booke of Songes or Ayres. Here, the speaker thinks the signifiers of old age, 'teares, vowes, praiers, and sacrifices', as 'good' as the trappings of youth and manhood, 'showes, maskes, iustes, or tilt deuises'.[104] Music-related devotional practices are used here to symbolise a turning, in age, to behaviours, actions and cultural practices appropriate to the speaker's 'time and season'.

It is, perhaps, no coincidence that as Dowland 'entered into the fiftieth yeare' of his age, his final collection of songs, *A Pilgrimes Solace*, shifted in theme from his previous songbooks towards devotion, repentance and contemplation; the collection is, he writes, 'in mine opinion furnished with varietie of matter both of Iudgement and delight'.[105] The 'Iudgement' to which he refers can be read in relation to the disclosure of his age. In musical terms – he had used his address to the readers to attack the younger generation of musicians – Dowland inherently draws on associations between age and judiciousness, often figured through musical metaphor: 'Young people ... may sooner *apprehend* a business', writes Richard Steele, but the '*Old man* by comparing and weighing all circumstances can make a better judgment of it', just as 'young *Musicians* ... may *Sing tunes* better, but the *Old Musician* can *set lessons* better'.[106] Yet, 'Iudgement' here seems also to infer the judiciousness of the chosen lyrics, reflected in the devotional connotations of the book's title. Certainly, by this time Dowland was figured by his contemporaries as an old man. His son, Robert, describes him in 1610 as 'being now gray, and like the Swan ... singing towards his end', and in 1612 his friend, Peacham, portrays him as '*Philomel*', sitting alone in silence, 'In depth of winter', noting 'thy yeares haue made thee white'.[107] Both Lee's lyric self-portrait and Dowland's turn towards themes of repentance and devotion in his final collection of songs draw on musical practice as a cultural marker of exemplary old age. Through such musical self-fashioning, Lee and Dowland – despite the social schism between them – make claims to continued patriarchal manhood into old age by displaying 'appropriate behaviour' beholden to their life stage, drawing on tropes of 'wisdom and authority, temperance and piety'.

Conclusions

At all stages of an early modern gentleman's life, musical practice could figure as a cultural marker of masculine status. The strictures underpinning attitudes to gentlemanly music-making were based on the values of moderation and judgement, both in terms of choosing appropriate music and the contexts and

---

[104] Text as in the Cantus part of John Dowland, *The Second Booke of Songs or Ayres* (London, 1600), Sigs Diiv–Fr.

[105] John Dowland, *A Pilgrimes Solace* (London, 1612), Sig. A2v.

[106] Richard Steele, *A Discourse Concerning Old-Age* (London, 1688), 93.

[107] Robert Dowland, *Varietie of Lute-Lessons* (London, 1610), Sig. A2v and Peacham, *Minerua*, 74.

company in which it was practised. These precepts were, however, inflected by attitudes to age. In childhood, music-making, for many boys, formed part of their education; its role was to instil in boys the skills and knowledge required in manhood. Attitudes to music and youth were the most complex and conflicted, as was youth the most unstable age. While love songs, and 'effeminate' music, were considered, in Puritan ideology in particular, most dangerous in the 'stripling age', such music was also primarily associated with, and considered most apt for, the young lover. Such music could further emasculate already 'effeminate' youth, but was also – as one of the *'the joyes of love'* – a tool of the lover in his suit of marriage, and a channel through which boys and men might affirm and express sexuality and bravado among their peers.[108] While the ideal for youth, as at all stages, was the use of grave and sober music, the wealth of literature that advised against immoderate indulgence in 'light' music, the literary commonplace of the 'light *inamorato*' and the musical evidence provided in printed songbooks and manuscript collections suggest that these strictures were frequently ignored. For socially elite men who continued music into manhood it could be employed, when seasoned with 'discreation', to affirm patriarchal status through moderation and good judgement alongside, in familial and social contexts, the assertion of their patriarchal positions as heads of household. Such ideals – mediated particularly through devotional music – were continued in the affirmation of masculinity in old age, though this was, perhaps, more often a literary trope than a lived reality. Music – in practice and in discourse – was a well-understood cultural signifier through which socially elite boys and men could fashion their identities in early modern England. The identities they would fashion through musical practice, or its representation, were determined, among other things, by hierarchically driven attitudes to age. In following the dominant cultural strictures about music or contravening them, moreover, they could – particularly in youth – exert their claims to patriarchal masculinity or could undermine, resist or ignore the 'patriarchal imperative'.[109]

---

[108] Phillips, *Mysteries*, 182.
[109] Shepard, *Meanings*, 249.

Chapter 4
From Castrato to Bass: The Late Roles of Nicolò Grimaldi 'Nicolini'

Anne Desler

In 1727, Abbé Conti wrote to his Parisian correspondent, the marquise de Caylus, to whom he routinely communicated Venetian news, 'Cavaliere Nicolini has mounted the stage of the Teatro San Giovanni Grisostomo at the age of 75.'[1] It would be hard to come by a 75-year-old opera singer nowadays; in the early eighteenth century, when opera singers commonly retired before they turned 50, it would have been sensational. Indeed, Conti was mistaken. The castrato Nicolò Grimaldi (1673–1732), known by his stage name Nicolini, was aged 54, and Conti's senior by only four years. However, Conti evidently perceived him as unusually old for a singer.

By 1727, Nicolini had been taking principal roles in the leading operatic centres of Italy, Naples and Venice for thirty years.[2] Less than ten years into his career,[3] the Republic of Venice had recognised his artistic merit by inducting him into its only chivalric order, the Cavalieri di San Marco, an honour he shared with the legendary seventeenth-century castrato Baldassare Ferri.[4] Nicolini's spectacular success during his first engagement in London in 1708–12 had contributed significantly to the establishing of regular seasons of Italian opera in England. Albeit a fierce critic of Italian opera, the playwright and journalist, Joseph Addison, described Nicolini as 'the greatest performer in dramatic Music that is now living, or that perhaps ever appeared on a stage' (*The Spectator*, 14 June, 1712), and according to

---

[1] 'Le Chevalier Nicolini à l'âge de 75 ans est monté sur le théâtre de San Crisostomo [sic].' Letter of 29 September 1727. Antonio Conti, *Lettere da Venezia à madame la comtesse de Caylus, 1727–1729*, ed. Sylvie Mami (Florence: Olschki, 2003), 169. Conti was a famous natural scientist, philosopher, writer and literary critic.

[2] Chronological information regarding singers' roles is drawn from Claudio Sartori's *I libretti italiani a stampa dalle origini al 1800. Catalogo analitico con 16 indici* (Cuneo: Bertola & Locatelli, 1990–94), Eleanor Selfridge-Field's, *A New Chronology of Venetian Opera and Related Genres, 1660–1760* (Stanford, CA: Stanford University Press, 2007), the Catalogo del Servizio Bibliotecario Nazionale (www.snb.it) as well as individual libretti.

[3] Nicolini's title 'Cavaliere della Croce di San Marco' first appears in *Ambleto* (Venice 1705).

[4] Galliano Ciliberti, 'Ferri, Baldassare', *Grove Music Online. Oxford Music Online.* Oxford University Press, accessed 13 December 2013, http://www.oxfordmusiconline.com/subscriber/article/grove/music/09539.

the prominent violinist John Ernest Galliard, Nicolini 'acted to Perfection, and did not sing much inferior'.[5] In short, Nicolini was one of the most famous singers of the eighteenth century's most prestigious operatic genre, the *dramma per musica* (or *opera seria*) – that is, Italian serious opera.

But no matter how famous a singer was, being perceived as old constituted a considerable danger as evident from the inglorious end of the career of another star castrato, Francesco Bernardi 'Senesino'. After having been vastly admired in London for nearly fifteen years and creating the leading heroic roles in eighteen of Handel's operas, Senesino suffered a steep decline in popularity upon the arrival in 1734 of Carlo Broschi 'Farinelli', the most renowned castrato of all – not only because of the latter's extraordinary virtuosity, but also because of their respective ages. While Farinelli was praised for his handsome looks, Senesino, then about 45 years of age,[6] was publicly criticised for having 'at last grown old, Foggy and Fat'.[7] Senesino's illustrious international career ended only five years later after he had been poorly received in Naples in 1739–40 as reported by Charles de Brosses: 'When the celebrated Senesino appeared in Naples last autumn, people exclaimed: What is this? Here is an actor whom we have seen before; he will sing in an antiquated fashion; his voice is a bit worn.'[8] Indeed, age was not merely a matter of physical appearance but inextricably linked with the notions of fashion and style. In an operatic culture that did not yet recognise a canon of 'classics' and in which novelty was paramount, particularly with regard to music, being perceived as old and old-fashioned was usually detrimental. Hence, singers typically withdrew from the stage in their forties.

Not so Nicolini. He never retired at all, but died aged 58 during the rehearsal period for the production of *La Salustia* in Naples. Yet his popularity continued undiminished until his death; in fact, during the last decade of his career, he had more operatic engagements than in either of the previous two, all at prestigious or lucrative venues. This is all the more astonishing considering that by the 1720s, Nicolini's voice had greatly deteriorated, while the virtuosic Neapolitan singing style was taking Italy by storm, led by its foremost exponent, Farinelli. Conti was surely not mistaken when in 1727 he wrote that Nicolini 'speaks more than he

---

[5] J. E. Galliard's commentary on §31 of Pierfrancesco Tosi, *Observations on the Florid Song,* trans. Galliard (London: Wilcox, 1743), 152.

[6] Senesino's exact year of birth is unknown.

[7] 'Foggy' and 'fat' were synonyms in the eighteenth century. The two singers were compared in the salacious *The Happy Courtezan: Or, the Prude demolish'd. An Epistle From the Celebrated Mrs. C- P- to the Angelick Signior Far-n-li*, published anonymously in London in 1735. Quoted from Thomas McGeary's edition in 'Verse Epistles on Italian Opera Singers, 1724–1736', *Royal Musical Association Research Chronicle* 33 (2000): 73.

[8] 'Lorsque le célèbre Senesino parut à Naples l'automne dernier, on s'écria: Qu'est-ce que ceci? voilà un acteur que nous avons déjà vu; il va chanter d'un goût antique; il a la voix un peu usée.' Charles de Brosses, *Lettres historiques et critiques sur l'Italie,* vol. 3 (Paris: Ponthieu, 1799), 240. Regarding the end of Senesino's career, see also chapter 8 of William C. Holmes, *Opera Observed* (London and Chicago: University of Chicago Press, 1993).

sings';[9] according to Colley Cibber, Nicolini's voice had already been 'impaired'[10] during his second London engagement in 1715–17. Furthermore, certain aspects of Nicolini's singing were already judged old-fashioned in the 1710s. In reference to his appearances in London, Galliard commented that 'his Variations in the *Airs* were excellent; but in his *Cadences* he had a little of the antiquated Tricks'.[11]

This raises the question how Nicolini, bereft of the former beauty of his voice and no longer novel, could sustain his success, even more so as he frequently performed with the young, handsome, virtuosic Farinelli between 1727 and 1730. Even allowing for the exaggeration and distortion inherent in the genre, a caricature of Nicolini as Idaspe in Venice in 1730 suggests that he was no less rotund than Senesino and no longer looked young – the singer's face and throat show clear signs of ageing (see Figure 4.3, discussed later in the chapter).

Conti seems to provide the answer: 'He keeps himself going by means of his acting. In fact, he is the greatest actor in our theatres ... he is greatly applauded, for he vividly expresses all the passions.'[12] Indeed, Nicolini's acting elicited universal admiration. Addison went so far as to promote it as a model for the English spoken stage (*The Spectator*, 15 March, 1710–11):

> I have often wished that our tragedians would copy after this great master of action. Could they make the same use of their arms and legs, and inform their faces with as significant looks and passions, how glorious would an English tragedy appear with that action which is capable of giving dignity to the forced thoughts, cold conceits, and unnatural expressions of an Italian opera!

As Joseph Roach has shown, Nicolini did exert great influence on both the theory and the practice of English acting, setting in motion developments that led to the revolutionary ideas of David Garrick in the 1740s (see Figure 4.1).[13] So great was Nicolini's fame as an actor that it was still upheld as a model of perfection by the vocal pedagogue, Giambattista Mancini, in Vienna in the late 1770s,[14] even after Gaetano Guadagni, a student of Garrick, had brought the latter's aesthetics to the Viennese stage as Orfeo in Gluck-Calzabigi's 'reform' opera *Orfeo ed*

---

[9] 'Il parle plus qu'il en chante.' Letter of 29 September 1727. Conti, *Lettere*, 169.

[10] Colley Cibber, *An Apology for the Life of Colley Cibber*, 3rd edn (London: Dodsley, 1750), 317.

[11] Galliard's commentary on §31 of Tosi, *Observations*, 152.

[12] 'Il se soutient par son action. En effet, c'est le plus grand acteur de nos théâtres. Mais il parle plus qu'il en chante, néanmoins il est fort applaudi, car il exprime avec vivacité toutes les passions.' Conti, *Lettere*, 169.

[13] Joseph R. Roach, 'Cavaliere Nicolini: London's First Opera Star', *Educational Theatre Journal* 28 (1976): 202–5. See also Roach, *The Player's Passion: Studies in the Science of Acting* (Ann Arbor: University of Michigan Press, 1993), 68–70.

[14] Giambattista Mancini, *Riflessioni pratiche sul canto figurato* (1777), facsimile edition (Bologna: Forni, 1996), 232–3. Mancini, too, attributes Nicolini's popularity despite the poor quality of his voice to his excellence as an actor.

Euridice (1762).[15] However, Senesino too was considered to possess 'Excellence of *Theatrical Expression*'[16] and was both younger and in better voice than Nicolini when his career faltered. Evidently, outstanding acting as such did not suffice to sustain a career.

Figure 4.1　Nicolini (centre) during an opera rehearsal in London c. 1709; acting out his role in a musical rehearsal attests to the inseparability of musical and physical expression in his approach to operatic performance. Z13111, *The Rehearsal of an Opera* (Nicola (Nicolò) Francesco Leonardo Grimaldi ('Nicolini'), Francesca Margherita de L'Epine and twelve other sitters) by Marco Ricci, oil on canvas, c. 1708–1709. Photograph © National Portrait Gallery, London; unknown collection

---

[15] Daniel Heartz, 'From Garrick to Gluck: The Reform of Theatre and Opera in the Mid-Eighteenth Century', *Proceedings of the Royal Musical Association* 94 (1967–68): 124–6.

[16] [Richard Pickering], *Reflections Upon Theatrical Expression in Tragedy* (London: Johnston, 1755), 64. Senesino is praised alongside the leading English actors of the period, including Garrick.

The secret of Nicolini's continuing success resided in his role choices and his ability to utilise his assets as well as his liabilities to his advantage. Nicolini possessed an exceptional understanding of the taste of his audiences, which he had acquired through extensive experience not only as a singer, but also as an arranger and director.[17] Moreover, he was ostensibly acutely self-aware and self-critical. The keen interest in creating dramatic unity among the cast he had demonstrated as a director in Naples in 1721[18] seems to have developed into a quest for an unprecedented kind of verisimilitude in his late career that set his performances aside from those of other singers with excellent acting abilities. Exerting the influence concomitant to his professional status, he achieved this verisimilitude by exploiting and bending both the dramatic and the musical conventions of the *dramma per musica*.

The *dramma per musica*, based on historical, chivalric or mythological subject matter, was part of a theatrical tradition that predates dramatic realism and operated within the aesthetic framework of mimesis. Its performances were to represent or 'imitate' plots and characters with the greatest possible degree of verisimilitude – that is, plausibility and consistency – but did not aim at suspending the audience's disbelief and creating the illusion that the action unfolds before their eyes. Costumes were generally not specific to the period or location of a *dramma*, but often owned by the singers and worn in different operas. Similarly, stage sets, which consisted mainly of backdrops and side flats, were reused by theatres for operas set in various countries and periods, often for years.[19] As in contemporary comic stage genres,[20] characters in the *dramma per musica* fit into a limited number of role types. Star singers in particular specialised in a role type and retained it throughout their careers. These conventions served to realise the genre's purpose of representing universal principles, which, in keeping with Aristotelian drama theory, were to effect a moral improvement of the individual as well as society as a whole. However, differently from ancient Greek tragedy, the *dramma per musica* nearly always concluded with a *lieto fine* (happy end), at which virtue, demonstrated by characters' sacrifice of personal interests for the sake of the common good, was rewarded.

Casting in the *dramma per musica* followed a number of conventions. The cast was structured hierarchically according to the performers' professional status. As Figure 4.2 shows, the top tier consisted of the *primo uomo*, typically a castrato in the role of a heroic and/or virtuous lover, a female prima donna and often a

---

[17] Dennis Libby, 'The Singers of Pergolesi's *Salustia*', *Studi Pergolesiani* 3 (1999).
[18] Libby, 'Pergolesi's *Salustia*', 174.
[19] Jana Spáčilova, 'Libretto as a Source of Baroque Scenography in the Czech Lands', in *Theatralia/Yorick 2011/1*, ed. Christian M. Billing and Pavel Drábek (Brno: Masaryk University, 2011). Spáčilova compares the use of sets in Czech and Venetian theatres.
[20] See, for example, Gianni Cicali, *Attori e ruoli nell'opera buffa italiana del Settecento* (Firenze: Le Lettere, 2005).

male singer with a low voice (a tenor or bass),[21] who portrayed a ruler, a father and/or a general. The *secondo uomo* and *seconda donna* formed the second tier, and the singer of the least important role, the *ultima parte* (last role), the lowest tier. Differences in singers' professional status were evident from the number of arias they sang and the arias' placement within the acts. Whereas female singers frequently took male roles, especially when availability or budget constraints prevented the engagement of castrati,[22] male singers, both castrati and tenors, did not perform female roles.[23] This basic structure was adapted to each individual production. Depending on singers' availability, budget and patrons' preferences, the top tier could include an additional star castrato or prima donna, diminishing the tenor's position. Libretti might require several small roles or a third couple of lovers. Singers' positions in the cast hierarchy could be negotiated for each engagement; the singer of a *seconda donna* role in Venice or Naples might appear as a *primo uomo* role in a provincial theatre.

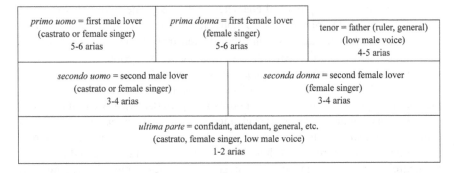

Figure 4.2   Typical structure of *dramma per musica* cast

---

[21] As eighteenth-century operatic roles were composed for or adapted to specific singers, there was less need for the categorisation of voice types, which was consequently less rigid than today. Singers' ranges were described according to the clefs in which their roles were notated (that is, soprano, alto, tenor and bass clefs). Parts for low male voices in the *dramma per musica* would be described as tenor or baritone roles in modern nomenclature; tenors predominated. Low basses appeared mainly in comic opera. Until the 1720s, Neapolitan *dramma per musica* casts contained two comic servant roles for a (female) soprano and a bass, but their scenes were only loosely connected to the main plot and eventually developed into independent *intermezzi*.

[22] The Teatro Sant'Angelo in Venice, for example, routinely engaged women for male parts to reduce expenses (Selfridge-Field, *New Chronology*, 350), and some women (for example, Diana Vico) specialised in male roles.

[23] Only in Rome, where women were prohibited from singing on stage, did castrati take female roles. The Roman prima donna castrato Giacinto Fontana 'Farfallino' sang women's parts in Perugia in 1725 and 1734 and Fano in 1731; however, both cities were part of the Papal States at the time.

An important aspect of *dramma per musica* casting is the association of the low male voice with middle or mature age and the authority engendered by it. Tenors often portrayed fathers of adult children (acted by castratos and/or female singers in the cast), whose weddings constituted the final resolution of operatic plots. Age was also implied in the roles of high-ranking generals and monarchs: advancing to a high military rank required long-standing service and succession to the throne often occurred at a mature age following the death or voluntary retirement of the father of the heir to the throne. The roles of young monarchs, especially those whose suit for a bride was thematicised, were often sung by castratos or female singers. Although, overall, star castrati and prima donnas attracted greater attention from the audience than famous tenors it is untrue that the latter were 'sidelined into walk-on parts in *opera seria* for much of the eighteenth century'.[24] Not only were tenor roles often equally, or almost as, large and dramatically weighty as *primo uomo* and prima donna parts, but, given that casts comprised mostly high voices, they provided an important sonic contrast.

Musically, the *dramma per musica* consisted mainly of an alternation of arias and recitatives. The latter (monologues and dialogues delivered in speech rhythm over a sparse accompaniment by the *basso continuo*) propelled the plot and led to situations of heightened drama. In these, characters expressed their emotional reactions in arias, in which the *basso continuo* was normally joined by string orchestra and sometimes woodwind or brass instruments. Arias enabled singers to demonstrate their quality of voice, ability at virtuosic singing, breath control and skill at ornamentation and improvisation. While the dramatic action could nearly cease in arias that explored strong passions such as sorrow, joy, rage and fear, the *aria d'azione* (action aria) furthered the plot. Star singers were expected to demonstrate command of the main singing styles, the *bravura* (fast and virtuosic), *cantabile* (long-breathed and ornate), *parlante* (with rapid and/or declamatory text delivery) and *grazioso* (graceful) styles, in different arias. Arias in key dramatic moments could be preceded by accompanied recitatives in which the vocal recitation was punctuated by orchestral interjections or underpinned by sustained chords. Accompanied recitatives were more frequent and of longer duration in roles of singers with very good acting skills because their dramatic importance and the intensifying effect of the orchestral part required correspondingly powerful dramatic delivery.

---

[24] John Potter and Neil Sorrell, *A History of Singing* (Cambridge: Cambridge University Press, 2012), 96. This view can partly be attributed to the circumstance that Handel, the best-known *opera seria* composer today, allotted low male voices comparatively small roles. However, in this regard (as in many others) Handel's operas are not representative of the Italian operatic mainstream. Moreover, the tenor has been overshadowed in modern scholarship due to the interest in the castrato and prima donna in current debates in gender, identity and feminist studies.

Nicolini embarked on his operatic career at age 24,[25] six to eight years later than most castrati. From 1697 to 1700, while gradually advancing from *secondo* to *primo uomo*, he appeared in a variety of role types. Once in a position to choose his roles, Nicolini showed a distinct preference for two types of dramatically challenging characters. First are heroic roles that offer the opportunity for onstage battles with human enemies, monsters or wild beasts. Nicolini's most famous among these was Idaspe's strangling of a lion with his bare hands in an amphitheatre, which was crucial in making *Idaspe* (London 1710) one of the most successful productions in London's operatic history despite raised ticket prices.[26] Second are roles that display Nicolini's dramatic flexibility and skill at characterisation, such as Ambleto (Hamlet),[27] whose pretended insanity and deceit his uncle tries to unmask throughout the *dramma*.

In such roles Nicolini continued until he turned 50 in 1723. So far, the course of his career had generally followed the pattern typical for star castrati, but at this point it diverged. Instead of retiring, Nicolini began to take on characters whose age approximated his own. In the first half of his late career, 1723 to 1727, these were still predominantly *primo uomo* lovers, but nearly all of his new *primi uomini* were middle-aged rather than young (see Table 4.1, at the end of this chapter). Their age is evident from the *argomento* (the preface introducing the plot printed at the beginning of each libretto) and, in the case of famous historical or mythical figures, it was common knowledge. Thus the marriage of Siface to Viriate (*Siface*, Naples 1723) seals a peace treaty after many years of war, and Siroe (*Siroe*, Venice 1726), who is set apart from his younger brother by means of his military merit and experience, is crowned king by his father who wishes to retire from the throne. Enea (*Didone abbandonata*, Naples 1724) encounters Didone after six years of journey following the ten-year Trojan War. Contemporary audiences, in whose education classical mythology and history[28] played an important part, would have been aware that Enea was middle-aged. Similarly, many would have known of the Roman general Flavius Aëtius, whom Nicolini portrayed in *Ezio* (Venice 1728), and who by the time of the episode related in that opera was aged 54. The parts in new *drammi* were expressly tailored to the dramatic profiles of the singers who created them and all these roles were newly written. The correlation between the singer's and his characters' respective ages was thus hardly coincidental.

---

[25] Previously he had made an isolated operatic appearance in 1685.

[26] Nicolini sang this role in four different productions of Giovanni Pietro Candi's libretto, respectively entitled *Gli amanti generosi* (Naples 1705), *L'Idaspe fedele* (London 1710), *L'amor generoso* (Naples 1714) and *Idaspe* (Venice 1730).

[27] According to the libretto's anonymous preface, the *dramma* is based on the Danish histories of Meursius, Pontanus and Saxo Grammaticus (not Shakespeare's play). Nicolini performed Ambleto in Venice (1705) and London (1712).

[28] Many figures that are considered mythological in the twenty-first century (for example Aeneas) were regarded as historical in the eighteenth century.

In the second half of his late career, 1727–31, Nicolini made a still more dramatic career move. Nearly all new roles during these years, some written specifically for him and some in pre-existing adapted libretti, were typical tenor roles.[29] All of these characters are the fathers of one or more young lover in the plot, leaving no doubt as to their mature age, and several of them too were well-known historical or mythological figures. This unusual casting significantly upset casting conventions because it did not affect Nicolini's part alone, but meant that the tenor was either replaced by Nicolini or assigned to a castrato role. A replacement could result in a complete or nearly complete absence of low male voices in the cast.[30] Especially interesting is the scenario in which Nicolini sang the role of a father and a tenor that of a young lover. In the *dramma per musica*, roles were distributed based on singer's professional status and dramatic preferences, not age. But in every case in which Nicolini exchanged roles with a tenor, the latter was significantly younger than he,[31] so that both roles aligned with their singers' biological age. This was all the more conspicuous as both Nicolini and the tenors appeared in role types untypical for their voice types.

The improbability of a castrato as a father, which might appear paradoxical from a modern perspective, did not pose a problem.[32] This can be explained both by the non-realist performance aesthetic of the *dramma per musica* and the circumstance that its casting conventions developed in the seventeenth century when gender was widely conceptualised within the framework of what Thomas Laqueur has termed the 'one-sex model'.[33] According to this model, children, castrati,[34] women and men constituted different points on the continuum of a single sex. Gender was understood as a combination of social constructs and an individual's amount of body heat: a higher degree of body heat resulted in a vigorous, decisive,

[29] In *Antigona*, he even changed roles, singing the *primo uomo* Osmene in Venice in 1723 and Osmene's father, Creonte, in Bologna in 1727.

[30] There were no low voices in *Antigona* (Bologna 1727) and *Artaserse* (Bologna 1730); in *Catone in Utica* (Venice 1729), the baritone, Giuseppe Maria Boschi, sang only one aria in the *ultima parte* of Fulvio.

[31] Annibale Pio Fabri, the *primo uomo* Zamiro in *Argeno* in Venice, was 31 in 1728. The respective years of birth of Filippo Giorgi (Artaserse in the eponymous opera, Venice, 1730), Antonio Barbieri (Costatino in *Massimiano*, Venice, 1731) and Francesco Tolve (Zamiro in *Argene* and Claudio in *La Salustia*, both Naples 1731) are not known. However, given that tenors debuted around the same age as castrati (at 16 to 18 years of age), they were probably between 23 and 28 years old at the time of the above-mentioned productions.

[32] In fact, a significant number of *primo uomo* characters are fathers of young children, for example Timante in Metastasio's *Demofoonte* and Farnace in Antonio Maria Lucchini's eponymous *dramma*.

[33] See Thomas Laqueur, *Making Sex: Body and Gender from the Greeks to Freud* (Cambridge, MA and London: Harvard University Press, 1990), chs 3–5.

[34] Wendy Heller applies Laqueur's model to the castrato in 'Reforming Achilles: Gender, "opera seria" and the Rhetoric of the Enlightened Hero', *Early Music* 26 (1998). However, Neoplatonism conceived of the castrato as a third sex.

strong personality and maturity, a lower degree in passivity, lasciviousness and immaturity; hence the association of female and castrato voices with the lovers' roles and that of low male voices with the 'masculine' qualities necessary to govern or achieve a high military rank.[35] Nicolini was widely admired not only for the vigorousness of his onstage battles, but also for his commanding stage presence and air of authority and nobility in his portrayal of princes and kings,[36] which fulfilled social expectations regarding conventional masculine behaviour.

Example 4.1 'Il nocchier che si figura', *Ezio*, I.5, Venice 1728
(N. Porpora-P. Metastasio), bars 67–74[37]

---

[35] That castrati were nevertheless cast as heroes can be explained with the Neoplatonic view of the high voice as perfect and transcendent.

[36] See, for example, John Steele's description of Nicolini's acting in *The Tatler*, 3 January 1709–10.

[37] Sung by Boschi as Massimo; GB-Lam, MS79, fols 42v–43r. '[A sailor] … shall not complain if he remains a mendicant fisherman.'

Example 4.2 'Pallido il sole', *Artaserse*, II.15, Venice 1730
(J. A. Hasse-P. Metastasio), bars 13–24[38]

---

[38] GB-Lam MS72, fols 133v–134r. 'Pale is the sun, turbid the sky, pain threatens, death awaits; everything breathes remorse and horror.'

Example 4.2 continued

Dramatically, Nicolini could thus feasibly take father roles, but a musical issue arose from the close association of this role type with the low male voice. As a castrato, Nicolini could not simply choose to sing in the tenor or bass range. This problem he circumvented by making use of characteristic features of bass idiom. Its perhaps most recognisable feature is a greater preponderance of melodic leaps, especially the root movement between the final tonic and preceding dominant chord at important cadences (Example 4.1, bars 73–4; cf. Example 4.2, bar 24 and Example 4.4, bars 71–2).

The angularity of bass idiom contrasts with high voices' stepwise approach to the final tonic, lending bass idiom a sense of 'masculine' vigour, which is further strengthened by the typical unison texture at the end of the phrase (Example 4.1, bars 70–74; cf. Example 4.4, bars 68/70–72). The use of bass idiom also contrasted Nicolini and his young tenor colleagues who sang arias in a virtuosic style not unlike that of some leading castrati.

Mature men's roles also helped Nicolini conceal his vocal liabilities (shortness of breath, diminished range and sound quality) as they lent themselves to situations in which characters express passions such as vengefulness, disdain, imperiousness, reproachfulness or remorse. These passions could suitably be conveyed in the only style Nicolini commanded comfortably at this time, the *parlante* style. Its declamatory nature did not require a beautiful tone, sustained lines, coloratura singing or a wide range, but clear, emphatic text projection as well as apposite action and stage presence. Accordingly, Nicolini's arias from this period, as, for example, 'Pallido il sole' (Example 4.2), are characterised by completely or nearly syllabic text setting, very short phrases and a narrow range.

Many arias also make ample use of the unison accompaniment commonly used in bass arias as its support of the vocal line was advantageous for Nicolini. Some of Nicolini's father roles even incorporate his vocal problems into the dramatic action. Weary from his flight on foot from the enemy army, the mature Chinese emperor Argeno rests at a fountain (III, 8). He begins to sing an aria but soon interrupts himself and reverts to recitative, saying 'but dry from breathlessness and exhaustion, my lips can hardly utter a sound'.[39]

However, Nicolini applied bass idiom discerningly, employing it to convey heroism, authority or negative passions. Departures occur in scenes in which Nicolini communicates either genuine or simulated *galant* or tender sentiments. For example, 'Stringi l'amata sposa' (I.12, *Argeno*, Venice 1728), in which Argeno pretends to give consent to his daughter's marriage to an enemy and only acknowledges his deceit in an aside, employs typical soprano style: all cadences are approached stepwise, the vocal line is decorated with elegant grace notes and the orchestral texture is characteristic of the fashionable Neapolitan style (Example 4.3).

Example 4.3 'Stringi l'amata sposa', *Argeno*, I.12, Venice 1728 (Leonardo Leo-Domenico Lalli), bars 51–7[40]

---

[39] 'Ma dall'ansia, e languore inaridite/Non san le labbra articolar più voci' (*Argeno*, III.8, Venice 1728, L. Leo-D. Lalli).

[40] GB-Lam, MS74, fols 63r–63v. 'How happy I am. (But you are deceived.).'

Example 4.4 'Dovea svenarti allora', II.13, Venice 1729 (L. Leo-P. Metastasio), bars 62–72[41]

---

[41] B-Bc 2194, 268–9. '[A daughter] as perfidious as you, a father as miserable as I.'

At times, Nicolini even ostentatiously displayed his antiquated musical style for the sake of dramatic characterisation. The G-minor aria[42] 'Dovea svenarti allora' (II.13), from *Catone in Utica* (Venice 1729), for example, employs frequent voice crossing between the first and second violins and a bare, syllabic vocal line to convey the anger of the Roman senator, Cato, on account of his daughter Marzia's love for his enemy, Julius Caesar (Example 4.4).

The style not only reinforces the austerity of Cato's pronouncement that he should have killed Marzia as soon as she was born: on a larger scale, it underpins the *dramma*'s core issue, the ideological conflict between the values of the Roman republic championed by Cato and the new, autocratic rule of Caesar. Additionally, the strong contrast between the old-fashioned style of Nicolini's Cato and the modern, virtuosic Neapolitan style of Domenico Gizzi's Cesare and Farinelli's Arbace differentiates the father, Cato, from Marzia's two suitors.[43]

That all these dramatic and musical decisions were not fortuitous, but intended to enhance the verisimilitude of Nicolini's characters is supported by the singer's unusual interest in character- and plot-specific costumes, which seems to have persisted throughout his career. The costumes worn in commercial theatres (such as those in Venice and London) by other early eighteenth-century singers typically reflected their personal tastes[44] rather than fitting into a visual production aesthetic. However, Nicolini seems to have exploited costume, possibly even make-up, for the sake of characterisation. For example, the two costume changes for Ambleto specified in the libretto (Venice 1705) serve to underpin the character's pretended insanity, and a letter by Lady Montague attests to the verisimilar effect of Nicolini's 'flesh-coloured doublet to simulate his nakedness in the gladiatorial arena'[45] in act III of *Idaspe* (London 1710): 'I was last Thursday at the New opera and saw Nicolini strangle a lion with great gallantry. But he represented nakedness so naturally, I was surprised to see those ladies stare at him without any confusion, that pretend to be so violently shocked at a poor *double entendre* or two in a comedy.'[46] Zanetti's caricature of Nicolini in the same role in Venice twenty years later (Figure 4.3), suggests that the singer might have used dark make-up earlier in the opera when he is disguised as a Moorish warrior. Such make-up would not

---

[42] Minor-key arias had become scarce by the late 1720s. In *Catone*, only four of the twenty-six arias are in minor keys.

[43] In actual fact, Julius Caesar was five years older than Cato. However, in the *dramma per musica*, politico-philosophical aims frequently override historical fact.

[44] A famous example is the dress worn by the prima donna Francesca Cuzzoni in Handel's *Rodelinda* (London, 1724), which was considered tasteless by conservative opera-goers, but a trendsetter among young ladies. Charles Burney, *A General History of Music*, vol. 4 (London: Burney, 1776), 299.

[45] Roach, 'Cavaliere Nicolino', 196.

[46] *The Complete Letters of Lady Mary Wortley Montagu*, ed. Robert Halsband (Oxford: Clarendon Press, 1965), vol. 1, 22–3; cited in Roach, 'Cavaliere Nicolino', 196–7.

only have made his disguise more verisimilar, but also have helped to conceal his age in one of the few young lover's roles late in his career.[47]

Figure 4.3   Nicolini as Idaspe in *Idaspe*, Venice 1730, with Francesca Cuzzoni as Berenice. Antonio Maria Zanetti the Elder, *Nicola Grimaldi detto Nicolini e Francesca Cuzzoni*. Venice, Fondazione Giorgio Cini, Gabinetto dei Disegni e delle Stampe (dall'album di caricature di Antonio Maria Zanetti, f. 12). Photograph: Venice, Fondazione Giorgio Cini, Matteo De Fina

If Nicolini occasionally portrayed young lovers late in his career, this occurred for good reasons. The choices of Arminio (*Arminio*, Florence 1725), Teseo (*Arianna e Teseo*, Venice 1727 and Florence 1728) and Idaspe (*Idaspe*, Venice 1730) were motivated by the success Nicolini had earned in these roles earlier in his career, a common motivation for reusing libretti.[48] All three roles exploit

---

[47]   Also, *Rosiclea in Dania* (Naples, 1721) was received enthusiastically because of Nicolini's direction and the costumes (Libby, 'Pergolesi's *Salustia*', 174). Nicolini may have been responsible for the costumes as the design of new costumes for celebratory court operas generally fell into the director's remit. See Roger Savage, 'Staging an Opera: Letters from the Cesarian Poet,' *Early Music* 26 (1998): 585–6.

[48]   Nicolini exerted great influence on the choice and adaptation of libretti. See Libby, 'Pergolesi's *Salustia*' and Stefan Brandt, '"...um die Oper der Aufmerksamkeit

onstage battles and *ombra* scenes ('shadow' scenes making reference to death or the underworld) for which he was famous and popular with audiences. The reason for Nicolini's singing Colmiro (*Girita*, Milan 1727) and Onorio (*Onorio*, Venice 1729) was simple necessity. In both instances, the casts included neither a tenor nor another castrato who was sufficiently reputable to fill the *primo uomo* role in Nicolini's stead.

Around his 50th birthday, Nicolini apparently realised that 'he had become less suited in middle age for some roles, that a fine young actor could more effectively portray an aged king than a fine old one could carry off the role of a young lover'.[49] In fact, it seems that Garrick, to whom the latter quotation referred originally, was not the first actor-director who pursued an ideal of greater specificity of character by all available means. The contemporary reception of Nicolini attests to the unsuitability of the still prevalent view of singers' interventions engendered by the traditional author- and work-centred approach to the *dramma per musica*, which regards singers' contributions as undesirable interference with composers' and poets' creative vision for the sake of mere vanity and self-display. Nicolini undoubtedly exerted his professional influence to shape both the musical and the dramatic aspects of his roles in order to further his career. However, it must not be ignored that not only singers', but also composers' and poets' careers, and thus their opportunities for continued artistic output, depended on a positive reception of operatic productions. In the star-centred *dramma per musica*, roles that suited star singers' artistic personae were crucial for success.[50] Moreover, Nicolini's choices evidently conformed to an aesthetic of verisimilitude of his own that was distinct across his career, consistent throughout his collaborations with all the leading librettists and composers of his time, recognised by his contemporaries and as widely acclaimed as any composer's or poet's. The approach of modern scholars who recognise singers' artistic contributions to the *dramma per musica* but limit them to performance[51] does not do justice to Nicolini, either, as he

---

des Publikums noch würdiger zu machen". Zum Einfluß des sängerischen Personals auf Arienkompositionen bei Porpora und Händel', *Barocktheater heute. Wiederentdeckungen zwischen Wissenschaft und Bühne*, ed. Nicola Gess, Tina Hartmann and Robert Sollich (Bielefeld: Transcript, 2008).

[49] George Winchester Stone, Jr. and George M. Kahl on Garrick in *David Garrick – A Critical Biography* (Carbondale: Southern Illinois University Press; London: Feffer & Simons, 1979), 320.

[50] See Berta Joncus, 'Producing Stars in *Dramma per musica*', in *Music as Social and Cultural Practice: Essays in Honour of Reinhard Strohm*, ed. B. Joncus and M. Bucciarelli (Woodbridge: Boydell, 2007).

[51] Cf., for example, Reinhard Strohm, 'Zenobia: Voices and Authorship in Opera Seria', in *Johann Adolf Hasse in seiner Zeit*, ed. Szymon Paczkowski and Alina Żórawska-Witkowska, Studia et Dissertationes Instituti Musicologiae Universitatis Varsoviensis, Series B, Vol. XII (Warsaw: Instytut Muzykologii Uniwersytetu Warszawskiego, 2002) and Thomas Seehofer, '"Wie ein gutgemachts kleid [sic]". Überlegungen zu einer mehrdeutigen Metapher (nebst einigen Randbemerkungen zu Mozart)', in *'Per ben vestir la virtuosa'*.

co-authored operas not only in live performance, but also by shaping their poetic and musical texts.

Nicolini's self-transformation from a young *primo uomo* lover to a father in his late career bears witness to his artistic imagination in using the conventions of the *dramma per musica* as a framework of reference that enabled audiences to discern and evaluate his unique profile by interpreting both his adherences and his departures from standard practice. In this manner, Nicolini achieved the near impossible in the context of the eighteenth-century audience's demand for the new, fresh and unheard-of. From the vocal and visual signs of ageing, he created something novel, eliciting the admiration rather than disapproval even of critical opera-goers such as Conti when he 'mounted the stage of the Teatro San Giovanni Grisostomo at the age of 75'.[52]

Table 4.1   Nicolini's late roles, 1724–31

Year, Season	City	Title	Role	Young lover	Middle-aged lover	Father
1724, carnival	Naples	*Didone abbandonata*	Enea		X	
1724, autumn	Venice	*Antigona*	Osmene	X		
1725, carnival	Venice	*Didone abbandonata*	Enea		X	
1725, spring	Reggio	*Didone abbandonata*	Enea		X	
1725, summer	Milano	*Arsace*	Arsace		X	
1725, summer	Florence	*Arminio*	Arminio	X		
1725, spring	Reggio	*Didone abbandonata*	Enea		X	
1726, carnival	Venice	*Siface*	Siface		X	
1726, carnival	Venice	*Siroe re di Persia*	Siroe		X	

Die Oper des 18. und frühen 19. Jahrhunderts im Spannungsfeld zwischen Komponisten und Sängern, ed. D. Brandenburg and T. Seedorf (Schliengen: Edition Argus, 2011).

[52]   Conti, *Lettere*, 169.

Year, Season	City	Title	Role	Role Type		
				Young lover	Middle-aged lover	Father
1727, carnival	Milan	*Girita*	Colmiro	X		
1727, carnival	Milano	*Siroe re di Persia*	Siroe		X	
1727, summer	Bologna	*Antigona, ovvero la fedeltà coronata*	Creonte			X
1727, autumn	Venice	*Arianna e Teseo*	Teseo	X		
1728, carnival	Venice	*Argeno*	Argeno			X
1728, summer	Florence	*Arianna e Teseo*	Teseo	X		
1728, summer	Faenza	*Arsace*	Arsace		X	
1728, autumn	Venice	*Ezio*	Ezio		X	
1729, carnival	Venice	*Catone in Utica*	Catone			X
1729, carnival	Venice	*Semiramide riconosciuta*	Scitalce		X	
1729, autumn	Venice	*Onorio*	Onorio	X		
1730, carnival	Venice	*Mitridate*	Mitridate			X
1730, carnival	Venice	*Idaspe*	Idaspe	X		
1730, carnival	Venice	*Artaserse*	Artabano			X
1730, summer	Bologna	*Artaserse*	Artabano			X
1730, autumn	Venice	*Didone abbandonata*	Enea		X	
1731, carnival	Venice	*Massimiano*	Massimiano			X
1731, carnival	Venice	*Siroe re di Persia*	Siroe		X	

Year, Season	City	Title	Role	Role Type		
				Young lover	Middle-aged lover	Father
1731, summer	Naples	*Argene*	Argene			X
1731, winter	Naples	*La Salustia*	Marziano			X

PART II
Gendered Musical Communities

Chapter 5
Music as a Lifelong Pursuit for Bandsmen in the Southern Pennines, c. 1840–1914: Reflections on Working-Class Masculinity

Stephen Etheridge

On 3 November 1886, a writer for *Musical World* noticed the attraction of brass bands to labouring people in the Southern Pennines:

> Now if there is one thing in the way of music that is dear to the heart of a Lancashire artisan, it is a brass band. It is the height of ambition with a lad to play in a band ... From many a small cottage in country villages, or in the back streets of a Lancashire town, may be heard the mournful sounds of a cornet ... as the mechanic struggles to make his evenings a preparation for harmonious concerts later on, when he shall have qualified for admission to the nearest amateur band he can find.

From the beginning of the movement, a player could be a member of a band for a lifetime. The invention of the piston valve – credited with the spread of a large brass band movement – and its application to brass instruments resulted in all the valved instruments using the treble clef and same system of fingering, which meant that a player could easily move between instruments during their career.[1] This was illustrated on 19 September 1937, when *The Observer* reported on the National Brass Band Festival:

> The young man in the factory town instinctively takes to the cornet ... Thence he gravitates to the local brass band, and finds that he can play almost any required instrument in it, for they are all the same 'family'. In old age he may end up with the BB flat bass, the deepest instrument of them all, requiring the lungs of a glassblower to fill it.

Clearly, brass musicians had the opportunity to perform music throughout their lifetime. This situation provides an arena to reflect on working-class masculinity

---

[1] Trevor Herbert and John Wallace, 'Aspects of Performance Practices: The Brass Band and its Influence on Other Brass Playing Styles', in *The British Brass Band: A Musical and Social History*, ed. Trevor Herbert (Oxford: Oxford University Press, 2000), 292.

in a period when observers were attempting to understand the wider habits and customs of the working class.[2] Moreover, as Keith McClelland argues, 'discussions of working-class life, in the media, between about 1850 and the 1870s were about the "working man" who was the representative artisan'.[3] Artisans who in good trade conditions could save a little money, and through a more secure and visible trade unionism, for at least a few workers, with the expansion of friendly and co-operative societies, and other means of collective security, became people who were secure enough to bring about a new legitimacy for the working class and its institutions in state and civil society.[4] Nevertheless, bands were present in the respectable and the rough. For the majority of middle-class observers, bandsmen were perceived as part of the respectable working class.[5] Yet, through their use of taverns for rehearsals, playing in competitions that contained rough elements, and living and working in working-class communities, bandsmen were not immune to rough behaviour.[6] In terms of understanding their masculinity, the question becomes how much rough or respectable masculinity was embraced; how much respectable masculinity – courtship, marriage, employment security and so on – was accepted by bandsmen as the natural progression for their lives? Were bandsmen, being practitioners of a respectable leisure pursuit, able to escape the influence of the rougher parts of working-class masculinity or did they display an amalgam of all aspects of working-class masculinity?

It is to the brass bands of the Southern Pennines I turn to examine the working class in a period when their lives and culture were under examination.[7]

---

[2] The work of the Journeyman Engineer Thomas Wright is significant here as an example of these observations. Titles such as *Some Habits and Customs of the Working Classes* (1867), *The Great Unwashed* (1868) and *Our New Masters* (1873) reflected an interest in observing and understanding lives of labouring people. Wright started work with a seven-year engineering apprenticeship in Liverpool. By attending journalism classes at mechanics' institutes he eventually became a journalist and gave the middle-class reader what was effectively an insider's view of working-class life. See Alistair J. Reid, 'Wright, Thomas (1839–1909)', *Oxford Dictionary of National Biography* (Oxford, 2006), accessed 1 August 2013, http://www.oxforddnb.com/view/article/4426.

[3] Keith McClelland, 'Masculinity and the Representative Artisan in Britain, 1850–80', in *Manful Assertions: Masculinities in Britain since 1800*, ed. Michael Roper and John Tosh (London and New York: Routledge, 1991), 74.

[4] McClelland, 'Masculinity and the Representative Artisan', 84.

[5] Dave Russell argues that the popular music societies of the West Riding were conservative in nature, embracing self-respect and class collaboration. Dave Russell, 'The Popular Music Societies of the Yorkshire Textile District: A Study of the Relationship between Music and Society' (PhD diss., University of York, 1979), 5.

[6] For an example of the rough and the respectable in nineteenth-century Lancashire, see Shani D'Cruze, 'Sex, Violence and Local Courts: Working-Class Respectability in a Mid-Nineteenth-Century Lancashire Town', *British Journal of Criminology* 39 (1999).

[7] Patrick Joyce was emphatic that that 'the manufacturing districts of Lancashire and the West Riding of Yorkshire were the cradle of factory production, and it [was] to them that

As Ruth Finnegan has observed of amateur music-making traditions elsewhere, a band practice, a trip to a competition, a day in the park or an evening concert became more than just time allocated to music: they were also a social occasion.[8] In April 1892, the *Magazine of Music* illustrated the eclectic range of events bands took part in, writing:

> There is scarcely a public function of any kind at which there is not a band to dispense sweet harmonies. As one looks through the record of a month's work, one sees social gatherings of all kinds – teas, suppers, dances, cricket or football matches, presentations, festivals, demonstrations, camp meetings and anniversaries. It would seem as if nothing human were complete without a band, for this week, a band has to play at a marriage and a funeral.

The Southern Pennines: A Dense Social Network of Bands

On 23 May 1903 the *British Bandsman and Contest Field* (hereafter, *British Bandsman*) commentator 'Shoddythorpe' reflected on the growth of the brass band movement in the North. Shoddythorpe estimated that there were approximately 250 bands in the West Riding of Yorkshire alone. The brass band historian Arthur Taylor illustrated the density of brass bands on the Southern Pennine's Lancashire side by saying that 'the whole area of Saddleworth could almost be designated a national park for brass bands, with Dobcross as the centerpiece'.[9] Music in the Southern Pennines was highly localised. Slaithwaite, a village in the Colne Valley, was an example of a type of musical life replicated throughout the region, and was indicative of music's popularity in the region. In 1819, Slaithwaite Old Band formed and, according to an article in the *Huddersfield Chronicle and West Yorkshire Advertiser* (14 June 1851), was active until 1822. Local publications give a picture of a thriving musical culture in the village. In the 1850s, surviving members of the Slaithwaite Old Band were playing with the Slaithwaite Union Band. Slaithwaite Victoria Band was a brass-and-reed band formed in 1840; it was active between 1856 and 1872 (*Huddersfield Chronicle and West Yorkshire Advertiser*, February 1856–11 May 1872). By 17 April 1898, the *Slaithwaite Guardian and Colne Valley News* was reporting the prominence of Upper Slaithwaite Brass Band. By 1900, Slaithwaite boasted four choral societies, a brass band and an amateur orchestra.[10]

---

posterity ... looked in seeking to discern the nature of the class structure to which the new system of manufacture gave rise'. Patrick Joyce, *Work, Society and Politics: The Culture of the Factory in Later Victorian England* (London: Methuen, 1982), xiii.

[8] Ruth Finnegan, *The Hidden Musicians: Music-Making in An English Town* (Cambridge: Cambridge University Press, 1989), 47.

[9] Arthur R. Taylor, *Brass Bands* (London: Hart-Davis MacGibbon, 1979), 211.

[10] Dave Russell, *Popular Music in England 1840–1914: A Social History*, 2nd edn (Manchester: Manchester University Press, 2004), 208. Russell points out that in 1901

The Southern Pennines were readily associated with choral groups and brass bands. Many reasons were given for the high quality of musicianship in this area. One argument that became popular from the late nineteenth century into the first decades of the twentieth was that because of the physical exercise involved in walking around such a hilly area, northern musicians were fitter, had better lung capacity and, therefore, a better quality of tone for singing and playing in brass bands. From 1900 onwards this argument gained currency in the brass band journals to explain why bands from the Pennines were more successful than bands from other parts of the country, in particular, London, the Midlands and the South.[11]

However tempting it is to subscribe to these arguments – and there is indeed a substantial area of research to be undertaken around this theme to understand the similarities, differences, regional attitudes, friendships and antipathies between Pennine bands and bands in other areas, most notably London and the home counties – Dave Russell rightly argues that they were somewhat fanciful, and that the real reason the area was renowned for its musical prowess was that 'an inter-relationship of several factors operating in the late eighteenth and early nineteenth centuries generated a climate propitious to musical endeavour'.[12] What were these factors? First, Methodism was a powerful influence in the area, and the influence of Methodists on music is well known. Nevertheless, Methodists did not dominate local musical activity and Anglicans were also influential in the area's early choral groups. Roman Catholic influence should also be acknowledged as, in the mid-nineteenth century St Patrick's church was a well-known musical centre in Huddersfield.[13] Additionally, often under the ethos of rational recreation, the local elite supported local working-class musical groups. Music was arguably the best of all rational recreations, many Victorians believing that the performance and appreciation of music could lead to social harmony and have a refining influence upon people.[14] Finally, as Russell argues, the development of musical life in

---

Slaithwaite had a population of around 10,000. Bacup, in east Lancashire, is indicative of towns in the Southern Pennines; its population rose significantly from 10,315 in 1861 to 23,498 in 1891. Official census, cited in Jeanette Edwards, 'Ordinary People: A Study of Factors Affecting Communication in the Provision of Services' (PhD diss., University of Manchester, 1990), 22.

[11] See, for example, *The Cornet*, 15 February 1900, 4; *The Cornet*, 15 June 1901, 4.

[12] Dave Russell, 'Music in Huddersfield, c. 1820–1914', in *Huddersfield: A Most Handsome Town: Aspects of the History and Culture of a West Yorkshire Town*, ed. Hilary A. Haigh (Huddersfield: Kirklees Metropolitan Council, Cultural Services, 1992), 655.

[13] Russell, 'Music in Huddersfield', 655.

[14] In its most elaborate form the notion of music as a rational recreation was developed by the High Church Theologian Hugh Reginald Haweis. His influential book *Music and Morals* was published in 1871 and by 1903 it had reached its twentieth edition. It became an important text for individuals who were interested in the relationship between music and social reform, being widely read in socialist circles. Chris Waters, *British Socialists and the Politics of Popular Culture, 1884–1914* (Stanford, CA: Stanford University Press, 1990), 98.

the Pennines was helped by the flexible working patterns of people in the late eighteenth and early nineteenth centuries. Textile workers largely had control over their working environment to allow for rehearsal time. The final elements in the growth of the popularity of music were the rivalries and competition that grew between musical groups, often expressed through competitions, in an effort to match the excellence of 'rival' towns.[15]

The Membership and Training of Pennine Brass Bands

Bands were composed almost entirely of working-class members. By May 1889, *Brass Band News* was in no doubt that bands were working class, writing:

> Our amateur bands are composed of horny-handed working men exclusively ... I mean factory-men, forge-men, colliers and so on. We never expect to have a man as a member who 'gets his living with his coat on', and this class are, as a rule (there are honourable exceptions), such 'superior persons' that would rather have their room than their company.

In the 1889 edition of *Amateur Band Teacher's Guide and Bandsman's Adviser*, Wright and Round advocated the training methods in use among northern bands: theirs was 'a synthesis of the systems on which the celebrated prize bands of Lancashire and Yorkshire [were] taught'.[16] From the late 1860s onwards, the most successful 'crack' bands – Black Dyke Mills, Besses O' Th' Barn, Meltham Mills and so on – were from the manufacturing districts of the North. This period saw a national consistency of instrumental technique that was heavily influenced by the imitation of the playing styles of the championship bands, which were often conducted by the northern triumvirate of band trainers, John Gladney (1839–1911), Alexander Owen (1851–1920) and Edwin Swift (1843–1904). From 1875 to 1895, there were few major contests when one, two or all three of them did not conduct one of the winning bands.[17] The working-class culture that emerged from brass bands became associated with the industrial North. By 1914, the *British Bandsman* reflected that, 'it could not be denied that the cradle of the brass band was on the slopes of the Pennine Chain' (18 April 1914). While the brass band was a national musical experience that was also popular in the rest of the country, most notably the industrial areas of Cornwall, Scotland and Wales, it was most readily associated with, and indeed has become a cliché of, northern working-class

---

[15] Russell, 'Music in Huddersfield', 656.
[16] *Wright and Round's Amateur Band Teacher's Guide and Bandsman's Adviser* (Liverpool, 1889), 1.
[17] J. L. Scott, 'The Evolution of the Brass Band and its Repertoire in Northern England' (PhD diss., University of Sheffield 1970), 248.

culture.[18] Moreover, the years 1870–1914 are of fundamental importance in any study of recreation and leisure. These years saw the fruition of previous trends and the emergence of a fully formed working-class style of leisure. This period witnessed the evolution of some small public houses into fully fledged music halls, the professionalisation of sports, the emergence of the seaside holiday and the coming of the cinema.[19] In short, this era saw the birth of classic working-class leisure, which created widespread working-class attitudes and experiences. Therefore, the appreciation of masculinity of bandsmen adds to the understanding of a period when both men and women were taking part in leisure activities that came to define working-class cultural identity.[20]

Martin Francis has argued that feminists have rightly asserted there is no shortage of histories of men, histories that were principally about war, diplomacy and statecraft. Francis maintains that 'the study of men as gendered beings has been a relatively recent departure in historiography'.[21] Moreover, Karen Harvey and Alexander Arnold observe that that 'the bulk of research into the history of masculinity has inevitably concentrated on culturally and commercially dominant groups of men not least because records relating to them are most profilic'.[22] Michael Roper and John Tosh argue that making men visible as gendered subjects had major implications for all historians' established themes: for family, labour and business, class and national identities, religion, education and institutional politics too.[23] Thus, an analysis of bandsmen's social networks, in a period when working-class leisure was highly visible, answers a call to examine masculinity in this period outside the more dominant models of middle-class education, power and politics.[24]

---

[18] In 1892, for example, the South Wales and Monmouthshire Brass Band Association held its first annual meeting, which incorporated 26 bands and 641 members. *Magazine of Music*, 9 (April 1892): 62.

[19] Martin J. Childs, *Labour's Apprentices: Working-Class Lads in Late Victorian and Edwardian England* (McGill: Queen's University Press, 1992), 143.

[20] See Eric Hobsbawm, 'The Making of the Working Class, 1870–1914', in *Uncommon People: Resistance, Rebellion and Jazz* (London: Abacus, 1999).

[21] Martin Francis, 'The Domestication of the Male? Recent Research on Nineteenth- and Twentieth-Century British Masculinity', *Historical Journal* 45 (2002): 637.

[22] Karen Harvey and Alexander Shepard, 'What Have Historians Done with Masculinity? Reflections on Five Centuries of British History, circa 1500–1950', *Journal of British Studies* 44 (2005): 277.

[23] Michael Roper and John Tosh, eds, *Manful Assertions: Masculinities in Britain Since 1800* (London: Routledge 1991), 1.

[24] See J. A. Mangan and James Walvin, eds, *Manliness and Morality: Middle-Class Masculinity in Britain and America, 1800–1940* (Manchester: Manchester University Press, 1987).

The Novice Bandsman: Reflecting Early Industrial Experiences

When bandsmen came together to practice they transferred working-class identities found elsewhere to their practice space. Indeed these spaces became a place to continue and develop traditions labouring people had established in the early industrial period. The term 'band room', used as a dedicated rehearsal space, could embrace the room in a public house, the room above a restaurant, the room in a hotel and even a bedroom. In the late nineteenth century independent band rooms, such as Batley Old Band's band room, were often nothing more than wooden sheds. More dedicated spaces, designed by architects, with extensive facilities, including catering spaces, did not emerge until the first decade of the twentieth century.[25]

In early industrialisation, industrial centres exhibited traditionalism together with outstanding technical progress. As matrices of small workshops they developed rhythms of labour that lasted for decades and the influence of these rhythms resonated through the working class, the brass band movement being no exception to these working memories. The workplace was where a boy in a trade established essential identities associated with that trade. Responsibilities included being sent out for beer at break times, as before more efficient manufacturing methods emerged an apprentice was often expected to run errands, not only for essential items for the manufacturing of goods, but also for items for the other men in the workplace; this willingness to run errands was an essential element in gaining acceptance as an apprentice in the peer group. In addition, apprentices bonded, and reinforced acceptance, with other labouring men by engaging in chat and horseplay. In late eighteenth-century Birmingham workshops, for example, the *Birmingham Journal* (26 September 1855) reported that:

> The industry of the people was considered extraordinary; their peculiarity of life remarkable. They lived like the inhabitants of Spain ... Three or four o' clock in the morning found them at work. At noon they rested; many enjoying their siesta; others spent their time in the workshops eating and drinking, these places being often turned into taprooms and apprentices into pot boys; others again enjoyed themselves at marbles or in the skittle alley.

Echoes of these traditions from the workplace can be found in the band room, where the 'work' of making music was often ignored in favour of the social interaction. In an article published in the *British Bandsman* on 15 March 1913, J. Eaton, Bandmaster of Batley Old Band, reminisced about the early practices of the late 1870s:

---

[25] See the account of the building of Hebden Bridge Band's band room in the *Hebden Bridge District News* (3 December 1909), complete with two snooker rooms, a reading room, kitchen, cellar and a large practice room.

> We used to have some pleasant hours in the old bandroom. There were plenty of cracks and holes about the place, and I remember that when it was frosty the gas meter used to be frozen. All used to sit around chaffing and telling tales until the fire burnt up; the meter ... would be placed on the fire to thaw.

Eaton does not say whether they concentrated on music afterwards. Evidence suggests that by 1900 Batley Band was using the band room as a place for chatting, smoking and drinking rather than performing music. One observer at a rehearsal wrote to the band journal *The Cornet* (15 February, 1900):

> Tobacco smoke so thick one could cut cakes of smoke ... There was much larking around ... The music started late, then they only played for twenty minutes before stopping ... All hands gathered around the stove ... and the snare drummer was sent for a pail of beer, and with the beer, more stories, and beer again, until it was too late to do any work, so all went home with the idea that they had done their duty as band boys ought to.

By 1909, more dedicated band rooms had been built, often with extensive facilities. Nevertheless, on 31 January 1914, the *British Bandsman* featured a cartoon called 'Scenes in a Band Club' that saw bandsmen playing billiards, smoking, drinking and playing cards and darts. The practice space was empty, the instruments lying unused. On 21 March 1914, the same journal admonished bandsmen who used the band rooms as social clubs and who had moved away from the serious business of making music. Critics were missing an important point, which was that bandsmen used the rooms as social spaces that bonded bandsmen together. Socialisation brought players under one roof, reinforcing rules, rituals and customs that, for socialisation, had their roots in early industrialisation and apprenticeship.

As John Tosh has argued, these spaces illustrated two powerful arenas where masculinity was expressed. The first was homosocial contact, the need for men to associate with other men outside the home. Moralists argued that this was just sinful pleasure-seeking, but clubs and alehouses and indeed band rooms were areas where gender and masculine status were both recognised and assessed. An array of social groups and committees also reinforced masculine status outside the home. In moral terms these often philanthropic groups were easy to justify; nevertheless, critics accused these groups of diverting men from domestic responsibilities.[26] Aspirations to masculine independence were not new in this period. Keith McClelland, however, argues that the *dominance* and *visibility* of independent masculinity was new. Like middle-class institutions, the working class sustained masculine independence because of the 'building of the institutions of collective social defence'.[27] In other words, working-class institutions such as

---

[26] John Tosh, *A Man's Place: Masculinity and the Middle-Class Home in Victorian England* (New Haven: Yale University Press, 2007), 6.

[27] McClelland, 'Masculinity and the Representative Artisan', 84.

the co-operatives, friendly societies and trade unions, and brass bands, were places where masculinity was respectable in surroundings outside domesticity.

Even though McClelland rightly argues that working-class masculinity sustained itself by building collective defence arenas, the areas where masculinity was practised outside domesticity can be traced to early industrialisation and the celebration of Saint Monday. Saint Monday was the trait of taking the first day of the week off, and this could extend into Tuesday and Wednesday. Evidence suggests it lingered longest in the North.[28] Skilled workers could command high wages, but they would often elect to take moderate wages in exchange for flexible leisure. Such flexible working followed not from weekend drinking but from the workers' deeply held traditional expectation of the surplus of wages. Saint Monday became associated with the lowest forms of labouring people's entertainment: cock fighting and pugilism were common on Monday afternoons up to the 1830s. The tavern was the primary venue for drinking, bar games and entertainments of various sorts in this period.[29]

Throughout the 1840s to 1860s the tradition of Saint Monday was still being kept against the emerging rational recreation ethos. It was against this background that the Journeyman Engineer, Thomas Wright, viewed the brass band movement, not, as many Victorians viewed music, as one of the finest rational recreations, which improved the morals and soul, but as a reflection of earlier, rougher labouring traditions. Indeed, in Wright's opinion, the brass band became a vehicle that led respectable men away from the family unit of home, wife and child, into drinking and the resultant poverty which that created. In 1870 Wright wrote a sketch called *Willie Tyson's Turkey*.[30] It was the story of Willie Tyson, a worker who had 'good-looks, good-humour and a nice-manner'. Willie was a good singer and in general a good musician: with these skills 'he was voted good company and much sought after'. Before Willie got married, he belonged to a choral society where, even though other members were in better positions, they considered him good company, and a valuable asset. The choir members hosted many social events, and this is where Willie met, and courted, his future wife, but also where he liked to socialise with a drink. Willie's fiancée thought that every young man needed to enjoy himself and that after they were married he would not drink so much. However, after getting married, they did not attend so many parties, and Willie craved a drink, so he began going to the pub. As Wright warned, 'He was already beginning to be spoken of as what among working men is styled

---

[28] George Davis, *Saint Monday; or Scenes from a Low Life* (Birmingham, 1790), 7–8, cited in Douglas A. Reid, 'The Decline of Saint Monday 1766–1866', *Past and Present* 71 (1976), 78. The situation was never clear cut, as it is probable that some putting out work was done on Mondays as 'reckoning time' was late on Saturday and this too would encourage a day out of work.

[29] Reid, 'Decline of Saint Monday', 79.

[30] Thomas Wright, The Journeyman Engineer, 'Willie Tyson's Turkey', *Leisure Hour* 991 (24 December 1870).

a "lushington".' Some ten months later, the factory where Willie worked started a brass band, which he joined. 'Now, a workman's band was a very good thing in a general way; but to a man inclined to drink, it often afforded both excuse and opportunity for drinking', remarked Wright. The band proved a snare to Willie, as the bandsmen often celebrated Saint Monday, and together with other outings, and the drinking that accompanied them, Willie started to have days off work. Willie lost his job, spent all his wife's money and they had to pawn all their belongings. His reputation as a drunkard meant he could not find a job, and 'the once bright little home became shabby and bare and comfortless'.

Extending Social Networks and Social Roles

Wright's view was cautionary. The writer was reinforcing a view of alcohol held by other advocates of rational recreation and social improvement, most notably the temperance movement. Nevertheless, as Peter Bailey recognised, in this period the consumption of alcohol, with certain exceptions, became less of a total experience and more of a social lubricant.[31] Drinking and making noise seemed natural accompaniments to popular recreation and bandsmen were not immune to them.[32] They were not just reactions to the ennui of industrial work; these were part of the sociability and public nature of working-class recreation.[33] Throughout the 1830s the *Bolton Press* showed the wide range of activities on offer, highlighting activities that encouraged communal bonding, such as bowling, quoiting, glee clubs and free and easies, amateur and professional dramatics, fruit and vegetable shows, flower shows, sweepstake clubs and the meetings of friendly societies.[34] Peter Bailey has argued that 'the pub remained a centre of warmth, light and sociability for the urban poor, a haven from the filth and meanness of inadequate and congested housing'.[35] Therefore, Wright's negative view of the drinking, and disreputable, bandsman is not that clear cut. What emerged in this period was that the pub and the band room were social spaces that encouraged, developed and created nuanced relationships between bandsmen, their friends, their wives and sweethearts, and the wider community.

---

[31] Peter Bailey, *Leisure and Class in Victorian England: Rational Recreation and the Contest for Control, 1830–1885* (London: Routledge & Kegan Paul, 1978), 174.

[32] On the 5 June 1875 the *Accrington Times* reported on Church Brass Band, near Accrington, in east Lancashire, which had lost a regional competition that day, and whose members, after drinking too much, were said to have fallen into the Leeds and Liverpool Canal.

[33] Bailey, *Leisure and Class in Victorian England*, 9.

[34] *Bolton Press*, cited in Peter Bailey, 'The Victorian Middle Class and the Problem of Leisure', in *Popular Culture and Performance in the Victorian City* (Cambridge: Cambridge University Press, 1998), 21.

[35] Bailey, *Leisure and Class in Victorian England*, 9.

Brass bands affirmed the inn's place in their traditions by using it for annual suppers: these were opportunities to bring together families and other supporters to celebrate the year's achievements. The annual bonding of the supper was where the bands reaffirmed their traditions, rules, rituals and customs. Reported in the press, such events assured the band's identity within the milieu of community life. These rituals can be seen from records of Bacup Band's annual supper (1870) held at the New Inn, Bacup, in east Lancashire's Rossendale Valley (see Figure 5.1). The bandmaster, John Lord, and the trainer, George Ellis, were honoured, their skills as mentor and trainer supported by the prizes that the band had won under their leadership. Photographs of other band members showed that the band's success was a group effort and, finally, these wins had their roots in a musical tradition that had been practised by now-deceased bandsmen, highlighting the lineage of brass band custom. On 5 September 1870, the *Bacup Times* reported:

> The occasion being graced with the presence of all members of the band; with their wives, sweethearts and several friends. The room was very tastefully decorated for the occasion. In the centre of the table, at the higher end of the room, stood the beautiful gilt marble timepiece, presented to John Lord, Bandmaster ... The table was adorned with a variety of prize instruments ... Above the table, and suspended against the wall, was the splendid drum won ... at Belle Vue, in 1869, it was adorned with banners etc. In front of the drum was suspended an excellent life size photograph of the old and respected tutor of the band, George Ellis ... Amongst other decorations were mottoes, banners ... photographs of members of the band, intermixed with evergreens. In one corner of the room a mourning card was suspended, bearing the following inscription: 'In memory of our deceased friends', over which hung the instruments which belonged to those friends, whose services were so highly prized; and who were so feelingly remembered after death.

This article reveals that the band had an extended network of friends and relations that were important in supporting the band. The bandsmen were heavily reliant upon a network of women who were as enthusiastic about running the band as the bandsmen themselves. It is to these women I turn to highlight more subtle relationships in the life of the bandsman.

Accounts of ladies' committees are sparse, yet the accounts are significant.[36] Brass bands came with a wide range of expenses and raising money was always

---

[36] One of the first accounts of women organising themselves into a group dedicated to helping a band was in the industrial North, when the Ladies' Committee of Upper Slaithwaite Brass Band arranged a cricket match between themselves and the Ladies Committee of Slaithwaite Cricket Club, where, during and after the match, the band supplied music. There was a tea, and dancing carried on late into the night (*Huddersfield Daily Chronicle*, 30 August 1899).

Figure 5.1   Bacup Old Band, c. 1860

one of the main activities. The *Brass Band News* recognised women as being the best at selling tickets to raise funds, reporting on 1 December 1901:

> Ask the ladies to organise a tea, and they will give what they can, and beg borrow or steal (figuratively speaking) all the rest. Moreover, they can sell tickets when a man would have no chance. A grocer in a Lancashire village once told us that in one of these ladies teas he gave a ham towards the feed, and then the lady he gave it to asked him to take half-a-dozen tickets, although she knew he could not go. Get the ladies interested in the band, and in what it wants and half the battle is over. Mr H. Clegg of Birstall Old Band [in the West Riding of Yorkshire] mentions their own band in point, he says, "the ladies gave a tea ... and the funds benefited by about £5".

In September 1901, Bacup Change Band, in Lancashire's Rossendale Valley, held a 'British Empire Bazaar'. The *Rossendale Free Press* reported that 'the object of [the bazaar was] to raise about £200 with which to pay for uniforms, and to form a nucleus for tuition and instruments'. The bazaar stalls 'were laden with a variety of useful and fancy goods, tastefully arranged'. There were at least eleven stallholders. Fundraising committees demonstrated the extent of the support shown by the wives, partners and female relatives of the band members, but also that the women had become part of the band by organising themselves into a ladies' committee, a formal structure that represented the band outside musical performance. Ladies' committees became essential in negotiating, arranging and supporting ways of raising finance for bands. Women, as *The Cornet* illustrated, could bring the band to the attention of the public in arenas to which bandsmen could not, or, as *The Cornet* (14 January 1899) pointed out, would not want to have access.

By 1914, it was clear that women were an important element in the social networks of brass bands, so much so that they had become the subject of columns in the *British Bandsman*, highlighting the difference in gender roles at this point in band history. In 1914, the *British Bandsman* featured a column called 'A Little Gossip: written by a bandsman's wife'. A fictional column written in a humorous style, it nevertheless shows the importance of bands' support networks. Reflecting the needs of Bacup Change Brass Band, and others, it shows the importance to these women of raising funds for instruments. The character Mrs Quickstep said in the column, dated 17 January 1914:

> The band got a new set of instruments, and like everything else they could not pay for them ... The members suggested they get up a bazaar ... Twenty women promised to do all they could to make the bazaar a success. The things we made would have stocked the Co-operative store: mats, carpets, shirts, blouses, fancy cushions, tea cosies ... I couldn't tell you one quarter of the work we did.

Moreover, what emerged was that women were not content with their roles as fundraisers but wanted more recognition as organisers. On 23 May 1914, in *A Little Gossip*, Mr Jones read aloud to his wife from a newspaper report that featured him being such a fine band secretary, saying he was 'a born leader, a remarkable organizer, and was one who was untiring in his efforts on behalf of the band'. Mrs Jones replied to her husband that 'it's a good job for you that I'm not [in the band], or I'd let them in for a peep behind the scenes.' When he asked what she meant, Mrs Jones said:

> I mean those who think you do all the work. How long would you keep the position if I didn't help you? You'd often be in arrears in your work, if you had to do it yourself. Who sold the most tickets for your concert? Who made the most articles for the bazaar? Who does all the work when you show your hospitality to the 'roamers' who come here? Who mends the uniforms damaged by careless bandsmen? [Raising her voice] Who takes care of the instruments when bandsmen leave the band? Who canvassed the women-folk when you wanted their help? Who did the cooking for the band supper? Not the Secretary? Oh no. He gets all the honour but where would he be without his wife?

Nevertheless, the essential nature of the brass band movement was to perform music and it was the band contest that was prominent in the region. Local band contests were popular from the 1840s onwards, often attracting crowds of thousands. In August 1888, the *British Bandsman* noted that, 'the northern counties were "all alive" with brass band contests'. Writing in 1901, *Good Words* reported that 'brass band contests evoked white-heat enthusiasm in local people; they were important factors in the social life of the people, thousands of people took the keenest interest in them'.[37]

---

[37] T. W. Wilkinson, 'Brass Band Contests', *Good Words* 42 (December 1901): 593.

Naturally competitions attracted elements of the respectable, the romantic and the rough. In other words, the milieu of community life was concentrated in one relatively small space.[38] This aspect was illustrated by one trombone player's experience with Shipley Band, after a competition in 1882, when his trombone was stolen. Indeed, these were places not just for musical competition but where the bands' larger social networks could develop. The band wrote to *The Yorkshireman* on 7 January 1882, saying:

> One of our band chaps got fresh on Saturday night, and while he wor doing a bit of sly courting, he put his trombone on a wall, and a chap wor peeping, and when he wor telling woman how hard he loved her, this other chap ran off with his play. Please warn all pop shops not to pop it.

This mixed-sex environment meant that the bandsman moved away from purely homosocial environments and, as we have seen, became reliant on partners for support. It was inevitable that these new social networks would weaken the homosocial dominance of the bands' environment. By 1914 some women were clearly expecting to be part of the contest day. One bandsman wrote to the *British Bandsman* saying: '"Missus" had been spouting again, now she wants to go to band contests – the very idea! Why the bandroom and the contest field were the only places on earth where a bandsman is comparatively safe from feminine interference' (7 March 1914). The reply from the Bandsman's Parliament in the *British Bandsman* sympathised, moreover the reply revealed not only that bands had become reliant on networks of women but that this reliance could improve the band movement's status in the eyes of the world.[39] What was important was that the bandsmen were seen to be moving away from being rough working-class men. The Bandsman's Parliament wrote, on 7 March 1914, that:

> The member for Queensbury thought the honourable member was taking an extreme view on the matter. There was one thing he would always give the ladies credit for. He thought they were able to go to a contest and keep right in their heads, and that's what a lot of band chaps couldn't do. He thought they would keep sober, and their husbands too, probably ... He thought their influence would refine us, and some of us could do with it, and be the means of elevating our social status in the eyes of the world.

---

[38] On the morning of the 1893 Belle Vue Competition, train excursions from Bacup were packed with people and most of the mills were obliged to stop. Two special trains were run, with local bookings as follows: Bacup 1,093, Stacksteads 200, Newchurch 519, Rawtenstall 323. Isaac Leech, *Reminisces of The Bacup Old Band, Which Appeared in the Columns of the Bacup Times in 1893* (Bacup: L. J. Priestley, 1893), 59–60.

[39] The Bandsman's Parliament was an occasional column that ran in the *British Bandsman* from 1912. It was a space where bandsmen could write in to a group of experts asking questions about any aspect of brass band life.

From Young Novice to Responsible Bandsman

The band contest was where players could obtain one of the most defining aspects of working-class masculinity, that of independence, which relied on money, to be able to supply security, and spending money, for himself and his dependents. What came to have dominance in the working class from the 1870s onwards was a distinctly masculine interpretation of what it meant to be 'independent'. Men were often dependent on women when cyclical and seasonal employment meant they lost their jobs. London bricklayers, joiners and plasterers depended on their wives' earnings as ironers in a collar factory when out of work in the winter.[40] Dependence on wives, family and other charitable foundations only resulted in economic and psychological depression. Too little is known about how men coped with these issues, but given the central role work took in the construction of men's identities it probably led to a sense of incompleteness and shame as men coped with a loss of dignity and status that could not be contemplated when they lost a job.[41]

The key point of a man's employment may seem obvious; nevertheless, it was central to defining masculinity that no man would 'expect, or be expected, to leave work on marriage or at the birth of a child, seek employment because his wife's earnings were too low, or look for work that was reconcilable with his domestic duties'.[42] Men found it difficult to ask for help when they were short of money. By playing in competitions, bandsmen could find funds to support the need for recognition as the breadwinner. Contest rules stated that all members of a band must have been a member of the competing band for at least three months prior to the day of the contest, and that they should live not more than 4 miles from the town where the band resided.[43] This rule was often broken, and it gave players the opportunity to earn money outside the workplace.

The minute books of Helmshore Brass Band (see Figure 5.2) showed that money was available for deputies to perform at local contests. In June 1903, they voted to enter the Rishton contest as long as they could get the same players that they had at the Ramsbottom contest.[44] In August 1903, they voted to have Hibert and Hoyle for the Goodshaw contest, and on 31 August, they voted to ask J. P. Broadwood and John Heskey to play at Crawshawbooth contest.[45] The back

---

[40] Gareth Steadman Jones, *Outcast London* (Oxford: Oxford University Press, 1971), 84, cited in McClelland, 'Masculinity and the Representative Artisan', 78.
[41] McClelland, 'Masculinity and the Representative Artisan', 78–9.
[42] McClelland, 'Masculinity and the Representative Artisan', 79.
[43] For example, see rules four and five of the Crystal Palace Contest, September 1902, in Trevor Herbert, ed., *The British Brass Band: A Musical and Social History* (Oxford: Oxford University Press, 2000), 317.
[44] Helmshore Brass Band Minute Book (18 June 1903). Thanks to John Simpson, of Accrington Local Studies Library, for allowing access to this source in his private collection.
[45] Helmshore Brass Band Minute Book (13 and 31 August 1903).

pages of the minute books from 1889 to 1920 contain thirty-three names of players who could deputise for them, including the amount of money they charged for rehearsals and contests.[46]

Figure 5.2   Helmshore Brass Band, c. 1909

Bandsmen could command economic independence from the norms of factory work. If they lost their jobs they could earn money on the contest circuit.[47] Money, and the security and status it brought, was important in defining masculinity; moreover, it was important in defining a man's ability to sustain a family life. When Black Dyke Mills toured America in 1906, it was written into the contract that the majority of their salary, which was two pounds a week, was given to their wives and partners, leaving the bandsmen with two shillings a week pocket

---

[46]   Helmshore Brass Band Minute Book (1889–1920). Albert Lonsdale, soprano cornet, 3 Albion Street, Wingates, charged twelve shillings and sixpence for all expenses and the contest, as well as five shillings and five pence per rehearsal; E. J. Woodhead, trombone, 23 Lyon Street, Shaw, charged fifteen shillings and fares for contests; Louis Wilson, cornet, reflecting his status as a soloist, charged one pound per contest plus train fares, and seven shillings and sixpence per rehearsal.

[47]   From the 1880s onwards there were a growing number of players, trainers and conductors linked with the 'crack' bands that were professional in all but name. This professionalisation should not be confused with the fact that the majority of bands were composed of working-class men who undertook 'banding' as a hobby.

money. This reflected a working-class experience for men of relying on their wives to manage the household.[48]

An examination of the financial records of Todmorden Old Band, in West Yorkshire's Calder Valley, reveals that it was able to supply work to bandsman and even assist when bandsmen were in financial distress. From 1899 to 1911 the band paid R. Cunliffe a monthly salary of one pound and fifteen shillings to clean the band room and be the librarian.[49] In 1908, the committee paid ten shillings to a 'distressed bandsman'.[50] These amounts paid to bandsmen were seasonal and one-off payments, and, on occasion, altruistic. They gave bandsmen an element of security when a man's independence depended on how much spending money – or 'spends' – he had for himself. The economy of the working-class household was rooted in the collective earnings of father, mother and children. Jose Harris has highlighted the importance of the financial contribution of the wives and children to the household, for, as social surveys of the period recognised, how much the man contributed from his wages could vary wildly. Indeed, the management of the household fell to the wife, and in what were considered the more respectable households the man would hand his wages over and the wife would often give the husband his 'spends' after the essential items – food, bills and so on – had been budgeted for. In spite of observers disagreeing about the significance of the amounts the husband gave, one thing that all observers agreed on was that it was the wife's skill, or ineptitude, in making ends meet that determined the comfort or neglect of working-class homes.[51]

With the rise of competitions, the homosocial element of banding, although still present, declined. Bandsmen became reliant upon their networks of wives and sweethearts. Indeed, band events became arenas that reflected how bandsmen had become reliant upon women and their extended networks. Fairs, bazaars, lunches and suppers were not additions to the life of the bands but an essential part of it. Consequently, domesticity, and the social networks that grew from it, was equal to the homosocial networks developed in the inns and band rooms. Men could still have independence, most often acted out in the band room, but joint ventures, carried out in public, now implied respectability and domesticity.

The final words, however, belong to Willie Jeffrey, a flugal horn player with Black Dyke Mills Band. In 1906 the band undertook a three-month tour of Canada and the United States. In spite of the excitement and glamour of the tour, Jeffrey only wanted to get home; he wrote in his diary:

---

[48] Queensbury Historical Society, Legal Agreement, regarding the Canadian and American tour of 1906 (1 June 1906), 2.
[49] Todmorden Old Brass Band Ledger Books (June 1897–March 1912), held by Todmorden Community Brass Band, Wellington Street, Todmorden.
[50] Todmorden Old Brass Band Ledger Books (9 June 1908).
[51] Jose Harris, *Private Lives, Public Spirit: Britain 1870–1914* (London: Penguin, 1994), 72–3.

> At last, the great American tour is over, and in looking back, I can say we have seen and learnt some wonderful things. It has been a tour full of interest, a tour of education and experience which could never possibly been got in any other way, still I for one am glad that it is now over, and that we have all been spared to return to those at home we hold so dear.[52]

Jeffrey showed that bandsmen had grown from the novice, who drank and bonded with other men, and had moved through courtship, and the bands' social events that reinforced these courtships, to maturity. In the final analysis the bandsman was a respectable working-class man, something the *British Bandsman* wanted all bandsmen to be, when, on 1 January 1915, it reported:

> It is good to be a working man, whatever the sphere of work – manual or menial; but it is not good to be only a working man. Why not be a working man and a gentleman? That is the noblest combination on earth.

---

[52] Queensbury Historical Society, 1906 Diary of Willie Jeffrey, cited in John H. Clay, *Black Dyke: An Inside Story* (Stockport: Jargen's, 2005), 49.

Chapter 6
Intergenerational Relationships: The Case of the Society of Women Musicians

Laura Seddon

I was not born into the sisterhood: I closed a line of sons.[1]

Old women are your future.[2]

On the cusp of the twenty first century Germaine Greer asserted that 'even more questionable than the suggestion that sisterhood unites women across class and ethnic lines is the claim that sisterhood binds women of different generations. Sisters, by definition, belong to an age set.'[3] As third-wave and, we might argue, emerging fourth-wave feminists grapple with conflicts of the individual, the collective and their relationship to women of older generations, a century earlier a group of creative women had already instigated similar debates. The Society of Women Musicians (SWM) was formed in 1911 to improve the position of women in musical society and the music professions as well as to provide a creative, critical and educational outlet for women who did not have access to mainstream musical avenues.[4]

Groups of mothers, daughters, sisters and other family members joined the SWM together; in the early years there were twenty-six groups of sisters and fifteen groups of mothers and daughters.[5] Here, the SWM will be used as a case to explore the nature of intergenerational relationships and notions of collective age within women's music by arguing that, although musical movements certainly do not always map social and political 'waves', in this case the history of the SWM aligns with the entire period of first-wave feminism, disintegrating at the point of the explosion of second-wave feminist activism. This discussion ultimately then leads to the question of how these historical attempts to engage with issues of

---

[1] Elizabeth Mitchell, 'An Odd Break with the Human Heart', in *To Be Real: Telling the Truth and Changing the Face of Feminism*, ed. Rebecca Walker (London: Anchor Books, 1995), 55.

[2] 'The Old Women's Project, T-Shirt Campaign', accessed 12 August 2013, http://www.oldwomensproject.org/index.htm.

[3] Germaine Greer, *The Whole Woman* (London: Anchor Books, 2000), 292.

[4] Papers of the SWM are housed in the SWM Archive, Royal College of Music, London, hereafter SWM-A-RCM.

[5] SWM Membership Lists, Annual Reports, Box 178, SWM-A-RCM.

intergenerationality and creative relationships with precursors might influence approaches to contemporary women's musical practice.

The SWM was the product of a conversation between three friends: Gertrude Eaton (1861–?), Marion Scott (1877–1953) and Katherine Eggar (1874–1961). The three founders were women of music-college background who were well connected and persuasive in attracting others to their cause. Eaton was a graduate of the Royal College of Music (RCM), was involved with the Women's Institute and the suffrage movement, and later was vocal on prison reform. Eggar studied composition with Frederick Corder at the Royal Academy. She exerted considerable influence in the early years of the SWM, becoming president in 1914. Scott was a music critic writing for the *Musical Times* and the *Christian Science Monitor*, among other publications, a violinist leading her own quartet and a composer.

Eaton, Eggar and Scott wanted to raise the profile of women in musical society, at a time when although the conservatoires were flooded with female vocal and piano students, the numbers of women able to pass the harmony and counterpoint test to enter composition classes was very low. The SWM provided an alternative network by organising meetings and composing seminars, lectures and concerts to promote and support women's work. For many years, the SWM attracted influential women and men with differing levels of involvement. These included composer and educator Nadia Boulanger (1887–1979), writer Rosa Newmarch (1857–1940), composers Elizabeth Maconchy (1907–94) and Elizabeth Poston (1905–87) and musicologist Edward Dent (1876–1957). It continued to have regular meetings and concerts featuring works by members but the focus on the search for a female musical aesthetic dwindled. Instead, the Society concentrated on a series of campaigns to increase the position of women within the music industry generally. There were lengthy correspondences in the 1920s over the lack of women in university departments, the lack of female trustees on boards of musical associations and the lack of female members of the Philharmonic Society. The society weathered the feminist backlashes in the musical community after both world wars, such as women musicians losing their orchestral positions as male troops returned, the most widely reported being the Hallé Orchestra's dismissal of its female players in 1921.

The process of collective ageing emerges between the lines of the formalised and corporate language of sixty years' worth of correspondence, minutes of committee meetings, programmes and annual reports in the SWM archives. The eventual disbanding of this group followed almost twenty years of discussion about the nature of the Society's work, the changing position of women in musical society and the possibility of changing the Society's name. The dissolution was finally voted upon in 1972 – ten years after Eggar's death – by the members of the SWM with a result of 141 votes to continue and 119 to disband.[6] The remaining 286 members who did not return their ballot papers, however, were – as stated

---

[6] Minutes of SWM Council Meeting, Tuesday 22 February 1972, Box 175, SWM-A-RCM.

in the constitution of the Society – automatically added to those who voted to disband and the disappointment of the committee is evident in the minutes when this decision was confirmed. The effect of this lengthy and bureaucratic process, which lasted well into 1973, is illustrated in a letter from Treasurer Muriel Dawson to Secretary Grace Barrons Richardson: 'perhaps it's SWM and its unmentionables that makes us feel old and frustrated!'[7]

Underlying members' apparent apathy about the mission of the SWM resulted in a series of problems that developed after the Second World War. These included financial difficulties and raising of membership fees and the loss of the chamber music room in a building in St James's Square which had been occupied by the Arts Council and also housed the SWM's grand piano, but certainly most worrying was the decline in audience numbers for SWM concerts. In the 1930s and 1940s annual reports state that finances were in good health and that membership was continuing to increase, yet by 1951 the committee had opened a dialogue with members about the future of the Society and in 1962 a sense emerges of the fight having been won for women in music.[8] This is not to suggest that members stopped engaging with feminist debate entirely, for example in 1971 the Society sent a delegation to a meeting of the Six Point Group where Barbara Castle outlined her proposal for equal pay for women, however, at the very point at which second-wave feminist thinking was being developed through the political left, Margaret Patterson the President of the SWM stated in a letter to RCM Principal Keith Faulkner that 'women seem to have been accepted on equal terms with men in the music profession for a long time now ... we felt that our particular contribution to musical life has become something of an anachronism'.[9] This viewpoint is a development of a statement to SWM members by the Committee in 1962: 'The status of professional women musicians is now no longer questioned, although there is still some discrimination against women in certain orchestras, an inevitable result of our family and domestic responsibilities.'[10]

The amount of academic literature on intergenerational conflict between the different 'waves' of the feminist movement – if indeed we choose to use the problematical term 'wave' – is primarily negative in tone, highlighting the harmful effects these perceived disagreements have on the feminist cause. The majority of this discourse concerns itself with the relationship between second- and third-wave feminists and raises very few examples of women from different familial or political generations working productively. Thus it is necessary for the 'sisterhood' in the case of the second wave and the 'daughterhood' in the third to renounce what has come before – what Phyllis Chesler describes in her

---

[7] Letter from Muriel Dawson to Grace Barrons Richardson, 11 March 1973, Box 175, SWM-A-RCM.

[8] SWM Annual Reports, 1911–73, Box 178, SWM-A-RCM.

[9] Letter from Margaret Patterson to Keith Faulkner, undated c. 1972, Box 175, SWM-A-RCM.

[10] SWM Annual Report 1962/63, Box 178, SWM-A-RCM.

letter to a young feminist in 1997 as psychologically committing matricide.[11] Perhaps somewhat unfortunately the most intense activity of the second and third waves of feminism are separated rather neatly by thirty years, the length of time which, in the 1950s, Karl Mannheim defined as a familial generation, basing his work on cycles of birth, reproduction and death.[12] This binary of the seemingly fractious rather than supportive mother–daughter relationship does not necessarily apply to the first wave which had a much longer time frame of activity from the mid-nineteenth century to the 1920s, although this would be to dismiss earlier feminist activity as well as that which occurred despite the backlash between the 1930s and late 1960s, in fact arguably spanning over a century. Thus intergenerational relationships within the first wave incorporate grandmother/grand-daughter discourse as well as a relationship to precursors no longer alive. Perhaps overly simplistically Mannheim identifies two models of generational conflict: a positivist approach where each generation improves upon the previous and a romantic-historical nostalgia for a historical moment that has past.[13] More complex combinations of relationships within the first wave, however, could be models for a less confrontational or sycophantic sense of the collective in contemporary musical feminist practices.

The early years of the SWM incorporate both these models but primarily are an example of those from different familial generations working in creative collaboration. Women from different generations taught each other – many in the composer group, for example, were the same age or older than Katherine Eggar who ran the group – had works played in the same concerts and were given career advice by a panel which included Eggar and composers Thomas Dunhill and Adela Hamaton. This sense of harmony, which did not necessarily continue in the same form in the 1920s and 1930s, can be attributed partly to the notion of the Society itself being young in terms of its collective age, and also to the lack of rebellion and lack of confidence of younger members. For example, the pianist Kathleen Dale recalled her relationship with Marion Scott: 'She was the co-founder of the Society, of which I was an untried new member ... I stood in awe of her.'[14]

Concern about engaging younger women in SWM activities occurred from the late 1930s, considerably earlier than debates on the future of the Society as a whole. In the 1940s, which was a decade of stability for the SWM despite many members being involved in war work – indeed a larger concert venue had to be found to accommodate audiences – there were a number of initiatives to encourage a more youthful membership. The formation of a junior committee appears not to have played a significant role in the following years but other longer lasting schemes

---

[11] Phyllis Chesler, *Letters to a Young Feminist* (New York: Four Walls Eight Windows, 1997), 55.

[12] See Astrid Henry, *Not My Mother's Sister: Generational Conflict and Third-Wave Feminism* (Bloomington: Indiana University Press, 2004), 4.

[13] Henry, *Not My Mother's Sister*, 5.

[14] Kathleen Dale, 'Memories of Marion Scott', *Music and Letters* 35 (1954): 236.

included introducing student membership rates in 1946 and programming concerts with a balance of old and new works to appeal to those whose musical education had taken place after the First World War.[15] The problem of appearing collectively youthful continues in the proceeding decades and mirrors the twentieth century's burgeoning obsession with youth culture, as expanded upon by Patricia Meyers Spacks who describes this time period as 'the age of adolescence'.[16] This was a period where ageing – particularly for women – was and indeed continues to be seen as a traumatic process defined 'in terms of decline and disintegration rather than accumulation and growth'.[17]

The pressing need to engage with younger generations later recurred in second-wave feminist organisations and, similarly to the SWM, this tended to be by altering organisational structures. 'I see older organizations that have made a number of very earnest but unsuccessful attempts to create structures within them that might engage young women but I don't think that model of organization is appealing to young women.'[18] Contemporarily the phenomenon of girls' rock camps – primarily in the US – has developed a more facilitated rather than instructional model of engagement with girls' musical development:

> volunteers refuse to be *the* authority on feminism – punk rock and otherwise – and instead prefer to act as mentors who help to guide, but not determine, the girls' thoughts and actions. This way of teaching recognizes girls' agency to think critically and highlights the importance of dialogue between generations.[19]

While pedagogy has in general become more dialogue based, in the case of the rock camps this does not appear to have led to an expansion of women of different generations actually performing together or forming bands, which did occur within the SWM.

As a collectively young society the SWM systematically incorporated different familial generations into one political generation, as feminist theorist Astrid Henry argues:

---

[15] SWM Annual Reports 1911–73, Box 178, SWM-A-RCM.

[16] Discussed in Kathleen Woodward, 'Inventing Generational Models: Psychoanalysis, Feminism, Literature', in *Figuring Age: Women, Bodies, Generations*, ed. Kathleen Woodward (Bloomington: Indiana University Press, 1999), 163.

[17] Sadie Wearing, 'Subjects of Rejuvenation: Aging in Postfeminist Culture', in *Interrogating Postfeminism: Gender and the Politics of Popular Culture*, ed. Yvonne Tasker and Diane Negra (Durham, NC and London: Duke University Press, 2007), 280.

[18] Sarah Maddison and Rosemary Grey, 'New Feminist Generations: The Intergenerational Conversation Continues', *Australian Feminist Studies* 25 (2010): 488.

[19] Kristen Schilt and Danielle Giffort, '"Strong Riot Women" and the Continuity of Feminist Subcultural Participation', in *Ageing and Youth Cultures: Music, Style and Identity*, ed. Andy Bennett and Paul Hodkinson (London and New York: Berg, 2012), 152.

> Generational units must bring themselves into being through an active identification with their particular historical moment. For political generations, in particular, this active identification is crucial. Within recent feminist writing, however, such a vision of political generations is rarely articulated. Rather, it is all too frequently assumed that feminists of a certain age will, *naturally*, share a generational identity. Political generations, unlike familial ones, require intentional identification.[20]

The process of political identification in the case of the SWM is highlighted in copies of speeches in the archives. Eggar was particularly instrumental in rallying women to their cause, using techniques and language from the suffrage movement while maintaining a separate identity from political movements, as can be seen in extracts from her inaugural speech in 1911:

> We want to get women to sharpen their wits, to criticise things that are happening. I think one of the greatest reproaches against musicians is that they are so thoughtless, that is the 'bane' of musical beings, they are not 'brainy' in the best sense.
>
> Secondly we believe that the benefits of co-operation might be very great, we hope that those of expertise will be willing to help the in-experienced and to advise them; we hope to have on our council women who have proved themselves to be leaders.[21]

If the SWM is defined as a political generation, then a necessary part of its creation and continuing cohesion was to be aware of its own historical narrative – whatever the flaws in its construction – part of which was the process of archiving, both written documentation and scores/performance. As Beth Sneider argues 'a generation must be self-conscious about its own role in history' and the SWM took this part of its remit very seriously.[22]

As is the case for many societies – as part of identity creation – the SWM kept extensive records of activities, but also created a library of works: not only of members' works but of works by male composers (mainly contemporary) which members could consult or perform. Marion Scott collected press clippings sometimes sent by members, apparently indiscriminately, with archly critical reviews alongside those that were encouraging, sentimental and abusively patronising. The rate at which material was collected and the range of the material itself slowed in the 1930s; no clippings in the albums are dated after 1933. While the 1930s was a period of stability for the Society both financially and in terms of

---

[20] Henry, *Not My Mother's Sister*, 6–7.

[21] Extracts from Katherine Eggar, Address to the SWM Inaugural Meeting, Saturday 15 July 1911, SWM-A-RCM.

[22] Beth E. Sneider, 'Political Generations and the Contemporary Women's Movement', *Sociological Inquiry* 58 (1998): 7.

membership and audience numbers, the Society started to be concerned about the ideological direction of its work and engaging younger members.

Within the seemingly cohesive political generation that the SWM maintained as its public identity in the early years there were factions. In her work on the second-wave feminist movement in Columbo, USA, Nancy Whittier identified 'micro-cohorts' of women who entered the movement every few years whose 'presentation of self, use of language and participation in political culture' were distinctive from other cohorts who became politicised at different times.[23] In Columbo she classifies four micro-cohorts: *initiators* (entering the movement 1969–71) who visibly critiqued the status quo, formed initial organisations and networks, were militant and saw themselves as revolutionaries but were part of a broad movement having been politicised by the New Left and the civil rights movement; *founders* (entering 1972–73) who founded formally structured organisations not linked to the New Left or other institutions, were active and started to use the term 'radical feminism' but saw minimal conflict within the movement; *joiners* (entered 1974–78) who were part of a large increase of membership becoming politicised within the women's movement rather than outside institutions, were optimistic, with broad goals, were increasingly linked to lesbianism, worked both outside and inside mainstream structures particularly relating to government funding, and felt both admiration and resentment towards initiators and founders; *sustainers* (entered 1979–84) who redefined feminism as the social/political climate became increasingly conservative, experienced internal conflict relating to sexuality, class and race, were pessimistic about sweeping social changes, thus having more moderate goals, and had problems recruiting new members.[24] Indeed, for Whittier, 'age is less important in shaping political outlook and actions than the time one enters a movement and the experiences one has as an activist'.[25]

Whittier's analysis of the US women's movement is a useful tool in considering the 'micro-cohorts' of the SWM, and while the specific issues or time spans are different – sixty-one years in the case of the SWM compared to fifteen years in the Columbo study– some similarities in attitudes of the cohorts emerge. Eggar, Scott and Eaton (entered 1911) share the qualities of *initiators*, forming initial networks, seeing themselves as revolutionary in that nothing similar had been done on such a scale before. Rather than coming from the political left, they were involved in the temperance movement and prison reform, with broad political aims. They expanded into *founders* (entered 1912–18) with women such as Liza Lehmann, Kathleen Schlesinger, Lucie Johnstone, Adine O'Neill and May Mukle helping to articulate their musical and political message and to form the constitution. Notably these women were often involved in the suffrage movement or had extensive

---

[23] Nancy Whittier, *Feminist Generations: The Persistence of the Radical Women's Movement* (Philadelphia: Temple University Press, 1995), 56.
[24] Whittier, *Feminist Generations*, 59–79.
[25] Whittier, *Feminist Generations*, 226.

experience as musicians or published composers and were musically politicised before entering the SWM. The steady increase in membership after the First World War, incorporating the Second World War until 1950, marks the extended period of *joiners* such as Elizabeth Maconchy, Elizabeth Poston and committee member Rachel Fell who were positive and active in their campaigns for women in the music industry, took advantage of the opportunities afforded them and, despite having benefited from a much broader musical education, became musically politicised through the organisation. They were not, however, always in accord with initiators' and founders' musical tastes and in particular the SWM composer concerts were less centred around Katherine Eggar's composer group.

The point at which the SWM starts to consider its position in musical society in 1951 marks a period of what we might term *consolidators* who tended to be politically more conservative and were considerably less allied to the feminist movement, having come of political age in the post-war feminist backlash. They attempted to redefine the purpose of the SWM and were conflicted in that they felt the need for an activist element to the Society but placed higher value on the social aspects of membershie. This was a period of conflict with longer-standing members who were more overtly feminist in their concert programming and campaigning. Those members joining the movement between 1961 and 1972, *sustainers*, tended to be apathetic in their musical politics instead valuing the performing opportunities the SWM provided, were musically and politically conservative, had much less broad aims for women within music and had problems recruiting new members, indeed 1961 marks the period where for the first time membership numbers started to fall.

The supposed generational conflict does not seem to have been as evident in the SWM as in Whittier's study. Instead, the concept of creative conflict is generationally further removed – the musical version of Chesler's 'matricide' in being able to destroy tradition and forebears has infamously been described by Harold Bloom as the anxiety of influence 'the creative anxiety one feels when confronting one's precursors. It proceeds much like an Oedipal killing. The male needs to remove the onus of the (male) precursor's style and presence, and the only way to do so is to destroy, to kill that ontological weight.'[26] There is, however, surprisingly little attention given to the researching or reclaiming of a female past – musically or otherwise – by the SWM both initially and in later decades. Thus the male construct of anxiety of influence was replaced by a relationship with a future woman who would achieve greatness.

In this particular era of first-wave feminism, of which the SWM was part, the perceived lack of female precursors could be argued to have acted as a buffer for this kind of inhibitive anxiety, where even acknowledgement of the predicament does not exempt the artist. Bloom assesses the extent to which this affects the poet William Blake: 'To be enslaved by any precursor's system, Blake says, is to be

---

[26] Marcia J. Citron, *Gender and the Musical Canon* (Urbana: University of Illinois Press, 2000), 69.

inhibited from creativity by an obsessive reasoning and comparing, presumably of one's own works to the precursor's. Poetic influence is thus a disease of self-consciousness; but Blake was not released from his share in that anxiety.'[27] This is not to argue that SWM members did not consider male composers to be their precursors – indeed Marion Scott considered herself indebted to Haydn and Beethoven and displayed detailed interest in the lives of both – rather that in the early years of the SWM a sense of freedom to create a female aesthetic prevailed, moving away from mainstream romanticism. The creative energy that this attitude fostered, however, was recognised by Eggar and Scott as merely a starting point, not futile, but instead necessary for the next generation, as a long-term project.

Kathleen Woodward observes that as generations live longer we subsequently participate in wider interactions and relationships between the generations become more complex (often being portrayed in the media as also increasingly more disengaged and hostile).[28] Arguably the members of the SWM were not able to negotiate this increasing complexity as they aged in terms of their relationship with previous generations of women, resorting instead to a pre-established engagement with the generalised western musical canon. Their initial creation of a female canon where we can see the process of carving out a place for themselves in British musical history – what, as will be discussed later, Julia Kristeva might define as a 'signifying space' – is highlighted in their programming of the twenty-fifth anniversary in 1936 of the formation of the SWM.[29] This was a celebratory micro-history of the compositions created under the auspices of the SWM with works by contemporary composers Ethel Smyth, Lilian Robinson, Alma Goatley, Elizabeth Maconchy, Imogen Holst, Dora White and Phyllis Tate, and those who were deceased (Jane Joseph, Dorothy Fox, Hilda M. Grieveson and Kathleen Bruckshaw). It was a claiming of ground and a statement on the SWM's role in musical society, although they did not acknowledge or even show curiosity in their implied relationship with earlier generations of women composers.

By the SWM's Golden Jubilee celebrations in 1961 the relationship to the past had become more historical but less feminist in terms of programming, organising a young member's concert where female performers including Jacqueline and Iris du Pré played works by Bach, Brahms, Wolf, Ravel, Albeniz and Beethoven, as well as a Wigmore Hall recital, which included the contralto Nancy Evans and the English String Quartet, who played works by Duparc, Faure and Schumann but also by SWM members Elizabeth Maconchy and Elizabeth Poston.[30] Ten years later at the Diamond Jubilee concert at the Queen Elizabeth Hall, the positioning of women in the canon had been reduced to a premiere of Margaret Lucy Wilkins's prize-winning work *The Silver Casket*, alongside works by Mozart, Ibert, Gordon

---

[27] Harold Bloom, *The Anxiety of Influence: A Theory of Poetry*, 2nd edn (New York and London: Oxford University Press, 1997), 29.
[28] Woodward, 'Inventing Generational Models', 164–70.
[29] Programme for 25th Anniversary Concert, Box 175, SWM-A-RCM.
[30] Programme for Golden Jubilee Concert, Box 175, SWM-A-RCM.

Jacob, Lennox Berkeley, Ivor Walworth, Brahms and Dvorak.[31] This dilution of their previous claiming of political ground is incongruous with the committee's assertion that women had achieved equality in the music profession and was justified by statements that the Society wanted to look towards youth and the future, although this is certainly not reflected in the selection of composers.

Issues in Contemporary Discourse

The increasing complexity of intergenerational relationships, relationships with musical forebears and with future audiences is a vital consideration when curating and presenting works by contemporary women composers and those working in sound. Claiming, evaluating and placing historical women's works has of course happened via a multitude of programming techniques, with examples of recent activity in the UK ranging from the single composer recitals such as the Chaminade recital as part of the Brighton Festival in May 2012, performances combining the historic and the contemporary such as composer Rhian Samuel being programmed alongside Liza Lehmann (1862–1918), Rebecca Clarke (1886–1979) and Muriel Herbert (1897–1984) as part of the 2012 London English Song Festival, to contemporary intergenerational performances and interactions such as Fatoumata Diawa and Angelique Kidjo at the Women of the World Festival at London's Southbank in March 2013, where Diawa referred to Kidjo as her 'musical mother'.

The issue of a non-teleological presentation of a 'site' of resistance was pertinent in the curation of *They Clapped Until She Bowed Once More*, a 2011 project to celebrate the centenary of the formation of the SWM.[32] By commissioning contemporary composers – of different familial and political generations including Amy Cunningham, Lynne Plowman and Rhian Samuel – to directly respond to historical works by members of the SWM, works which would have been heard at SWM concerts and discussed in seminar-like groups in a variety of decades in the twentieth century, the nature of intergenerational relationships – up to four generations removed – emerged and was questioned. The programming of both historical works followed by responses as well as responses leading into historical works enabled cross-generational conversations to sound across the concert space.

A more interwoven exploration of intergenerational connections combining re-enactment and remixing was *The Brilliant and the Dark* project initiated by Eileen Simpson and Ben White in 2010, based on the 1966 score of the operetta of the same title composed by Malcolm Williamson with a libretto by Ursula Vaughan Williams, which was commissioned by the National Federation of

---

[31] Programme for Diamond Jubilee Concert, Box 175, SWM-A-RCM.
[32] 'Contemporary Connections, They Clapped Until She Bowed Once More', accessed 30 August 2012, http://contemporaryconnections.weebly.com/index.html.

Women's Institutes.[33] The work documented women's lives through history and was performed at the Royal Albert Hall by 1,000 women in 1969. With permission from the original publishers, lyrics, melodic phrases and rhythms from the work were incorporated into a new multimedia piece combining live performance of women chorus and pre-recorded elements alongside a film re-enacting the parts of the original performance but in the setting of the Women's Library, London. Thus both historical stories of women as perceived by Ursula Vaughan Williams and 1960s women performers sounded through contemporary women's bodies.

By contrast and in common with many first-wave women's organisations the SWM had a teleological, progressive sense of history, a sense of certainty that the next generation would develop from their work in the present. Rather than the heightened levels of anxiety perceived by Bloom in relation to poetic influence or contemporary debates on the supposed irreconcilable differences between second- and third-wave feminists, Julia Kristeva argues for a less chronological and more inclusive approach:

> My usage of the word 'generation' implies less a chronology than a *signifying space*, a both corporeal and desiring mental space. So it can be argued that as of now a third attitude is possible, thus a third generation, which does not exclude – quite the contrary – the *parallel* existence of all three in the same historical time, or even that they be interwoven one with the other.[34]

Thus, rather than completely eradicating notions of generational time advocated by philosophers such as Robyn Wiegman or a conception of a narrative of time where there is no debt to precursors, as conceived by Judith Roof, Kristeva suggests a utilisation of current structures.[35] Indeed Jennifer Purvis argues that 'the tripartite generational model is so firmly entrenched [within contemporary feminist debate] that it may function as a productive site of resistance'.[36]

Unlike the suffragettes – as a political movement – the SWM did not refer to themselves as 'sisters' or the 'sisterhood' and rarely used familial language as part of their rhetoric; this may or may not have been a deliberate strategy. Indeed this study is in agreement with Purvis that purely familial generational language is

---

[33] 'Open Music Archive, The Brilliant and the Dark', last modified 19 November 2012, http://www.openmusicarchive.org/projects/index.php?title=The_Brilliant_and_the_Dark.

[34] Julia Kristeva, 'Women's Time', trans. Alice Jardine and Harry Blake, *Signs* 7 (1981): 33.

[35] Jennifer Purvis, 'Grrrls and Women Together in the Third Wave: Embracing the Challenges of Intergenerational Feminism(s)', *NWSA Journal* 16, 3 (Fall 2004), accessed 11 November 2012, http://go.galegroup.com/ps/i.do?id=GALE%7CA125488656&v=2.1&u=west&it=r&p=GPS&sw=w.

[36] Purvis, 'Grrrls'.

fundamentally reductive; as she argues, it 'reinscribes heteronormative principles in its assertion of both hegemonic social structures and a heterosexist narrative of reproduction'.[37]

Both the feminist movement – with its plurality of forms – and more specifically the feminist musical community need to consider the possible damage politically and creatively of generational conflict (whether constructed internally or through external agencies) as well as notions of time. Within the SWM archival material, a rare expression of familial relationship occurs in comments by Kathleen Dale and Elizabeth Poston after the death of Katherine Eggar in 1961. Dales wrote:

> To SWM members of my generation, Katherine Eggar stood as a symbol of ageless continuity ... It was as the youngest member of a little group of the Society's composer members who used to assemble periodically at Katherine's flat in Kensington during the First World War for discussion and criticism of their work, that I first came under the spell of this uniquely gifted woman, my senior by twenty one years ... in old age still youthful and erect in figure her mind still open to new currents of thought.[38]

In addition Poston saw Eggar as 'a great civilising influence in the world. How many of us realise this now, with lifelong gratitude for the dedicated loving care she had for us all. Her children rise up and call her blessed.'[39]

The above comments at once place Eggar within a particular generation – a motherly figure – and yet now that she had died, release her as an ageless concept able to move beyond a particular numerical age. This accords with Kathleen Woodward's argument that we each contain different aged selves within us, what she defines as psychic age as differing from psychological, social, cultural and chronological age.[40] As she points out, psychic age is more difficult to 'perform' than other aspects of age, yet it could be suggested that psychic age becomes more easily visible after death. How the performance of age links with the performance of gender is a complex issue, neither one remaining static or teleological, yet Eggar appears to have been successful – at least in the early years of the SWM – at moving between these temporal spaces to create a political and creative generation of women rather than a Society based on the hierarchy of individual age. This did not mean, however, that all members avoided this; rather some such as Kathleen Dale constructed individual hierarchies for themselves either in the moment or as part of reminiscences.

Yet how might 'signifying spaces' or 'sites of resistance' challenge generational stand-offs and more specifically apply to contemporary feminist musical practices?

---

[37] Purvis, 'Grrrls'.
[38] Kathleen Dale, SWM Annual Report 1961/62, SWM, Box 178, SWM-A-RCM.
[39] Elizabeth Poston, SWM Annual Report 1961/62, SWM, Box 178, SWM-A-RCM.
[40] Kathleen Woodward, 'Performing Age, Performing Gender', *NWSA Journal* 18 (2006): 166.

The Brilliant and the Dark and *They Clapped Until She Bowed Once More* are examples of programming where multiple generations share aural space and in that moment co-exist. Similarly to archiving, the performances stake a claim in historical narratives, questioning the political category of 'woman composer' in the case of *They Clapped* and 'woman in history' in the case of *The Brilliant*. Both projects use the generational model as scaffolding on which to question supposed miscommunications between generations and attempt to move beyond 'familial' conflict portrayed as being detrimental to the feminist movement in general.

To return to Greer's statement, arguably women composers do not need to be of the same familial or political generation to experience interaction with forebears or to influence future descendants. The complexity of these relationships and temporal spaces – gaps within gaps – can be overwhelming, and thus lead to a collective evasion of a musical feminist past by contemporary women practitioners. If you happen to fall between pre-defined 'generations' or bouts of feminist action, or if your musical education does not include works by women or an analysis of its cultural significance – for example the set works lists for the music A-level syllabus in the UK for the four main exam boards for 2013 only included one woman, the contemporary jazz musician Norah Jones – then this is a reasonable strategy.[41]

At its most extreme, however, Audre Lorde argues that this sense of historical amnesia regarding women's history in general – which can also be identified more specifically in musicology – is 'an important social tool for a repressive society'.[42] The processes of archiving, carving out a historical space and the later construction of a feminist musicological narrative therefore become political acts. Within these processes, an *identity* for women as creators, makers and engagers of music emerges which does not necessarily pre-exist or flow naturally from the political category of 'woman'. As Joan Wallach Scott argues in her work on feminist history: 'The identity of women, I argue, was not so much a self evident fact of history as it was evidence – from particular and discrete moments in time – of someone's, some group's, effort to identify and thereby mobilize a collectivity.'[43] The individual or group alluded to in the above quotation could (and perhaps should) be women themselves – as was the case with the SWM – and should be seen as interacting with aspects of gender, age, ethnicity, race and class.

The case of the SWM, therefore, highlights the productive possibilities of intergenerational creative 'action-based' relationships but also shows the tensions and ultimate flaws of collective ageing. As contemporary women negotiate these same issues – arguably in more complex ways than previously – it is worth

---

[41] See set works lists for A-level Music Syllabi for AQA 2013, Cambridge 2013 and 2014, OCR 2013 and Edexcel 2009–2014.

[42] See Lorraine Code, 'Age', in *Encyclopedia of Feminist Theories*, ed. Lorraine Code (London: Routledge, 2000), 13.

[43] Joan Wallach Scott, *The Fantasy of Feminist History* (Durham, NC and London: Duke University Press, 2011), 47.

considering moving away from a Freudian model of Oedipal parental relationships and looking towards further removed predecessors, through historical research and contemporary music programming that is sensitive to the implications of generational issues.

Chapter 7
Professionalism and Reception in the New York Composers' Forum: Intersections of Age and Gender

Melissa J. de Graaf

The New York City Composers' Forum, a series of weekly concerts of new music, was one of the New Deal's most successful endeavours, showcasing composers like Aaron Copland, Henry Cowell, Amy Beach and Ruth Crawford. Question-and-answer sessions followed the concerts, inspiring comments, critiques and, often, attacks from the public. Transcripts of these question periods are a rich source of information on female composers' experiences, so often ignored in more mainstream dictionaries and other music resources. During her 1937 Composers' Forum Concert, composer Marion Bauer was asked to explain the scarcity of women composers. Bauer replied: 'There are a great many more than you think. What many women composers need is encouragement and an opportunity to work and to be taken seriously ... Just think of us as composers and never call us lady composers.'[1] Forum sources indicate that numerous female composers were active during the 1920s and 1930s, but have simply been written out of history. They include fifteen professional female composers and several dozen female students from institutions of higher learning in the greater New York area who took part in special student concerts beginning in the third season of the Forum.

This chapter examines the intersection of age and gender in the reception of female composers – student and professional – in the Forum. Comments from the audience were often coloured by assumptions based on both age and gender. I analyse the reception of female composers within the context of the Great Depression, addressing in my discussion the interlocking systems of oppression of gender and age, as well as other factors such as marital status and musical style. The harshest, most sarcastic comments were reserved for those women composing in an ultra-modernist style. I also explore comments by Forum director Ashley Pettis, by composers and by audience members that show an at times hyper-awareness of age. Female students experienced a unique reception in the Forum, treated differently from both their male counterparts and the professional female composers. Finally, I consider the reasons behind the sharp decline in female

---

[1] Composers' Forum Transcript, 8 January 1937.

representation during the later seasons of the Forum, and the different impacts that decline had based on age and professional status.

Female Composers and Employment during the Great Depression

Female composers, like their male counterparts, received no direct financial assistance from the Composers' Forum. Women were far less likely to hold teaching or conducting jobs than men – most female composers eked out a living giving music lessons to private students. In fact, only one woman in the Composers' Forum, Marion Bauer, held a permanent teaching position at the time. Some women, like Ruth Crawford, had husbands who earned enough income to support the family. Although Crawford and her husband, Charles Seeger, struggled for years to make ends meet, he eventually was hired to work for the Resettlement Administration in 1935 – Crawford referred to it as 'their' job and shared in the labour. Other women, like Johanna Beyer, struggled desperately to stay afloat financially, scraping by with a handful of piano students, settlement house work and, eventually, home relief. Her letters are filled with anxious details about bill payments, cheques, poor heating in her Greenwich Village apartment and, in the end, lack of money for food and for hospital and medical needs.

Female college students and recent graduates also suffered. Many college graduates were out of work, fighting for jobs they had gone to college to avoid. Their own institutions failed to give them support. Deans at women's colleges urged graduates not to look for jobs.[2] This argument was underscored by Labor Secretary Frances Perkins, an important if conflicted role model for professional women. Most college graduates were not considered heads of households and were therefore thought to have been working merely for 'pin-money', money used for unnecessary luxuries. Perkins criticised the pin-money girl, calling her a 'menace to society, a selfish and short-sighted creature who ought to be ashamed of herself'.[3]

Age and Identity in the Composers' Forum

While feminist scholars have long considered the intersection of gender, race and class, the factor of age is usually conspicuously absent. Toni Calasanti and

---

[2] Laura Hapke, *Daughters of the Great Depression: Women, Work and Fiction in the American 1930s* (Athens: University of Georgia Press, 1995), 184.

[3] U.S. Department of Labor, *Annual Report of the Secretary of Labor* (Washington, DC: Government Publication Office, 1930), quoted in Nancy Woloch, *Women and the American Experience* (New York: McGraw-Hill, 1984), 452. For a discussion of the tenuous relationship between Perkins and Anderson and Perkins's attitudes towards women and labour, see Lillian Holmen Mohr, *Frances Perkins: 'That Woman in FDR's Cabinet!'* (Croton-on-Hudson, NY: North River Press, 1979).

Kathleen Slevin, in their introduction to *Age Matters: Realigning Feminist Thinking*, suggest that feminist theorists have in fact perpetuated the cultural devaluation of ageing by neglecting this factor.[4] Feminist theory has seen several decades of quite successful application in musicology, but music scholars have not as yet incorporated theories of age into their analyses. Calasanti and Slevin's model of age relations may prove a useful starting point for my discussion here. They organise their approach into three main inquiries: 1) how a society organises by age; 2) how groups within a society are defined in relation to and in opposition to one another on the basis of age; and 3) how age intersects with gender and other factors to form interlocking systems of oppression.

The Composers' Forum certainly organised programmes by age. In addition to the clearly demarcated student concerts beginning in the third season, there was also a 1938 concert of the Alumni Association of the Juilliard Graduate School (consisting of very *recent* alumni) and a 1940 Young Composers Concert. Moreover, the regular concerts often featured programming based on age, whether extremely disparate (oldest and youngest composers together) or similar (usually two young composers). For instance, Morris Mamorsky was 27 when he appeared in the Forum alongside Henry Holden Huss, age 76. Norman Cazden and Frederick Woltmann seem to have been paired more according to their youth than to a shared aesthetic. Cazden was 23 and Woltmann 29 at the time of their concert, making them two of the youngest composers programmed.

Individuals in the Forum were frequently defined by labels of age. Pettis several times alluded to Huss's age, proclaiming him more than once as the oldest composer in the Forum. William Schuman, on the other hand, was one of the Forum's 'discoveries', first appearing on a 1936 programme at age 26. Pettis conveyed the distinction of the occasion with the following introduction: 'I am sure that Mr. Schuman is unknown to most of those present. I feel that while we would not experience the thrill of a midwife, at least we have the pleasure of being either godfather or godmother at a christening.'[5] At subsequent concerts and in the associated Forum materials, Pettis continued to promote Schuman as a Forum prodigy.

Youth and old age – represented in the Forum by Schuman and Huss – also mapped onto that most heated of oppositions: modernism versus traditionalism. Scholars have explored associations between modernism and masculinity, as well as female composers' challenges to the masculinist paradigm of modernism, but we forget that perceptions of modernism have as much to do with youthfulness as with masculinity and 'virility'.[6] 'Virility' itself is as much about age as it is

---

[4] Toni M. Calasanti and Kathleen F. Slevin, 'Introduction', in *Age Matters: Realigning Feminist Thinking*, ed. Toni M. Calasanti and Kathleen F. Slevin (New York: Routledge, 2006), 2.

[5] Composers' Forum Transcript, 21 October 1936.

[6] For discussions of modernism and masculinity, see Catherine Parsons Smith, '"A Distinguishing Virility": Feminism and Modernism in American Art Music', in

about gender, implying youth as well as masculinity. In one of the most balanced and admirable defences of new music in the Forum transcripts, composer Henry Hadley stated:

> The modern tonality is extraordinarily interesting. It is all very interestingly worked out and if some of us are not as yet trained enough to hear them, nevertheless we must have the patience to listen to everything that is going on in our country because the younger men are reaching out and doing things. We are not standing still but going ahead harmonically and in every way musically.[7]

Modernism fell clearly under the purview of young men. Howard Hanson, though not much older than many of the modernists, responded to the critique of romanticism with some well-appreciated self-mockery, replying, 'I am, of course, absolutely "old hat" in this matter. I am 16th century. Oh! way back – maybe the 15th or 14th', before seriously defending his position, arguing against the use of music for political aims.[8]

Intersections of Gender and Age: Reception of Female Composers in the Forum

Bauer's request to be taken seriously was of primary concern for female composers, whose music was too often received with good-natured cordiality but without respect. Female students in the Forum were frequently condescended to – audiences did not take them seriously and often questioned their intentions towards pursuing careers in music. Questions and comments were written on slips of paper, to be handed up and read by Pettis. To the students of Vassar College and The Women's College of the University of North Carolina: 'Are any of you planning to follow music as a profession and continue composing upon finishing college?' The replies from the first several women were 'I am', but Helen Garth, perhaps annoyed by what she perceived as condescension, answered tongue-in-cheek: 'It's a secret.'[9] Pettis, too, allowed condescension to creep into his tone:

Cecilia Reclaimed: Feminist Perspectives on Gender and Music, ed. Susan C. Cook and Judy S. Tsou (Urbana: University of Illinois Press, 1994); and Judith Tick, 'Charles Ives and Gender Ideology', in *Musicology and Difference: Gender and Sexuality in Music Scholarship*, ed. Ruth A. Solie (Berkeley: University of California Press, 1993). For more on female composers challenging patriarchal alignments of modernism, see Ellie Hisama, *Gendering Musical Modernism: The Music of Ruth Crawford, Marion Bauer, and Miriam Gideon* (Cambridge: Cambridge University Press, 2001); and Melissa J. de Graaf, '"Never Call us Lady Composers": Gendered Receptions in the New York Composers' Forum, 1935–1940', *American Music* 26 (2008).

[7] Composers' Forum Transcript, 9 December 1936.
[8] Composers' Forum Transcript, 17 March 1937.
[9] Composers' Forum Transcript, 15 March 1939.

'Would the audience please come forward? These girls are not accustomed to speaking in public.' The students of Hunter College faced scrutiny, doubt and mockery. Listeners wondered whether they had ever written a fugue and if they had even heard any contemporary music. One member of the audience inquired, 'What is your gossip on polyphony?' The strange query was met with silence, until Pettis finally commented, 'Evidently there is no gossip on polyphony.'[10] The term 'gossip' connotes, of course, femininity, frivolity and youthful silliness – not the kinds of associations serious female students would have desired. Another listener posed this withering question: 'Why bring your exercises and homework to the Composers' Forum-Laboratory. Where is your creative music?' After a short silence, Pettis prompted, 'What, no response?' to which one student admitted, 'We are crushed.' One last condescending barb rounded out the evening: Pettis announced that somebody had written two words on a slip of paper: 'Baby Talk'.

The professional female composers were not exempt from condescending attitudes. Audiences frequently complimented the professionals (though *not* the modernists) on their charm and good looks. One composer who was particularly vulnerable to such 'compliments' was Mabel Wood-Hill. Almost completely forgotten today, Wood-Hill was quite successful in her day, particularly in the music club circuit. She and her husband, Frederick Trevor Hill, a prominent lawyer and author, had homes in Irvington on Hudson and in the city; Wood-Hill had a studio on West 86th Street, where she entertained. She was, in other words, a society lady, viewed more as a patroness than a serious composer. Her orchestral works were frequently and successfully performed, and she won several national prizes, but they were from amateur associations or groups associated with feminised musical culture – from the Associated Glee Clubs of America and Canada and from the National Penwomen's League.

Wood-Hill's Forum experience seems laced with unspoken accusations of dilettantism. In her 1936 Forum, some admirers found her music 'delightful', 'beautiful' and 'such a treat after the last three male composers'. Other listeners criticised her dependence on programmatic elements in her music. One audience member challenged: 'Is not music, as a means of expression, sufficient unto itself without literary appendages?' to which the composer replied, 'It certainly is. In choosing a program it is very difficult to know exactly what should be on it. I should have liked to put on some transcriptions of Bach or Scriabine but Mr. Pettis would not let me.' Finally, she was asked whether she thought '"charm" [was] more important than musical content'. She responded defensively that they would 'have to have another Forum of [her] works'.[11] There were other, presumably worse, comments that Pettis declared he was not reading – questions 'written under the cloak of anonymity'. Perhaps Wood-Hill regretted her programming choices, most of which reflected her accessible, at times sentimental, style, with two of the works based on children's literature: *Wind in the Willows Suite* for orchestra and

---

[10] Composers' Forum Transcript, 24 May 1939.
[11] Composers' Forum Transcript, 25 November 1936.

Aesop's Fables (1925) for voice and orchestra. She may have felt that different, less light-hearted selections – even if mere transcriptions or arrangements – would have been taken more seriously by listeners, particularly fellow composers.

Other women in the Forum also fell victim to 'charm' comments. An audience member pronounced after a concert of Bauer's works, 'We may not have many women composers but what there are, have written most charming music.'[12] The audience at Alda Astori's concert appears to have been so overwhelmed by Astori's good looks that all musical considerations were overlooked, or at best regarded in relation to her pretty face. Several members of the audience commented on her charming style, and one listener wrote: 'Your music is indeed reflective of your beautiful self. Charming and delightful.'[13] There were, of course, no compliments for 'handsome' male composers, and very few instances in which their music was labelled as charming. The seemingly innocuous term 'charming' of course connotes a stereotypically feminine, vacuous, superficiality – certainly nothing to be taken seriously.

Undoubtedly adding to Astori's problems that evening was the prominence of the harp in nearly all of her selections. The harp had been considered an emblem of middle-class, feminine gentility since the early 1800s and was often taken less than seriously by composers. According to Samuel Milligan's blog post on the Harp Column Blogs (21 April 2006), it was thought that the 'inherent beauty of the harp would enhance the beauty – real or imagined – of any young lady sitting behind it'.[14] Astori was not a harpist herself and had, ironically, composed the works for her husband, Salvatore de Stefano, who performed them that evening.

Far from being isolated examples, these comments reflect a tenacious Victorian ideology surrounding gender, genre and form. The ideology of separate spheres held that women belonged in the domestic environment of the home, while men could function in the public sphere, working outside the home. Professional, public music-making, as well as the creative enterprise of composition, was the role of the man.[15] Beginning in the late 1800s, the growing number of female music teachers and the appearance of the first generation of female composers

---

[12] Composers' Forum Transcript, 8 January 1937. Works performed that evening included the *Fantasia Quasi una Sonata*, Op. 18 (1928), Four Poems, Op. 16, on texts by John Gould Fletcher (1924) ('Through the Upland Meadows', 'I Love the Night', 'Midsummer Dreams', 'In the Bosom of the Desert'), Viola Sonata, Op. 22 (1935) and String Quartet, Op. 20 (1927).

[13] Composers' Forum Transcript, 22 January 1937.

[14] For further reading on the gendering of harp performance, see Olga Gross, 'Gender and the Harp. I', *American Harp Journal* 13 (1992); and Olga Gross, 'Gender and the Harp. II', *American Harp Journal* 14 (1993).

[15] Masculinity had long been viewed as the ultimate and only creative force. Men were defined as creators, while women were procreators, limited to imitating or inspiring. Women who did aspire to artistic creation were perceived as masculine, lesbian or pseudo-males. Christine Battersby explores masculinity as a creative force in *Gender and Genius: Towards a Feminist Aesthetics* (Bloomington: Indiana University Press, 1989).

of American classical music contributed to what many modernists perceived as a 'feminisation' of American music and musical life, which they believed needed to be attacked and eradicated. Deems Taylor wrote, in the music article for *Civilization in the United States* (1922): 'This well-nigh complete feminization of music is bad for it ... [Women's] predominance in our musical life aggravates our already exaggerated tendency to demand that art be edifying.'[16]

Perhaps as a reaction to the increased visibility of women in public musical life, particularly as composers, critics took up the debate over the 'man-tone' in music.[17] This 'man-tone' had less to do with the actual sound of the music and more to do with a certain ideology of genre and form. Suitable forms for women composers included songs, piano pieces and small chamber works, while the man-tone consisted of the larger forms: symphonies, operas and other large-scale orchestral music. As the composer Mary Carr Moore wrote: 'So long as a woman contents herself with writing graceful little songs about springtime and the birdies, no one resents it or thinks her presumptuous; but woe be unto her if she dares attempt the larger forms!'[18]

The idea of the man-tone put female composers in a double bind. A woman could either avoid the large forms, retaining her femininity but relinquishing respect as a composer, or pursue the large forms in an attempt to be taken seriously as a composer, while relinquishing her femininity. Women who chose to write in the larger genres were accused of 'seeking after virility'. Women who followed the first path were rarely taken seriously by critics and other male composers. This double bind and the Victorian gender ideologies behind it help account for the condescending and patronising reception most female composers received in the Composers' Forum. They fail to explain, however, the much harsher criticism and sarcasm directed towards Crawford, Beyer and other 'ultra-modern' female composers.

Reception of the Ultra-modernists

The transcripts from Beyer's Forum record sessions that degenerated into sometimes vicious attacks on the composer both professionally and personally. At

---

[16] Deems Taylor, 'Music', in *Civilization in the United States*, ed. Harold Stearns (New York: Harcourt, Brace, 1922), 205–6. For a discussion of the feminisation of mass culture, see Andreas Huyssen, *After the Great Divide: Modernism, Mass Culture, Postmodernism* (Bloomington: Indiana University Press, 1986).

[17] For a discussion of the 'man-tone' and the concept of virility in the early twentieth century, see Tick, 'Charles Ives and Gender Ideology', 91–2.

[18] Mary Carr Moore, 'Is American Citizenship a Handicap to a Composer?', *Musician* 40 (1935): 5, 8 (an interview by Juliet Lane), quoted in Catherine Parsons Smith and Cynthia S. Richardson, *Mary Carr Moore, American Composer* (Ann Arbor: University of Michigan Press, 1987), 173.

her first concert in 1936, her music was described as chaotic and weird, containing 'pathological sounds and noises'. The final question brought gender tensions to the surface: 'Miss Beyer, you seem to have gone your male preceptors one better in search for strange and ineffective tonal combinations. Have you consciously adopted Rudyard Kipling's statement, "The female of the species is deadlier [sic] than the male" as a guiding principle in your composition?'[19] At her second Forum concert the following year, Beyer's style of piano playing caught the attention of the audience. One audience member asked, 'How can you explain your music and your playing with your fists?' Another asked, 'Did you strike your elbows and fists at random?' Pettis omitted the second half of that question: 'Did you intend your pantomime to be part of the effect? How are your elbows?'[20]

This last, sarcastic remark reflects one of the major differences between criticism of male modernists and that of female modernists. The men were almost entirely exempt from sarcastic taunts, while sarcasm was a defining characteristic of the transcripts of female modernists. One audience member asked Baetz who had written the 'delightful vocalizations' of her Vocalizes. Another listener suggested that Baetz's compositions for Violin and Piano 'could very well do without the Piano and might do without the Violin as well', and that her 'variations on "doom-de-doom" are really not sufficiently infantile'.[21] One critic suggested she write a piece for 'toothless player on a comb', to which she replied that it had already been done. At Crawford's concert, one of the less kind attendees commented: 'Did you try hard to be original? Did you succeed?' This was followed by yet another sarcastic jibe: 'Do you really believe that your music is the future music of America? If so, then I pray for its deliverance.'[22]

While some of the criticism Beyer endured was directly in reference to her status as a female composer, Crawford's 1938 transcript is remarkably free from overt references to her gender. The only direct reference to her sex was one she raised herself. Asked whether she had written any music lately, she responded, 'I have been composing babies the past five years.'[23] The sarcasm directed at Crawford was no match for the antipathy endured by Beyer. One likely factor for this was Beyer's German nationality, at a time when anti-Fascist sentiment in the New York music world was running high. It is also quite possible that Beyer's status as a single woman, without the protection of a man, made her more vulnerable

---

[19] Composers' Forum Transcript, 20 May 1936.
[20] Composers' Forum Transcript, 19 May 1937. There is some discrepancy between these comments and the pieces listed on the programme for the 1937 concert, none of which include tone clusters. It is quite possible that Beyer and Baetz performed the *Movement for Two Pianos* again, which does contain tone clusters.
[21] Composers' Forum Transcript, 15 December 1937.
[22] Composers' Forum Transcript, 6 April 1938.
[23] Crawford's first child, Michael, was born in 1933; Peggy followed in 1935, Barbara in 1937 and Penny in 1943.

to the type of attacks Crawford managed to avoid.[24] Beyer lived alone and was perceived as a solitary figure. Single women in the Forum were occasionally heckled, with such questions as, 'Have you read *Live Alone and Like It?*' Marjorie Hillis, a writer for American *Vogue*, wrote the bestseller *Live Alone and Like It* in 1936, intending it as a self-help, inspirational book for the countless new 'working girls' who had flocked to the cities in the 1920s and 1930s. Throughout the 1920s and into the 1930s, popular media represented the unmarried urban woman as a threat to men. As single women got older, the perceived threat shifted from the pin-money girl to the spinster figure, an unnatural character. Psychologists and psychoanalysts, jumping on the Freudian bandwagon, declared that a woman was 'not a complete being or a "normal" woman if she was not partnered with a male and reproductively successful'.[25] The possibility that such a woman might be a lesbian further contributed to the stigma. Like the 'lack of emotions' attributed to Beyer, the lack of a husband was an unnatural state for a woman at that time.

Decline of Women's Participation in the Forum

Professional women's participation in the Composers' Forum fluctuated dramatically in the five seasons under discussion. The first two years were steady, at 14 per cent and 12 per cent participation. Year three saw a sharp increase, to 21 per cent, followed by a dramatic decline in the fourth and fifth seasons, at 2 per cent and 7 per cent. The third season inaugurated a number of concerts devoted exclusively to student composers from various schools and colleges in New York and the surrounding area. Schools represented included a number of all-women colleges like Vassar, the Women's College of the University of North Carolina and Hunter College, as well as co-educational institutions such as Eastman, NYU and Juilliard. This change seems to have had an impact on the participation of professional female composers. While the female student composers experienced a high point in participation in season four (68 per cent of total student composers), professional women virtually disappeared from the programmes in the fourth and fifth seasons.

Perhaps the social repercussions of the Depression influenced the selection committee to give the few opportunities to men.[26] The last few years of the Forum saw a change in administration. The new, more academic members on the selection committee may have been less tolerant of 'lady composers'. Possibly the director

---

[24] Crawford's husband, Charles Seeger, influential musicologist, educator and sometime composer, would have been well known to many in the Forum audience, particularly through his work in leftist musical circles.

[25] Trisha Franzen, *Spinsters and Lesbians: Independent Womanhood in the United States* (New York: New York University Press, 1996), 7.

[26] For an in-depth discussion of gender bias in the Depression era, see Hapke, *Daughters of the Great Depression*.

and selection committee felt the committee had already done its duty or filled some unspoken quota in the earlier seasons, and that there was nothing unusual in the absence of women in the late 1930s. Or perhaps they thought the inclusion of so many female student composers was sufficient in representing the genders. It is also possible that women composers stopped submitting selections. Perhaps the atmosphere of the Forum, with its frequent attacks and often gendered criticism, discouraged women from taking part.

The only comments during Forum sessions on the representation of women composers occurred during the second season. Prior to Mabel Wood-Hill's concert, Pettis apologised for the lack of women composers in the Forum, stating: 'I am not ready to offer an explanation for this. It certainly is not because of any prejudice on the part of the Committee, but women composers seem to be infrequent occurrences.'[27] A month and a half later, at Bauer's second Forum, Pettis announced: 'Tonight is the first evening that a composer has had a second appearance. To some extent I feel that it makes up for the lack of woman composers featured in the Composers' Forum-Laboratory. This is beyond our control, however. There seems to be a dearth of women composers.'[28]

Several key pieces of evidence suggest that the inclusion of female composers was well within the control of the committee, whose selection process may not have been as blind as official documentation indicates. Paolo Gallico mentioned being asked by Pettis to participate, and Henry Brant remembered being invited, if you knew someone. If it is true that some composers were simply invited by Pettis or by another member of the committee, then the lack of women in the Forum was certainly not 'beyond [their] control', as Pettis claimed at Bauer's Forum session.

Bauer, one of the few female composers of her time active as a professor, music critic and leader in the musical community, expressed her own opinion about the 'dearth' of women composers during her second season Forum, as quoted at the beginning of this chapter. She flatly contradicted Pettis's statement, maintaining that there were many more women active as composers than was apparent from Composers' Forum concerts, and that women needed support, opportunities to have their works performed and, above all, to be taken seriously.

Conclusions

The importance of the Composers' Forum records for female composers of the time period cannot be overstated. These documents show the unique obstacles women faced – the challenges resulting from intersections of gender, age, class, marital status and musical style. The transcripts show how these factors became tools by which to criticise and attack women for dilettantism, unconventional behaviour or

---

[27] Composers' Forum Transcript, 25 November 1936.
[28] Composers' Forum Transcript, 8 January 1937. Although Pettis called it her second appearance, Bauer had actually appeared in three Forums the previous season.

a modernist aesthetic. Analysing these composers' experiences through the lens of intersecting systems of oppression gives us valuable new insight into the ways in which women of different ages negotiated the tricky landscape of musical culture in the 1930s. Despite the commonly held belief that female composers were few and far between in this period, it is clear from these sources that women were not only expressing themselves through music, but also fighting back to claim their rightful place in musical modernism.

PART III
Contemporary Creative Practices and Identities

PART III

Chapter 8
Urchins and Angels: Little Orphan Annie and Clichés of Child Singers

Jacqueline Warwick

Flute and harmonica echo one another with a wistful phrase, and the camera pans slowly upward from a brass plate reading 'The Hudson Home for Girls' as a child's voice is heard singing softly. We see the little girl perched in an open window, gazing out on the New York city skyline as she sings lyrics about the parents she dreams will come back to claim her one day. Her sweet voice soars hopefully through the arpeggiated tune, demonstrates a bit more grit in the short phrases of the song's B section and then returns to the longer melodic lines and gentle melancholy of the opening verse. The song is 'Maybe', in the first scene of the John Huston-directed film *Annie* (1982), and the young actress, Aileen Quinn, is the envy of every girl watching, either during the film's original 1982 theatrical run or in its long life in various formats for home consumption.

Hundreds of girls have learned the song 'Maybe', and the anthemic 'Tomorrow' featured later in the score, in service to a production of *Annie*, but the song – and, indeed, Annie herself – has also become a staple for young girls studying voice and dreaming of acting careers. The plucky orphan girl seems to combine just the right amount of softness and sass, and her musical language is beautifully suited to the female pre-pubescent voice. What is more, the Tony Award-winning musical play of *Annie* offers several other roles for little girls; indeed, it is the Broadway musical which most heavily relies on pre-pubescent girls as actors and singers, and thus girls' daydreams of the stage are most likely to come to fruition via a production of *Annie*. So what can Annie teach us about what girls are? What is the secret of her decades-long appeal to girls, most of whom have no acquaintance with their heroine's hard knock life?

Carolyn Steedman argues that the figure of a child in art often symbolises human interiority, so that the prospect of a performing child is suffused with nostalgia and wistful introspection for the adult viewer. She notes that the performing child embodies the 'search for the self and the past that is lost and gone ... since the end of the eighteenth century, the lost object has come to assume the shape and form of a child'.[1] For audience members who are themselves children, of course, the child performer may represent inspiration and potential, modelling an ideal of

---

[1] Carolyn Steedman, *Strange Dislocations: Childhood and the Idea of Human Interiority, 1780–1930* (Cambridge, MA: Harvard University Press, 1995), 174.

childhood ability to be striven for. These are but two of the ways in which a child performer simultaneously conjures both the past and the future.

The performing child is often presented as a redemptive figure, the magical child who gives us wonder, love and joy, by re-awakening our childish wonder and delight in the world. This notion is summed up neatly in the trailer for the 1982 film of *Annie*, which proclaims: 'She is the child in all of us'. As with any roles, the parts available to child performers are shaped by clichés and stereotypes, and these govern our thinking about what children are like. For girls, the two most prominent archetypes have been the angelic, delicate and wan girl who arouses our impulse to console and protect, and the feisty, spunky girl of the street who teaches us to know ourselves. These archetypes are often assigned to singing girls as 'the little girl with the voice of an angel' and 'the little girl with the great big voice'. I will argue that a crucial aspect of Annie's success is her blurring of this distinction through combining vulnerability with toughness.

These sweet and sassy characterisations of girls are invariably shaped by hegemonic understandings of race and class; and here, the figures of Topsy and Eva serve as paradigms. These two girls originate in Harriet Beecher Stowe's famous 1852 novel *Uncle Tom's Cabin*, a bestseller in its day, and often credited with galvanising the movement to abolish slavery in the United States. Eva St. Clare is presented as an ethereal golden child, deeply religious, compassionate and kind, in spite of being fatally ill. Eva's angelic virtue is contrasted with the wilful, savage, slave girl Topsy, whose wicked ways and rough language are eventually tamed at the deathbed of her young mistress. The characters of Topsy and Eva gained a life beyond the page, however, enjoying many escapades on the vaudeville stage and in the early days of film, most famously through the work of the Duncan Sisters, who performed the roles for decades (one sister with a wig of golden ringlets, the other in blackface). Furthermore, it is possible even today to find Topsy and Eva dolls, which have two heads and no legs: when the doll is held up, the full skirt conceals either the face of sweet, saintly Eva or that of impish, wild-haired Topsy.[2]

These sentimental characterisations of children as either wild and close to nature or demure and (over-)civilised predate Topsy and Eva, of course, and began to appear in European culture with the rise of Romantic ideals in the eighteenth century. Indeed, the figure of Topsy in Beecher Stowe's work may have reminded some readers of the wild, unsettling child acrobat Mignon, whose death is an important plot device in Goethe's 1795 *bildungsroman*

---

[2] I have written further about Topsy, Eva and the Duncan Sisters in my *Girl Groups, Girl Culture: Popular Music and Identity in the 1960s* (New York: Routledge, 2007). Consideration of Topsy and Eva is a major theme in Robin Bernstein's excellent *Racial Innocence: Performing American Childhood from Slavery to Civil Rights* (New York: New York University Press, 2011). See also W.T. Lhamon's analysis in his *Raising Cain: Blackface Performance from Jim Crow to Hip Hop* (Cambridge, MA: Harvard University Press, 1998), 140–45.

Wilhelm Meister's Apprenticeship, helping the protagonist to understand himself through his grief over Mignon. Just as Topsy took on a life outside her original story, so Mignon survived as a stock character for girls on the stage, and also for girls making their living as street performers; Carolyn Steedman's *Strange Dislocations* explores the centrality of Mignon to both high and low art in Victorian Britain, considering iterations of the Mignon figure on the stage, page and canvas.[3] And just as Topsy's dangerous wildness is contrasted with and rendered safe by her gentle companion, iterations of Mignon can be seen as the foil to the doe-eyed, porcelain-skinned girls painted by Jean-Baptiste Greuze (1725–1805). Greuze's sentimental portraits of children in distress – weeping over the death of a pet, for example – fetishised the tender vulnerability of pampered children for the generation influenced by the work of Goethe, Rousseau, Diderot and other Enlightenment figures.[4]

The 'girl with the voice of an angel' and the 'little girl with the great big voice' are thus versions of these archetypes, assigned to the little girl on stage, and they confirm many class prejudices. Indeed child singers actually represent class groups in fairly specific ways through voice type ('angelic' or 'big'). A Victorian English study of the child's voice, still considered authoritative in the literature on vocal development, collected and presented the views of many choral directors and teachers of singing. One informant, a choral director at a church, draws a direct connection between a working-class, urban childhood and a strident vocal style, perhaps close to the musical theatre convention now known as 'belting', a twangy, nasal quality that is favoured in Broadway and other contemporary, commercial music styles:

> Rough play in the noisy streets, attended by loud shouting, I find to be, through forcing the tones of the lower register, the most frequent cause of failure in training boys' voices; so boys of superior classes make the best singers [in cathedral choirs].[5]

The class background of child performers is of huge significance in the twentieth and twenty-first centuries as well; Shirley Temple's mother insisted on the family's middle-class status, which made Shirley's 'play' very different from the breadwinning work of vaudeville kids. More recently, as Jane O'Connor reports, the producers of the *Harry Potter* film series explicitly sought to 'cast the parents'

---

[3] Steedman, *Strange Dislocations*.
[4] Emma Barker, 'Reading the Greuze Girl: The Daughter's Seduction', *Representations* 117 (2012).
[5] Mr Turpin, cited in Lennox Brown and Emil Behnke, *The Child's Voice: Its Treatment with Regard to After Development* (London: Sampson Low, Marston, Searle, and Rivington, 1885), 17.

of their child actors, believing that children with working-class 'stage mothers' would lack the unaffected naturalness they sought.[6]

The girl at the centre of my discussion here is explicitly working class, an urchin of the streets who has existed as a particular model of girl, in various media, for nearly ninety years. Little Orphan Annie made her debut in a 1924 newspaper comic by the artist Harold Gray, who continued to draw her until his death in 1968 (at which point other artists took over: the strip ran until 2010). The cartoon allowed Gray to express his fiercely held political views over four decades: supporting a free market conservativism, scoffing at state welfare and Roosevelt's New Deal, opposing restrictions on child labour and fomenting anxiety about communism. In this, her earliest incarnation, Annie was an almost Dickensian character, a model of toughness and determination whose serial adventures depicted the world of the underclasses but nevertheless had a broad appeal. Gray insisted that the girl show grit and sass, refusing sentiment and schmaltz as she made her way through the world. Her patron, Daddy Warbucks, whose fortunes rose and fell throughout the life of the series, often left her to manage on her own when he travelled for business, yet Annie never reproached him or expected to be cherished as a pampered dependent. In a 1947 plotline, for example, Annie worked as a grocery delivery girl, and offered the opinion that paid work for children was a good way to keep out of trouble. Gray made this philosophy more explicit in his own statements against regulating child labour: 'A little work never hurt any kid. Lord's sake, I was running a four-horse team in a field when I was nine years old. One of the reasons we have so much juvenile delinquency these days is that kids are forced by law to loaf around on street corners and get into trouble.'[7] Part of Annie's appeal for at least some of her readers, then, was her role as a level-headed, hardworking child in a climate where real children were perceived as spoiled, indolent and up to no good. When the cartoon strip was briefly cancelled in the 1920s, letters of protest proclaimed their love for Annie:

> First, she is the voice of the people; second because she is democratic in the true sense of the word, warm of heart, strong for the underdog; third because she is not dazzled by wealth or shoddy gentility; for because she is the eternal child that lives in the hearts of men and women ... children love her, adults sigh for their own lost spontaneity and initiative of youth, seeing them in her.[8]

During the 1930s, Annie was the focus of a popular radio serial, which aired in an after-school timeslot and was aimed at children, to the benefit of its sponsor Ovaltine. The voice of Annie was a 10-year-old Chicago actress, Shirley Bell,

---

[6] Jane O'Connor, *The Cultural Significance of the Child Star* (Abingdon: Routledge, 2008), 77.

[7] Bruce Smith, *The History of Little Orphan Annie* (New York: Ballantine Books, 1982), 65.

[8] Smith, *History of Little Orphan Annie*, 18.

who won the role after an audition process involving 500 children, and then held it for the entire nine and a half year run (1930–40).[9] This version of Annie's story had her living on a farm in the fictional town of Tomkins Corners and featured characters such as Ma and Pa Silo, the couple who care for Annie, and Annie's sidekick Joe Corntassel (voiced by a young Mel Tormé). It depicted Annie as 'much closer to Nancy Drew than Grey's [sic] streetwise scrambler'.[10] Gray's cartoon strip continued to run during Annie's radio years, of course, and there were two film versions (1932 and 1938), neither of which was successful with critics or audiences. Never a great believer in subtlety, Gray responded to Annie's 1930s film incarnations with a story line in his comic strip that saw Annie 'discovered' and sent to Hollywood, where she found herself exploited as the stand-in and stunt double for insufferable child star Tootsie McSnoots.[11]

The extent and complexity of Little Orphan Annie's biography will no doubt surprise readers who know her best through the 1977 Broadway musical, or – more likely – the 1982 film of the musical, which presents 'the iconic pop culture image of Annie' for contemporary fans.[12] The musical *Annie* positions the red-headed orphan explicitly in the Depression years, and drastically reimagines the political views of Gray and his characters, depicting Annie and Daddy Warbucks as friends to President Roosevelt and supporters of his New Deal. The stage play, first written by Martin Charnin and Tom Meehan in 1971, three years after Gray's death, would almost certainly not have met with Gray's approval.

The plot shows Annie in an orphanage run by the cruel Miss Hannigan, until she is chosen to visit the mansion of millionaire Oliver Warbucks as a sort of public relations stunt. She quickly wins the hearts of Warbucks and his entire household, but declines his offer to adopt her because she believes her parents are still alive. Miss Hannigan arranges for her con artist brother and girlfriend to pose as the long-lost parents in a scheme to get Warbucks' reward money, but Annie's orphanage friends reveal the plot and Annie is saved.

There are significant differences and continuities between Annie's cartoon world and her stage one. Gray's concept of the hero Daddy Warbucks is a man who has overcome humble beginnings and earned wealth selling munitions during the Great War, and he and his snobbish wife treat one another with contempt. Since in Gray's original conception it is Mrs Warbucks who brings home Orphan Annie for a vacation from poverty, it seems significant that this character is later erased (within the cartoon as well as in the musical), leaving Annie and Daddy as the ideal partnership.

---

[9] Smith, *History of Little Orphan Annie*, 42.
[10] Gerald Nachman, *Raised on Radio* (Los Angeles: University of California Press, 1998), 187.
[11] Smith, *History of Little Orphan Annie*, 44.
[12] Peter Hilliard, *Annie: A Rough Guide for the M.D.*, accessed 3 January 2014, http://peterhilliard.wordpress.com/2011/05/06/annie-a-rough-guide-for-the-m-d/.

The musical makes prominent use of girl performers, not just in the lead role, and so dozens of little girls were involved during the play's five-year run on Broadway, to say nothing of touring productions and community productions which continue to this day. The casting is a great challenge: the girl chosen to play Annie must act in virtually every scene, carry several songs and appear adorable and childlike, while also possessing the maturity to play the role of a neglected, streetwise 10-year-old whose sunny optimism carries her through some emotionally harrowing situations. Her unwavering cheerfulness is implausible, considering the wretchedness of her circumstances, and Joseph Zornado argues that

> In spite of her abandonment, her abuse, and her longing, or because of it, Annie sings, and she sings not about her sadness, anger, or confusion, but rather, about the promise of tomorrow: 'Tomorrow, tomorrow, I love you, tomorrow, you're always a day away.' These are not the child's words, but the adult's words put in the child's mouth. Annie's gleeful belief in tomorrow is the adult's nostalgia, the adult's longing for a Daddy Warbucks to save the day. Annie's story is a particularly pronounced version of how contemporary culture tells itself a story about the child in order to defend its treatment *of* the child. Annie's emotional state – her unflagging high spirits, angelic voice, and distinctly American optimism – grows out of the adult-inspired ideology of the child's 'resiliency.' This is self-serving, to say the least.[13]

The attraction of Annie, then, is her miraculous ability to find happiness against all reasonable odds and to serve as fictional evidence that children can survive unspeakable ill-treatment.

Martin Charnin and Tom Meehan devised the idea of a musical play based on the comic strip that would depict 'the lost, wandering child, brave, indomitable, a mythic figure in the annals of popular American culture, in contrast with the rough-hewn character of Oliver Warbucks – powerful, dynamic, ruthless', but retaining the style of the comic strip's arch humour and adult appeal. When they approached composer Charles Strouse, however, he disagreed with the direction: 'When Martin first brought it to me, he had this cartoon-y feel to it. His first idea was to do it with Bernadette Peters. The only way I could become interested in it was if it were done very much in the style of *Oliver!* or a Shirley Temple film.'[14]

Strouse, a conservatory-trained composer best known for his work on the 1960 musical *Bye Bye Birdie*, thus played a crucial role in recrafting the shape of the project, imagining the show as a child-centred drama combining pathos, comedy and child actors/singers. Whereas Charnin and Meehan perhaps anticipated an audience of adults reminiscing with irony about their childhood fandom of Little Orphan Annie, Strouse was able to imagine a cross-generational appeal,

---

[13] Joseph Zornado, *Inventing the Child: Culture, Ideology and the Story of the Child* (London: Routledge, 2004), 10.

[14] Cited in Smith, *History of Little Orphan Annie*, 89–90.

combining nostalgia for the 'pull together' spirit of the Depression years with a fresh-faced young cast and modern Broadway songs that did not merely pastiche 1930s music. Strouse was careful to include one musical number, 'You're Never Fully Dressed without a Smile', that was a fond recreation of 1930s popular music, but this could hardly be mistaken for an earnest attempt at historical authenticity. It features the orphanage girls play-acting the parts of a crooner and backing vocal trio, giggling, dressing up and hamming their way through an ostensibly improvised singalong with the radio. The number is strategically valuable in that it feeds the audience's sentimental wish for old-fashioned music, but also presents child performers brimming with immanence and youthful charm, and – because it is a self-conscious performance within the performance – it creates a certain distance from the 1930s period even as it emulates it. Other famous songs from the play, such as 'Maybe', 'Tomorrow' and 'Hard Knock Life', used unmistakeably contemporary musical language for Broadway in the 1970s.

Strouse's evocation of Shirley Temple, the most famous child star of 1930s Hollywood, was also shrewd, as Temple routinely played winsome tykes who charm older men in films such as *Little Miss Marker* (1934, directed by Alexander Hall) or *Curly Top* (1935, Irving Cummings), just as the stage version of Annie would have to do in her 1970s incarnation. In her study of iconic girls in popular culture, Valerie Walkerdine analyses the roles played by Temple as repetitive images of the 'poor girl whose main function is to charm the rich, persuade them through their love for her to love the poor and the unemployed, and to provide charity in the face of depression'.[15] The ideal stage Annie, then, would not only be cherubic and appealing, but also plucky and resourceful, and not too much a wan Eva St. Clare type. Thus the original Annie, Kristen Vigard, debuted the role at the Goodspeed Opera House in Connecticut, but was fired before the show opened on Broadway because it was felt she was too sweet and delicate. Strouse reports:

> It was hard for us to do, and of course very hard for her to accept ... We were all very, very guilty about doing it, it was very hard on her. Martin was particularly good, very thoughtful in the way he told her. But nevertheless she had to be told. Kristen was, and is, a very beautiful and gifted performer. But there was a built-in sweetness to her. It was making the show a little too saccharine. The audiences were buying it, but they were a little diabetic over it. It occurred to us that the tough girl, Andrea (McArdle), would give it that New York tough thing, and we wouldn't be asking the audience for sympathy ... she stood up to Warbucks, and the whole show became sassier.[16]

McArdle would be nominated for a Tony Award for her performance in the role and continues to be a well-respected performer in musical theatre, while

---

[15] Valerie Walkerdine, *Daddy's Girl: Young Girls and Popular Culture* (Cambridge, MA: Harvard University Press, 1997), 93.
[16] Smith, *History of Little Orphan Annie*, 94.

Vigard went on to a career including a recurring role on the 1980s tv soap opera *Guiding Light* and backup singing for bands such as the Red Hot Chili Peppers in the 1990s; she also recorded the vocals for many of the songs in the 1996 film *Grace of my Heart*, directed by Allison Anders and loosely based on the career of Carole King. In the immediate aftermath of the new casting, however, Vigard remained with the production as McArdle's understudy, a heartbreaking experience that would be faintly echoed by other Annies as they grew too old for the role and were pushed aside for younger actors. Some of those who played Annie or one of the orphans include Sarah Jessica Parker, Molly Ringwald and Alyssa Milano, mitigating somewhat the truism that child actors never go on to adult careers.

When McArdle stepped up to the role of Annie in 1977, she was nearly 14, but small enough to pass for a 10 year old. A studio recording by the Broadway cast was made that same year, and McArdle's vocal work is remarkable.[17] Given her age, it is likely that she had begun to experience at least pre-menarche, including the vocal changes that affect females, such as a quality of breathiness due to the 'mutational chink' caused by weak muscles not closing fully in the rear part of the glottis. According to vocal pedagogues such as Lynn Gackle, the female voice experiences change at puberty (though not as dramatically as the male voice) and is not fully mature until the early twenties; a child's larynx is approximately 5 mm long, but at adolescence it begins to lengthen to 17 mm in women and 23 mm in men, with this increase in length causing the 'Adam's Apple' bump in the male's throat.[18] During the years of puberty, many girl singers can manage the husky, airy quality of the voice by adopting a 'belting' technique. This approach to singing differs from the style taught in church choirs and used to sing classical choral repertoire, and it is also distinct from operatic technique, which requires healthy use of vibrato and is not generally encouraged for young voices (though to be sure, some young singers can manufacture a sound similar to vibrato by wobbling the jaw). McArdle sings with a strong belt style in 'Maybe', her opening number, with her forceful rhythmic precision and the syncopated orchestration creating a sense of energy and determination in the character of Annie.

By contrast, Aileen Quinn's 1982 film recording of the same song (discussed above, in the opening paragraph of this chapter) depicts a softer, more vulnerable Annie. Quinn was, importantly, four years younger than McArdle had been and actually the same age as the character she portrayed. The cinematic possibilities of close mic-ing and close up shots allow the audience to see and hear her in a more intimate way, permitting her more childlike voice to be heard. Quinn's singing is more breathy and tentative, and the song has been moved from B flat major to A flat to allow her pre-pubescent voice some comfort on the long-held high notes.

---

[17] Martin Charnin and Charles Strouse, *Annie*, with Andrea McArdle, Reid Shelton and Dorothy Loudon, LP, Columbia MasterWorks, 34712 (1977).

[18] Lynn Gackle, *Finding Ophelia's Voice, Opening Ophelia's Heart: Nurturing the Female Adolescent Voice* (Dayton, OH: Heritage Music Press, 2011), 12–14.

The orchestral arrangement has less rhythmic urgency and Quinn's phrasing is more fluid, creating a sense, perhaps, of a more passive, dreamy girl than her robust Broadway counterpart. If McArdle was a 'little girl with a great big voice' – or, more accurately, a teenager who could visually pass for a child – then Quinn veers closer to the 'girl with the voice of an angel' model of child singer.

Of course, the story of Annie depicts a girl of the streets, a child who is an old soul wise beyond her years, so Quinn's performance cannot be too sweet and waif-like. The second musical number of the show quickly demonstrates that Annie and her fellow orphans have spunk and sass, and 'Hard Knock Life' makes their drudgery seem charming and attractive. Although the girls are dressed in rags and forced to perform onerous chores, the theatrical exuberance of the number alleviates any worry that we are actually watching children suffer. As they complain about their hard lot, they dance, play and create more mess, apparently without fear of reprisal, and inspire the audience's sympathy and admiration for their pluck and cheeky high spirits.

The musical depiction of poverty as a thrilling adventure in 'Hard Knock Life' was obviously compelling enough for the young Shawn Carter (b. 1969) to find it moving and recall it in his adult work as Jay-Z. It may seem surprising to consider that a rapper associated with the thuggish, misogynist persona of a former drug dealer from the projects would have a sincere affection for the little girls in a Broadway musical, but he has stated that he found the Annie orphans moving and even inspirational, calling the song a 'ghetto anthem' in its own right and putting it at the centre of his own autobiographical hit song.[19] Jay-Z's 1998 'Hard Knock Life (Ghetto Anthem)' earned him a Grammy nomination and a gold certification from the Recording Industry Association of America, indicating sales in excess of one million. Certainly, the song allows Jay-Z to muse on his own triumph over adversity and rise to wealth and fame, in a life story that bears at least some similarities to Annie's. The chorus of the song (from the Broadway cast recording) is heard, in its entirety, six times through the course of Jay-Z's recording, and his video features different children lip-synching each time. Notably, however, the rapper himself never pretends to sing the chorus, perhaps indicating a reluctance to adopt the little girls' subject position fully, even as he identifies with their plight. Elsewhere, he makes his admiration for the girls' stoic endurance of hardship explicit by pointing out that 'If you notice the chorus, they're not singing like they're sad, they're singing like, "Yo, it's a hard knock life", just letting people know. It's a beautiful thing.'[20]

Although Jay-Z's song is explicitly autobiographical, and although he is of the generation that would have witnessed the height of *Annie*'s popularity in both stage and screen versions, the video does not nostalgically evoke the 1970s of his

---

[19] Michele Orecklin, 'Next Up: Big Daddy Warbucks', *Time* 152 (1998): 129; Nick Charles and Cynthia Wang, 'Street Singer: Jay-Z Makes the Switch from Hustler to Rap Star Look E-Z', *People Weekly* 51 (1999): 161.

[20] Jay-Z, quoted in Jacob Ogles, 'Samplin' Annie: "Hard Knock" Lyrics, Written to Last', *Vibe* (November 1999): 89.

childhood. The setting is quite clearly 1998, with actors dressed in contemporary styles, and none of the children featured is presented as Jay-Z's child self; indeed, the end of the video features the adult rapper sitting alongside children who are 'singing' (lip synching). In this way, he cannily disallows the viewer to consider childhood poverty merely a thing of the past, instead drawing a connection between underprivileged children in the 1930s, 1970s and 1990s while also acknowledging the differences in each generation's experience.[21]

The bravery and endurance of the Annie orphans does, perhaps, remind us of the realities of child labour and poverty in the past and the present day, even as we reassure ourselves that the little girls we are watching are all cherished, and rewarded for their performance.[22] Annie's suffering, and her cheerful determination in the face of her suffering, is crucial to the narrative that will see her rescued in the end by a kind older gentleman. 'Daddy' Warbucks is presented as a fierce and formidable man whose gruff demeanour is softened by his love for the plucky orphan, and it is Annie's charm that inspires Warbucks and his friend President Roosevelt to help the poor (in a blatant reversal of Harold Gray's strict anti-welfare politics). In the musical, 'Daddy' Warbucks is assigned a love interest in the form of his secretary Grace, but the final number clearly depicts Annie and 'Daddy' as the perfect couple. This scene works on one level as the acme of childish fantasy: a whole household has been put to work creating lavish Christmas delights for the hitherto deprived child, who can now bask in the love and security of a parent who will cherish and indulge her.

Yet I am surely not the only one who finds it harrowing viewing. I'm reminded of the plots of stage works such as Rossini's *Barber of Seville*, Molière's *Ecole des Femmes* and Sondheim's *Sweeney Todd*, stories in which wealthy men raise orphan girls and groom them to be their ideal wives. In her fascinating *How to Create the Perfect Wife*, furthermore, investigative journalist Wendy Moore traces the exploits of eighteenth-century gentleman Thomas Day, who took a girl from an orphanage and attempted to train her, according to the principles outlined by Jean Jacques Rousseau in his 1762 *Émile*, so that she might grow up to be his perfect bride.[23] This plot line is also seen in the real life relationship of Elvis Presley and his wife Priscilla; their romance began when she was 14 and he 24, and her parents

---

[21] The pastness of the 1970s childhood experience was made vividly clear to me when my own daughter, at age 10, chose to sing 'Maybe' in a local music festival in 2012. While memorising lyrics about how Annie's imagined parents 'collect things like ashtrays and art', she inquired: 'Mummy, what is an "ashtray" anyway?' Although my parents did not smoke, an ashtray was absolutely a standard item in my childhood home and the homes of most of my peers, yet it is a thing largely unknown to my child's generation.

[22] I examine the slippage between play and work more closely in *Musical Prodigies and the Performance of Childhood* (Routledge, forthcoming). I am intrigued by the extent to which child performance (musical and otherwise) can be recognised as child labour.

[23] Wendy Moore, *How to Create the Perfect Wife: Britain's Most Ineligible Bachelor and his Enlightened Quest to Train the Ideal Mate* (New York: Basic Books, 2013).

agreed to let her live with him from age 16 to 18 while she completed high school. The happy pairing of Annie with 'Daddy' after her trials and travails may therefore strike some as another uncomfortable blurring of the distinction between father and lover in connection to a vulnerable, adoring child.

Annie's fairytale ending may have a hidden lesson for girls that is sinister, recalling the assertions of children's literature scholars, such as Jacqueline Rose and Nina Auerbach, who have suggested that the function of works such as *Peter Pan* or *Alice in Wonderland* is to enable adult voyeurism.[24] But theatre historian Marah Gubar argues that this kind of response oversimplifies the many reasons adults love to see children perform, and she reminds us that children are themselves complex and discerning audience members for shows featuring child performers.[25] Gubar's study of the Victorian play *Peter Pan* uncovers the creative ways in which children incorporate the stories they see on stage into their own play-acting, story-writing and strategies of self-invention. The Annie who appears on stage and screen can speak to children in the audience in ways indecipherable to the adults watching alongside them.

It would seem, at any rate, that Annie is still a vital and vibrant part of mainstream music culture, still relevant to the ways in which we construct and negotiate girlhood. A new production celebrating the play's 35th anniversary was a success of the 2013 Broadway season. Perhaps more surprisingly, rapper Jay-Z and actor/rapper Will Smith have begun work on a film remake to air just in time for Christmas 2014. This film, originally planned as a vehicle for Smith's daughter Willow, will reimagine Annie as an African-American girl (played by Quvenzhané Wallis) with Oscar-winning actor Jamie Foxx playing a character based loosely on 'Daddy' Warbucks; the story will be set in the present day, with updated musical arrangements, presumably by Jay-Z.[26]

This is a thrilling new phase in Little Orphan Annie's already long life and potentially of great significance to our shared social understandings of what children are and the ways in which we depict them. A 2008 study of children's media by the Geena Davis Institute on Gender in Media concludes that 85.5 per cent of characters in children's films are white, and that three out of four characters are male. The symbolic impact of casting a black child in the single most-coveted musical theatre role for little girls is potentially tremendous. The redemptive power of the adorable street urchin, and all her complicated lessons about how to look at a performing girl, continues to be wonderfully resilient and adaptable as Annie is passed down as a heroine for new generations of girls.

---

[24] Nina Auerbach, 'Alice and Wonderland: A Curious Child', *Victorian Studies* 17 (1973); Jacqueline Rose, *The Case of Peter Pan, or, the Impossibility of Children's Fiction* (London: Macmillan, 1984).

[25] Marah Gubar, 'Peter Pan as Children's Theatre: The Issue of Audience', in *The Oxford Handbook of Children's Literature*, ed. Julia L. Mickenburg and Lynne Vallone (Oxford: Oxford University Press, 2011).

[26] *Annie* (dir. Will Gluck) went on general release in December 2014.

Chapter 9
'Across the Evening Sky': The Late Voices of Sandy Denny, Judy Collins and Nina Simone

Richard Elliott

In 2006, shortly before her 67th birthday, the American singer-songwriter Judy Collins undertook a tour of Australia and New Zealand, her first visit to the region in forty years. A number of press features and interviews accompanied Collins's visit, several of which were still featured at the top of the 'Press' section of the artist's website at the time of writing this chapter. One of the features, entitled 'Who Knows Where the Time Goes?' after one of Collins's 1960s hits, presented a reflection on the artist's career alongside observations on age and assertions of continued vitality.[1] Another, entitled 'Gem of a Voice Shines On', described some of Collins's most successful performances, including her recording of Joni Mitchell's 'Both Sides Now'. 'Its harpsichord tinkling has dated', wrote the journalist, 'but Collins' voice, warm and wise beyond its years, renders the song timeless.'[2]

I use these examples because they provide a foretaste of the themes of age, time and experience with which I wish to engage in this chapter, as well as a reference to the song upon which I will base my observations. The first aspect to note is the way in which an artist of Collins's longevity can afford to leave her website out of date in terms of publicity; the fact that the featured stories are seven years old at the time of access matters little when considering an artist whose performing career spans more than five decades. Second is the way in which age has become a factor in how Collins is discussed and promoted in the twenty-first century; it is both a calling card and a potential obstacle to overcome (seemingly not a problem for the age-affirming Collins). Third, and most important for this chapter, is the reference to the experiential mode of performing that the young Joni Mitchell tapped into in 'Both Sides Now', and which the 'wise beyond her years'

---

[1] Guy Blackman, 'Who Knows Where the Time Goes?', *The Age* online edition, 2 April 2006, accessed 5 August 2013, http://www.theage.com.au/news/music/who-knows-where-the-times-go/2006/03/30/1143441271278.html.

[2] 'Gem of a Voice Shines On', *The Age* online edition, 25 March 2006, accessed 5 August 2013, http://www.theage.com.au/news/music/gem-of-a-voice-shines-on/2006/03/24/1143083990392.html.

Collins introduced to the listening public in 1967. The 'timeless' song performed an early sense of lateness, an anticipation of experience normally associated with older people but surprisingly common among young songwriters.

Perhaps it shouldn't be so surprising to encounter such early lateness. As Kathleen Woodward observes, 'Age is a subtle continuum, but we organize this continuum into "polar opposites"', creating unhelpful distinctions between young and old, innocence and experience.[3] Imaginations, actual experiences and representations of age and ageing bodies get folded into each other through public discourse and popular culture. As Andrew Blaikie notes, there may be no denying the irreversibility of time and age, yet '"Maturity" itself is a term capable of many and varied definitions and the biological is but one of these.'[4] Such observations are useful when considering the possibility for, and even prevalence of, anticipated lateness in popular songwriting and singing, where strategies for dealing with age, time and experience are a constant (as they are in life), allowing multiple stages of reflection and multiple opportunities to feel 'late'.

Popular music artists, as performers in the public eye, offer a privileged site for the witnessing and analysis of ageing and its mediation, providing listeners with 'sounded experience', a term intended to describe how music reflects upon and helps to mediate life experience over extended periods of time.[5] Added to this is the fact that sound recording provides a rich space for exploring issues of memory, time, lateness and afterlife; in the brief examples cited above, it is the continued presence of Collins's recordings that allows for the stitching together of the artist's life narrative and the 'subtle continuum' of her public persona. This chapter engages the concept of anticipated lateness via discussion of the work of three female musicians whose work offers valuable insights into the interplay of history, biography and memory: Sandy Denny, Judy Collins and Nina Simone. It focuses specifically on the representation of innocence and experience via the 'late voice', a concept which is exemplified by these artists but which extends to a broad range of modern (post-mid-twentieth-century) popular musics and musicians. When referring to 'lateness', I have in mind five primary issues: chronology (the stage in an artist's career), the vocal act (the ability to convincingly portray experience), afterlife (posthumous careers made possible by recorded sound), retrospection (how voices 'look back' or anticipate looking back) and the writing of age, experience, lateness and loss into song texts. The song 'Who Knows Where the Time Goes', written by Denny and later performed by Collins and Simone, provides a case study for this discussion and is analysed in

---

[3] Kathleen Woodward, *Aging and Its Discontents: Freud and Other Fictions* (Bloomington and Indianapolis: Indiana University Press, 1991), 6.

[4] Andrew Blaikie, *Ageing and Popular Culture* (Cambridge: Cambridge University Press, 1999), 6.

[5] See Richard Elliott, *Fado and the Place of Longing: Loss, Memory and the City* (Farnham: Ashgate, 2010), 126–30.

terms of its representation of time and experience and in relation to the lives and works of its interpreters.

Sandy Denny

Sandy Denny (born Alexandra Elene Maclean Denny in 1947 in Wimbledon) established herself as a performer in the London folk scene of the mid-1960s. Denny had shown early promise as a singer, though a visit to the Royal College of Music with her mother had led to the verdict that her 'pretty little voice' would be best left untrained in order for her to concentrate on singing naturally.[6] Denny learned piano and guitar, focusing on the latter instrument as she entered the world of clubs associated with the folk song revival. As she frequented these venues and met other members of the scene, she built up a good knowledge of traditional song from the British Isles and North America and started to incorporate some of it into her own repertoire. Her early performances took place while she was pursuing other vocational possibilities – first as a trainee nurse, later as an art student – but by 1966 she was turning increasingly towards music as a profession and was developing a strong reputation for her singing. Following the standard folk practice of the time, Denny mixed traditional material with contemporary work authored by emerging writers; clear influences on her early style included Joan Baez and Anne Briggs – singers associated with the American and British folk revival respectively – and Bob Dylan, whose self-written songs had galvanised the American and British scenes.

From its initial stages, Denny's songwriting displays a sense of loss, melancholy and experience that suggests an early sense of lateness. Her first documented composition 'In Memory (The Tender Years)', written as an elegy for a former classmate who died young, includes references to 'the sighing of the wind', 'a murmur of regret', 'running with the dawn' and 'trees of green and gold'.[7] It features a mournful, elegiac arrangement, with fingerpicked acoustic guitar and fatalistic vocal lines that emphasise the passing of the seasons and of brief human lives and loves. The attachment of nature imagery to memory, nostalgia, longing and the passing of time would become a staple of Denny's writing, often complemented by allusions to water in the form of rivers, banks, shores or the sea.[8]

---

[6] Clinton Heylin, *No More Sad Refrains: The Life and Times of Sandy Denny* (London: Omnibus, 2011), 18; Philip Ward, *Sandy Denny: Reflections on Her Music* (Kibworth Beauchamp: Matador, 2011), 168.

[7] Sandy Denny, 'In Memory (The Tender Years)', on *The Notes and the Words*, CD, Island, 371 246-9 (2012).

[8] A number of writers have commented on Denny's obsession with water imagery, often reading it in gendered terms. Philip Ward, perceiving a particular emphasis on 'oceanic imagery' among female artists, supports his claim via reference to the work of Hélène Cixous; see Ward, *Sandy Denny*, 60–62, 183–5. Simon Reynolds and Joy Press connect

Denny's nature/time imagery would find its most famous setting in 'Who Knows Where the Time Goes', an early composition that initially bore the title 'Ballad of Time'. Discovered in Denny's notebooks, this early version does not refer in its opening line to either 'morning sky' or 'evening sky' as later versions would, but the remainder of the lyric, with its reflection on 'the storms of winter' and 'the birds in Spring again' remained the same, with its emphasis on seasonality and the transience of nature and human relationships. Denny's notebook poem opens with reference to a 'distant sky', across which 'all the birds are leaving'. The birds' seasonal migration is presented as an unconscious process; the question 'how can they know?' is left hanging, as is the repeated question of the refrain: 'who knows where the time goes?' The ballad's protagonist is safe beside 'the winter fire' and with 'no thought of time'. 'Thought' here must relate to concern rather than awareness, for the protagonist clearly has time on her mind, perhaps as a result of having time on her hands. This would seem to be supported by the echoes of this line in the ballad's other verses: 'I do not count the time' in the second, 'I do not fear the time' in the third. The second verse opens on a 'sad deserted shore' and refers to the departure not of birds but of 'fickle friends'. As so often in her writing, Denny here moves from nature imagery to the compromised world of social relations. The friends are presented as having no more knowledge or control over their actions than the migrating birds. The stoical protagonist remains rooted to the hearth, with the liminal space of the shoreline in mind if not in sight.

By the time Denny came to record the song in 1967, it had gained the title by which it would become famous and its first line had been changed to 'across the purple sky', providing a more poetic point of reflection from which to depart. Her first demo of the song finds her using a fast fingerpicking accompaniment and, although she elongates some of the key words ('leaving', 'go', 'dreaming', 'winter'), she sings the title refrain quite quickly, with little of the lingering reflection that she would subsequently adopt.[9] Denny recorded another version that same year during her brief tenure in The Strawbs, although the recording was a solo one, made during the group's trip to Copenhagen.[10] While of shorter duration than the first demo, this version sounds statelier, due to a less frenetic guitar style (a combination of slow strumming and spare picking) and Denny's more reflective vocal delivery. As a singer, she had, by this point found her style, one in which, as Philip Ward notes, her '*rubato* elongation of a line seems to make time stand still'.[11]

Denny's oceanic imagery with Carl Jung's 'feminine archetypes' in *The Sex Revolts: Gender, Rebellion and Rock 'n' Roll* (London: Serpent's Tail, 1995), 285. Rob Young does not focus solely on gender but is keen to read into Denny's work anxieties regarding her family, friends, husband and baby; see Rob Young, *Electric Eden: Unearthing Britain's Visionary Music* (London: Faber and Faber, 2010), 318–23.

[9] Denny, 'Who Knows Where the Time Goes', *The Notes and the Words*.

[10] Sandy Denny, 'Who Knows Where the Time Goes', *Where the Time Goes*, CD, Sanctuary, CMRCD 1181 (2005).

[11] Ward, *Sandy Denny*, 96.

Judy Collins

Sandy Denny's recording for The Strawbs would remain unreleased until 1973 and it was to be Judy Collins's version of 'Who Knows Where the Time Goes' that would propel the song to its greatest success when it appeared in three different formats in 1968: on a 7-inch single as the B-side to 'Both Sides Now', as the title track of Collins's eighth album and as the music played over the opening and closing scenes of Ulu Grosbard's 1968 film *The Subject Was Roses*. Born in Seattle in 1939, Collins was a piano prodigy who abandoned her classical music background when she became interested in folk music and switched to the guitar. She moved to New York's Greenwich Village in 1961, becoming part of the vibrant music scene that included Bob Dylan and Nina Simone. Following two albums of traditional music, Collins began to record contemporary songs by writers such as Dylan and Pete Seeger. As Johnny Rogan and Richie Unterberger both note, Collins's album *#3* was a vital link in the development of folk-rock, mixing the emerging pop sensibility with the rules and repertoire of the folk revival.[12] By the late 1960s Collins had moved far beyond most of her folk revival contemporaries, in terms of both the arrangements she was utilising and the range of material she was incorporating.

Collins discovered Denny's song when she was passed a tape of the recording made during The Strawbs' Danish trip. In her 2011 memoir, Collins writes of the happenstance of 'finding' this song at the time she was mourning her recently deceased father and how it fit so well with her own composition 'My Father', also included on *Who Knows Where the Time Goes*.[13] One obvious change to the song in Collins's version can be found in the opening words, which become 'Across the morning sky', a change from the 'distant sky' in 'The Ballad of Time' and the 'purple sky' of Denny's two early recordings.[14] It is unclear whether this was a change indicated by Denny at any point, though it is one she would briefly adopt when first performing the song with Fairport Convention. Collins further takes ownership of the song through her vocal treatment and the instrumental arrangement. The album version begins with the slowly strummed acoustic guitars of Collins and Stephen Stills before Collins's vocal enters, slightly later than might be expected, setting up a sense of dislocation that will continue throughout the recording. Collins's phrasing is different to Denny's, the syllables of most words delivered with a more regular stress, estranging some of the meaning established in Denny's versions. Like Denny, Collins dwells on certain words and sounds, for

---

[12] Johnny Rogan, liner notes to Judy Collins, *Judy Collins #3 & The Judy Collins Concert*, CD, Elektra/WSM, 8122 76505-2 (2004); Richie Unterberger, *Turn! Turn! Turn! The 60s Folk-Rock Revolution* (Milwaukee: Backbeat Books, 2002), 48–9.

[13] Judy Collins, *Sweet Judy Blue Eyes: My Life in Music* (New York: Three Rivers Press, 2011), 237.

[14] Judy Collins, 'Who Knows Where The Time Goes', on *Wildflowers & Who Knows Where the Time Goes*, CD, Elektra/Rhino, 8122 73393-2 (2006).

example by elongating the words 'go' and 'fire' and adding melisma to the first syllable of 'leaving' and second syllable of 'dreaming'. Following the first refrain (with its elongation of the word 'time' in the repeated line), there is another moment of dislocation as the rest of the band (bass, drums, electric guitar, piano) enter in a somewhat clunky manner. This is the first moment in the recorded chronology that 'Who Knows Where the Time Goes' becomes a rock song, with the potential for a gradual building up and layering of instruments. This introduces nuances to Denny's song, as instrumental fills appear between phrases, guitars build up at the climatic moments and the drum kit propels the verses and refrains forward with a new and appropriate relentlessness.

Nina Simone

By the time Nina Simone added Sandy Denny's song to her repertoire in the late 1960s, she had amassed a considerable amount of personal and professional experience. Of the three artists under consideration here, Simone was born first and her rendition of 'Who Knows Where the Time Goes' can therefore be considered as being most representative of a 'late voice' when lateness is associated mainly with biology and professional chronology. Born Eunice Waymon in North Carolina in 1933 to a working-class black family, Simone witnessed firsthand the cruelties and injustices of the segregated American South. While racial prejudice marked her from an early age, Simone also experienced opportunity when, in recognition of her precocious gifts as a keyboardist, she benefitted from private piano tuition, funded initially by her parents and later by a fund set up by the local community. The piano training continued though her teenage years, with everyone expecting Eunice to become a classical pianist. This dream died when, at the age of 18, she was rejected by the prestigious Curtis Institute in Philadelphia in a decision that Simone interpreted as racially motivated. Even as she continued with her classical training, Simone turned increasingly towards the performance of popular music, first as a pianist and singer in a variety of night clubs in Philadelphia and New York (at which stage she settled on her professional name), and, from the mid-to-late 1950s, as a recording artist. Following an ultimately unsuccessful contract with the independent Bethlehem label, Simone signed to Colpix and released a number of albums in quick succession, followed by an equally prolific period at Philips from 1964, where she released seven albums in three years. It was during this time, and her subsequent tenure with RCA, that she became strongly connected to the civil rights movement and to the revolutions taking place in art, music and social relationships.[15]

---

[15] Nina Simone and Stephen Cleary, *I Put a Spell On You: The Autobiography of Nina Simone* (New York: Da Capo Press, 2003); Nadine Cohodas, *Princess Noire: The Tumultuous Reign of Nina Simone* (New York: Pantheon, 2010); Richard Elliott, *Nina Simone* (Sheffield: Equinox, 2013).

Simone shared a significant amount of repertoire with Judy Collins, including songs by Brecht & Weill, Dylan, Pete Seeger, Leonard Cohen and Randy Newman. Simone also recorded Collins's own composition 'My Father', suggesting that Collins's repertoire may have been an influence on Simone's song choices. Certainly, Simone matched Collins in her eclecticism; like Collins and Denny, she was also a powerful songwriter, adding 'Mississippi Goddam', 'Four Women' and 'To Be Young, Gifted and Black' to the repertoire of classic 1960s protest/pride anthems.

The version of Denny's 'Who Knows Where the Time Goes' that Simone recorded at a New York concert in 1969, and which was released the following year on her album *Black Gold*, uses the 'morning sky' reference in its opening line, suggesting the additional influence of Collins. Regardless of her source, Simone takes absolute control of the song, treating it as an object to be manipulated to her desires. She begins this manipulation by introducing the song to her audience via a meditation on time and experience:

> Let's see what we can do with this lovely, lovely thing that goes past all racial conflict and all kinds of conflict. It is a reflective tune and some time in your life you will have occasion to say 'What is this thing called time? You know, what is that?' ... time is a dictator, as we know it: where does it go? What does it do? Most of all, is it alive? Is it a thing that we cannot touch and is it alive? And then one day you look in the mirror – how old – and you say, 'Where did the time go?'[16]

Simone delivers this introduction in a soft, reflective voice, creating an intimacy that invites her audience to think about time, age and experience. I have previously suggested that this spoken delivery, in combination with the subsequent performance, invites a heightened awareness of the passing of time.[17] A sense of inevitability is embedded into Simone's version of the song, when, during the second verse, percussion enters at one beat per second, offering a clockwork counterpart to the more free-flowing vocal and keyboard lines. Like Collins's band version, Simone's (which features acoustic guitar, piano, organ and light percussion) offers a sense of dislocation as it shifts instrumental textures and navigates between metric rigidity and fluidity. Unlike Collins, Simone doesn't use crescendo, largely avoiding the building up of instruments and vocal power. Instead, she sings the first verses in a soft, inviting register accompanied only by gently strummed acoustic guitar, later offering a modest piano solo before leaving keyboard duties to Weldon Irvine's ghostly organ. In a manner that recalls, and yet is distinct from, both Collins and Denny, Simone elongates certain key words, such as 'dreaming' in verse one, where her melisma on the /iː/ phoneme makes the

---

[16] Nina Simone, 'Who Knows Where The Time Goes', on *Emergency Ward/It Is Finished/Black Gold*, CD, Camden, 74321924802 (2002).

[17] Elliott, *Nina Simone*, 113–14.

word seem to flutter above the melody, emphasising the suggestion of dreaming, contemplation and reverie that pervades the song.

Lateness

While Sandy Denny first recorded her signature song as a solo performance, her subsequent recordings of the song would be in full band versions, most famously the version recorded by Fairport Convention in 1969 for the album *Unhalfbricking*. As she had found with her brief involvement in The Strawbs, and as she would later find with the post-Fairport group Fotheringay and the musicians who collaborated on her albums as a 'solo' artist, Denny welcomed the camaraderie and collaborative possibilities of a group. At the time of forming Fotheringay, Denny described her attitude towards collaboration via reference to a Judy Collins show she had attended in London. She described Collins as 'someone who was definitely a solo singer, who just happened to have a very good backing group. But that's all they were.'[18] While perhaps an unfair observation of Collins's collaborative process (described in rich detail in the latter's 2011 memoir and evident from listening to her recordings), Denny clearly felt a conflict between the role of solo artist and band member. The three performers discussed in this chapter are notable as female creators who mostly wrote solo while using all-male bands to flesh out their creations. Simone, who rarely performed or recorded solo, once bluntly described her collaborators as 'an extension of myself or they don't play with me'.[19]

Denny's work with Fairport Convention provides ample evidence of the collaborative process she valued. Fairport brought to Denny's songs a sense of drama achieved through the pacing and layering of additional instruments. To hear Fairport's recordings of 'A Sailor's Life' (a traditional song recorded by Fairport shortly after Denny joined the group and also previously recorded by Judy Collins) is to hear a decisive development of the British folk-rock template that would be adopted by Fairport and other groups during the genre's classic years.[20] The *Unhalfbricking* version of 'Who Knows Where the Time Goes' echoes the folk-rock template initiated by Collins's recording, while benefiting from a more fluid forward propulsion due to Richard Thompson's constant, subtle guitar work and the way in which the song's groove is established from the outset.[21] A version

---

[18] Cited in Heylin, *No More Sad Refrains*, 117.

[19] Arthur Taylor, *Notes and Tones: Musician-to-Musician Interviews* (New York: Da Capo Press, 1993), 157.

[20] Dave Laing, Karl Dallas, Robin Denselow and Robert Shelton, *The Electric Muse: The Story of Folk into Rock* (London: Methuen, 1975); Michael Brocken, *The British Folk Revival 1944–2002* (Aldershot: Ashgate, 2003); Britta Sweers, *Electric Folk: The Changing Face of English Traditional Music* (Oxford: Oxford University Press, 2005).

[21] Fairport Convention, 'Who Knows Where the Time Goes?', on *Unhalfbricking*, CD, Island/Universal, IMCD 293 (2003).

of the song by Fairport recorded for the BBC in February 1969 contains the 'morning sky' lyric used by Collins and Simone, though whether this is a Denny innovation or the influence of Collins is unclear. By the time the song appears on *Unhalfbricking*, Denny is singing of birds departed 'across the evening sky', as she will continue to do for the remainder of her career.

I have consistently noted the changes made to the opening line of the song by Denny, Collins and Simone because I think it helps to frame a reading of the song as an expression of time, experience and lateness. In an earlier interpretation of the song, I suggested that this switch between morning and evening as the point of reflection presented a paradox: if hearing Denny's song as an expression of 'youthful wonder', which I associated with the 'morning' of one's life, why start in the evening? And if hearing Simone's version especially as a reflective, retrospective song, why start in the morning?[22] Yet I also dwelled on the references to the turning of the seasons and it is this cyclical reading of the time of reflection which I am more inclined to pursue now. Where I previously associated evening with lateness and with the point of narration, the point at which one looks back at the 'day' of one's life, I now want to focus on the possibility of multiple opportunities for such retrospection, including morning with its bright exposure of what had previously been hidden by darkness. In her book *Relating Narratives*, Adriana Cavarero draws upon an anecdote recalled by Karen Blixen and subsequently analysed by Hannah Arendt. The anecdote concerns a man who works through the night fixing a leaking pond; on contemplating his work in the light of the morning he finds he has created the figure of a stork with his footprints. Blixen, Arendt and Cavarero use the story to offer reflections on how narratives make sense of the chaos of life and how, as Cavarero puts it, a story 'can only be narrated from the posthumous perspective' of one not currently engaged in the events of the story.[23] From my perspective, I am interested in the fact that, although the point of narrative must be late (or 'posthumous'), there is no obviously privileged time for this moment of late reflection; while evening invites contemplation of what Freud called 'day residues', morning brings fresh illumination on what has passed in the night, making sense of yesterday and last night, an ideal point for the interpretation of dreams.[24] Or, as Sandy Denny's song 'Dawn' has it, 'from the blackest night/ must come the morning sky'.

'Who Knows Where the Time Goes' is narrated in present and future tenses: birds and friends *are leaving*; birds and friends just *know* (permanently) when it is time to go; the protagonist *will be* dreaming, *will* still be here. The past is not explicitly mentioned, but this does not mean that there is no posthumous narrative, for the moment of storytelling is always in the present, as are the moments of

---

[22] Elliott, *Nina Simone*, 111–13.
[23] Adriana Cavarero, *Relating Narratives: Storytelling and Selfhood*, trans. Paul A. Kottman (London and New York: Routledge, 2000), 1–3.
[24] Sigmund Freud, *The Interpretation of Dreams*, trans. James Strachey, ed. James Strachey, Alan Tyson and Angela Richards (Harmondsworth: Penguin, 1991).

remembering and imagining. This present-tense realisation of what is in the process of disappearing and of what will come around again recalls Freud's essay 'On Transience', in which Freud recounts a walk in the countryside 'in the company of a taciturn friend and of a young but already famous poet'. The poet is dejected because of his awareness of the transient beauty of the nature surrounding them:

> The proneness to decay of all that is beautiful and perfect can, as we know, give rise to two different impulses in the mind. The one leads to the aching despondency felt by the young poet, while the other leads to rebellion against the fact asserted. No! It is impossible that all this loveliness of Nature and Art, of the world of our sensations and of the world outside, will really fade away into nothing. It would be too senseless and too presumptuous to believe it. Somehow or other this loveliness must be able to persist and to escape all the powers of destruction.[25]

Freud tries to convince his pessimistic companions that there is gain rather than loss in such things precisely because of their transience: 'Transience value is scarcity value in time. Limitation in the possibility of an enjoyment raises the value of enjoyment.' He asserts that nature, unlike human life, is eternal even though the seasons wreak temporary changes. As his companions fail to see his version of events, Freud surmises that they were experiencing 'a foretaste of mourning', the pain of which has 'interfered' with 'their enjoyment of beauty'.[26]

Freud's tale and Denny's song are connected not only through their shared emphasis on nature's transience and cyclical return, but also by the way in which time's passing is noted through visual evidence and the physical world. They are tales not only of time, but also of space, of tangible elements that can be held but not kept, that can be available to all the senses but cannot be fixed. That time is something locatable (and losable) is echoed in the question that provides Denny's refrain: *where* is time and where does it go?[27] Nina Simone makes such questions explicit with her framing of the song – the 'ballad of time' is both the beautiful object it will forever remain and also a way of reflecting on life and experience, a reflection (from morning or night, from Autumn or Spring) on what has been lost and may or may not return.

This possibility of return is not to deny the inevitable, unidirectional flow of age, however. As Jean Améry and Norberto Bobbio have emphasised, where

---

[25] Sigmund Freud, 'On Transience', *The Standard Edition of the Complete Psychological Works of Sigmund Freud*, vol. 14, trans. and ed. James Strachey (London: Hogarth Press, 1957), 305.

[26] Freud, 'On Transience', 305–7; see also Sylviane Agacinski, *Time Passing: Modernity and Nostalgia*, trans. Jody Gladding (New York: Columbia University Press, 2003), 13–14.

[27] For a fascinating exploration of such questions, see Eva Hoffman, *Time* (London: Profile, 2011).

biological age is concerned, life is not a cycle but a course that leads towards decrepitude and death. 'Those who believe they have what is called "time" *in front of them*', writes Améry, 'know that they are truly destined to step out into *space*, to externalize themselves. Those who have life within them, i.e., authentic time, have to be internally satisfied with the deceptive magic of memory.'[28] Améry pursues this distinction between the imagined time of the young and the 'authentic time' of the aged in order to make clear the irreversibility of the ageing process. Bobbio also dwells on irreversibility and decline, contrasting the romanticised image of 'wise old age' with the physical, mental and emotional realities of the ageing process.[29]

In Améry's terms, Denny's song, at least as first articulated by its young composer, could be heard as a precocious externalisation of the experience of time, a fearless throwing of oneself into the space of imagination and adventure rather than a submission of oneself to the prison of time. We might also hear it as a way of taming time and space, domesticating nature with its references to home and hearth and what we might call, after Susan Stewart, the miniaturisation of the gigantic. Stewart offers a reminder of the ironic stance and feigned distanciation inherent in the transformation of the sublime into the beautiful, or the feared into the tamed:

> The loneliness of nature spreads out before the solitary figure at the edge of the cliff as the stage of his consequent (and consequential) experience. But this beholder must always remain aware of the frame, aware of the encompassing role of nature. Hence the natural in the sublime is always a tamed beast, is always a transformation of action into object and distance into transcendence, and hence always sublimely ironic.[30]

The 'transformation of action into object' does not apply only to the objectification of time in Denny's song, but also to the objectification of the song itself. As object, the song becomes detachable from its source (hence, scores of cover versions of 'Who Knows Where the Time Goes') and the songwriter, as performer, also becomes detachable from the original artefact, be that the 'Ballad of Time' in Denny's notebook, the early home recording or the 'definitive' version of the song by Fairport Convention.

Though it may seem timeless, the song ages because of the various iterations it has undergone and because meaning is never fixed. Whether it is heard to age gracefully or otherwise is a matter of debate and depends on the emotional

---

[28] Jean Améry, *On Aging: Revolt and Resignation*, trans. John D. Barlow (Bloomington: Indiana University Press, 1994), 15.

[29] Norberto Bobbio, *Old Age and Other Essays*, trans. and ed. Allan Cameron (Cambridge: Polity, 2001), 3–31.

[30] Susan Stewart, *On Longing: Narratives of the Miniature, the Gigantic, the Souvenir, the Collection* (Durham, NC and London: Duke University Press, 1993), 78.

attachment the listener has to the song. Philip Ward notes how, in events commemorating Denny and her work, 'Who Knows Where the Time Goes' has inevitably become a rousing show closer rather than a meditative number.[31] Judy Collins writes, in her 2011 memoir, of weeping when she hears the song due to its associations with Denny's tragic death; here, what we might call the emotional life of the song, which for Collins must also include the role it played in her own career, is attached to the life (and death) of its writer.[32]

In terms of 'normal' lifespans, Denny did not age far, dying at 31 from complications following a fall. But in other ways she could be considered older than her years. A number of collaborators and commentators on her life noted the way that Denny's voice suffered as a result of her alcohol abuse and Denny herself expressed interest in replicating the 'shattered effects' of Janis Joplin's voice through emulating Joplin's drinking patterns.[33] Denny's last major concert took place in London in 1977 and was recorded and subsequently released as a live album. The performance includes a moving reading of 'Who Knows Where the Time Goes', a song that by this time had become an object with a separate life from its writer but that was also a part of her. Noting the changes in Denny's voice by this point, Pam Winters writes: 'Sometimes the voice wanders and wavers. It's worn fine like an old tapestry. It's not dewy and bright, but that's part of its beauty. It wears life; it contains mortality.'[34] Denny's friend Linda Thompson was less poetic about Denny's appearance after the London show, claiming that the 30 year old looked 50.[35]

While Denny did not reach the 'old age' that Améry and Bobbio write about, she provides an example of the singer who, like Billie Holiday, Hank Williams, Janis Joplin and Amy Winehouse, invites consideration of age, the body and experience due to an anticipated lateness and an abuse-scarred voice.[36] Voices, of course, can be put on and may or may not match the actual age of their owners. It is certainly not necessary for a voice to be singing about time, age or experience in order to convey these themes – vocal grain can be enough for that, while lack of vocal grain may leave us unconvinced by singers trying to convey songs of experience. But when 'experienced' or 'lived-in' voices attach themselves to lyrical evocations of passing time, the effect is amplified. The singing voices of artists are also given extra resonance by intertextual means, such as when they are heard speaking in

---

[31] Philip Ward, 'The Lady at the Barbican', *Sandy Denny* blog, 28 May 2012, accessed 30 August 2013, http://www.sandydenny.blogspot.co.uk/2012/05/the-lady-at-barbican.html.

[32] Collins, *Sweet Judy*, 242.

[33] Heylin, *No More*, 122–3.

[34] Pam Winters, liner notes to Sandy Denny, *Gold Dust*, CD, Island, 524493-2 (1998).

[35] Heylin, *No More*, 230.

[36] On Holiday and Williams, see Richard Leppert and George Lipsitz, '"Everybody's Lonesome for Somebody": Age, the Body and Experience in the Music of Hank Williams', *Popular Music* 9 (1990), 259-74.

interviews and concerts, or encountered in written form. Nina Simone's voice rings through her collaboratively written autobiography, adding extra layers of meaning to her recorded voice. Judy Collins, in her 2011 memoir, adopts a reflective and candid narrative voice that offers new insights into her emotional life. One brief chapter, entitled 'The Drinking Decades', offers a reflection on the point just prior to her decision, in 1978, to come to terms with her alcoholism:

> Where had the time gone? Where were the beautiful promises of my childhood, of my career, of my parents? ... There had been a time when the dream was bright. My memory, strangely undamaged, told me the story, over and over again, like the recollection of some far-off place, some fabled paradise to which I yearned to return.[37]

Layers of memory, loss and reflection must be added when we consider that these lines appear in a memoir written more than three decades after this realisation took place. Collins is using a framing mechanism that can only be constructed from a posthumous point of reflection as a way of making sense of the chaos of the events being recounted. Collins, who is using the narrative to set up the major event that was her return to sobriety, allows another sense of the emotional life of the song under discussion here by connecting her turmoil to its main lyric. Nina Simone also tapped into this emotional life when she introduced her version of Denny's song ('this lovely, lovely thing' as she called it), using it as an object to reflect on her own and her audience's awareness of time passing.

For Collins and Simone, such modes of reflection were possible as they enjoyed (or occasionally endured) longer careers and more opportunities for retrospection: late concerts, autobiographies, career reviews, interviews and features, songs of the ageing self or changes to versions of long-performed songs. Simone continued performing through her later years, more intermittently in the years leading to her death in 2003, at the age of 70. The meeting of her early sense of lateness with her chronologically late voice led to some rich, complex and sometimes infuriatingly uneven work.[38] Collins has continued making music while adding film directing, writing, painting and political activism to her accomplishments. As well as writing fiction and a book on the creative process, she has penned a number of memoirs, including an account of her attempt to come to terms with the suicide of her son. She has also retained Denny's song in her concert repertoire, allowing the emotional life of the song to articulate for Collins's fans their own understanding and appreciation of her continued presence in their lives.

---

[37] Collins, *Sweet Judy*, 310.
[38] See Elliott, *Nina Simone*, 104–45.

Chapter 10
Sanctuaries for Social Outsiders: A Queer Archive of Feelings in Songs by The Smiths[1]

Mimi Haddon

The past is hidden somewhere outside the realm, beyond the reach of the intellect, in some material object (in the sensation which that material object will give us) of which we have no inkling. And it depends on chance whether or not we come upon this object before we ourselves must die.[2]

Recent scholarship on Manchester's iconic indie balladeers The Smiths is rich in approaches that frame the band's music in terms of social identity. Issues of class, race, age, gender and sexuality have all been brought to bear on the band's output. Recent analyses have ranged from considering The Smiths' status as second-generation Irish immigrants, to studying their interpellation of British Muslims, to decoding their myriad articulations of unorthodox sexual desire.[3] Although in part attributable to the academic Zeitgeist, this scholarly interest in social identity has no doubt also been inspired by the eccentricities of The Smiths' lead singer Morrissey, whose undisclosed sexual orientation and xenophobic-seeming media faux pas have steered writers towards issues of sexuality and race.[4] But above all it is perhaps the ecstatic perversity coursing through many of the band's songs

---

[1] The title is based on the work of queer theorist Ann Cvetkovich whose development of the idea of an 'archive of feelings' informs parts of this discussion. Ann Cvetkovich, *An Archive of Feelings: Trauma, Sexuality, and Lesbian Public Cultures* (Durham, NC: Duke University Press, 2003).

[2] Marcel Proust, *Swann's Way, In Search of Lost Time*, vol. 1, trans. C. K. Scott Moncrieff and Terence Kilmartin, rev. D. J. Enright (London: Vintage, 2002), 51. This particular quotation also appears in Walter Benjamin's discussion of memory and poetic experience in Walter Benjamin, 'On Some Motifs in Baudelaire', in *Illuminations*, trans. Harry Zohn, ed. Hannah Arendt (New York: Schocken, 2007), 158.

[3] I am using French philosopher Louis Althusser's term 'interpellation' here to describe the way in which the subject is 'hailed' or called into being by ideology, or Ideological State Apparatuses, which can include literature and media. Louis Althusser, *Lenin and Philosophy, and Other Essays*, trans. Ben Brewster (New York: Monthly Review Press, 2001). For more on these individual examples, see the essays by Sean Campbell, Nabeel Zuberi and Sheila Whiteley, in Sean Campbell and Colin Coulter, eds., *Why Pamper Life's Complexities? Essays on The Smiths* (Manchester: Manchester University Press, 2010).

[4] It should be noted that Morrissey has keenly dismissed charges of racism in his recent autobiography. Allusions concerning his romantic encounters can also be found

that has fuelled this fascination with how The Smiths relate to processes of social identification.

A number of scholars have already begun to carve out an interpretation of The Smiths' music based on issues of queer identity specifically. These include Nadine Hubbs, Sheila Whiteley, Julian Stringer and novelist Benjamin Kunkel.[5] The Smiths' lyrics are saturated with queer name-dropping and personal pronoun play, and the characters chosen for their album art usually have queer connections or connotations. Drag-punks the New York Dolls, the androgynous Patti Smith and gay icons Oscar Wilde and James Dean are among those featured in The Smiths' or Morrissey's catalogue of inspiration.[6] Themes of secrecy, shame, hills 'alive with celibate cries', waiting, wanting and never having dominate the lyric content of their songs.[7] Irony and camp also abound, as in the above reference to enlivened hills that recalls 1965's camp classic musical *The Sound of Music*, directed by Robert Wise and starring gay icon Julie Andrews.

By choosing the idea of queer historiography as the primary hermeneutic strategy in this chapter I not only contribute to the existing body of identity and queer scholarship and The Smiths, but also aim at a close analysis of the band's aesthetic project. I propose that The Smiths borrow and bend pre-existing musical, visual and textual material that is marked, to borrow from Heather Love, by 'ruined or failed sociality'.[8] It is The Smiths' particular approach to intertextuality that lends their songs a queer air and in turn speaks to the issue of social exclusion. This queer aesthetic is, furthermore, characterised by a peculiar temporality that introduces the issues of age, generation and nostalgia into discussions of the band's artistry.

Love proposes seeking queer identification by looking 'backwards' to early twentieth-century queer figures whose tales of struggle, failure and trauma risk being lost or considered shameful as same-sex relationships become more

---

in the same book. Morrissey, *Autobiography* (London: Penguin Classics, 2013), 254–6, 273–9, 354–5.

[5] Nadine Hubbs, 'Music of the Fourth Gender: Morrissey and the Sexual Politics of Melodic Contour', in *Bodies of Writing, Bodies of Performance*, ed. Thomas Foster, Carol Siegel and Ellen E. Berry (New York: New York University Press, 1996); Sheila Whiteley, 'A Boy in the Bush: Childhood, Sexuality and The Smiths', in Campbell and Coulter, *Why Pamper*; Julian Stringer, 'Repressed (But Remarkably Dressed)', *Popular Music* 11 (1992); Benjamin Kunkel, 'Still Ill. The Smiths, *The Queen is Dead*', in *Heavy Rotation: Twenty Writers on the Albums that Changed their Lives*, ed. Peter Terzian (New York: Harper Perennial, 2009).

[6] Multiple references to the New York Dolls as well as James Dean pervade Morrissey's autobiography. Morrissey, *Autobiography*, 67–79, 292–6.

[7] 'The hills are alive with celibate cries' is a lyric from the song 'These Things Take Time'.

[8] Heather Love, *Feeling Backwards: Loss and Politics of Queer History* (Cambridge, MA: Harvard University Press, 2007), 22.

accepted and/or normative.[9] Love is keen to remind us that queer connections at the beginning of the twentieth century were often marked by unhappiness or failure in such a way that still brings to bear on experiences in the present. She argues, furthermore, that the whole idea of 'backwardness' fittingly characterises queer culture:

> Over the last century, queers have embraced backwardness in many forms: in celebrations of perversion, in defiant refusals to grow up, in explorations of haunting and memory, and in stubborn attachments to lost objects.[10]

Love proposes that the phrase 'impossible love' makes for a successful 'model for queer historiography', a historiography that focuses on queer histories marked by 'failed or interrupted connections' and 'broken intimacies'.[11] It is in this regard that the idea of the 'archive of feelings', as discussed by Ann Cvetkovich, is pertinent. As Cvetkovich describes it, fragments of cultural media that convey trauma (such as certain episodes of film and/or television) can be assembled together to figuratively articulate otherwise inexpressible personal stories or histories.[12] Bringing the two approaches together, then, I suggest that The Smiths look 'backwards' and use their songs and album art to archive instances of 'impossible love' found in other media.

Taking queerness as a trope that can be used to explore issues of marginality more generally is also an important aspect of this chapter. Indeed, my discussions of the influence of new wave drama/cinema and Motown engage with scholarly debate on The Smiths' complex relationship with matters of racial exclusion. It should be clear, however, that I do not directly equate queer and racial otherness and, in doing so, elide the historical and cultural specificity of subjective suffering. Rather, in the way that Love describes American writer Willa Cather's relationship with Valerie Ackland as 'part of a more general identification with social outsiders',

---

[9] For another critique of the normalisation or hetero-normalisation of queer relationships, see Lee Edelman, *No Future: Queer Theory and the Death Drive* (Durham, NC: Duke University Press, 2004). For more on the anti-social turn in queer theory, see Jack (Judith) Halberstam, *The Queer Art of Failure* (Durham, NC: Duke University Press, 2011).

[10] Love, *Feeling Backwards*, 7.

[11] Love, *Feeling Backwards*, 24.

[12] Cvetkovich discusses these ideas in relation to the work of filmmaker Jean Carlomusto specifically, whose work intersperses personal archives with 'Hollywood melodrama ... as a document of the emotions generated by stories that cannot be told and secrets that will never be uncovered'. Cvetkovich also writes, 'In the absence of the truth, the photographs, home movies, and films of popular culture, as well as temporary reconstructions of them, become trauma's archive'. Cvetkovich, *Archive of Feelings*, 261–2. For an exploration of a similar idea known as 'retrospectatorship', which denotes queer readings of Hollywood films, see Patricia White, *Uninvited: Classical Hollywood Cinema and Lesbian Representability* (Bloomington: Indiana University Press, 1999), 205.

this chapter also argues that The Smiths' songs speak to the trauma of social exclusion in its broadest sense.[13]

I therefore analyse three instances of intertextuality in The Smiths' music that transform their songs into sanctuaries or '[archives] of feelings' based upon empathy for 'broken intimacies' and social exclusion. Their use of pre-existing material or particular historical influences demonstrates turning 'backwards' and the recycling of 'lost objects' (and the trauma and sadness therein) to explore personal suffering, 'haunting and memory'. First, I analyse The Smiths' use of new wave (or 'kitchen-sink') drama/cinema. Second, I focus upon their romanticisation of abject landscapes and folk-style musical gestures. Finally, I propose a queer reading of the presence of soul music in the band's songwriting style. In short, The Smiths' music, lyrics, album art, dress and even performance style combine to form a multimedia scrapbook of failed connections from times past that codedly communicate the trauma of social exclusion.

'A Fascination with the Notion of the Past'

The Smiths' attraction to incorporating pre-existing material in their work, as well as their general interest in mid-twentieth-century trends and artefacts, is a noticeable theme in a handful of interviews and biographical accounts. Fellow artist and musician Linder Sterling, for example, remembers how she and Morrissey shared an interest in art of the 1960s and in excavating childhood memories. She recounts that they each had a 'fascination with Warhol's Factory, British cinema and the notion of the past' and that 'even though punk was rebelling against the present', she recalls, 'we had a fascination with the recent past of our childhood and our formative years'.[14] This idea of exploring and playing with the past also features in Morrissey's fabled first meeting with The Smiths' guitarist Johnny Marr. Presumably sometime around his 23rd birthday, in May 1982, Morrissey, who was notoriously shy, apparently only let 19-year-old Marr into his house on the basis of what he was wearing. Marr recalls his own outfit: 'a pair of fifties Levis ... with proper American bike boots and a Johnson's sleeveless jacket and a Johnson's shirt, and a real proper American flying men's cap and a superquiff which was faultless'.[15] Even though Morrissey's own account of this first meeting differs slighty from Marr's (Morrissey remembers seeing Marr for the first time at a Patti Smith concert in the late 1970s), the vintage look was noted: to Morrissey, Marr looked 'a bit rockabilly, a bit weird'.[16]

---

[13] Love, *Feeling Backwards*, 8.
[14] Linder Sterling quoted in John Robb, ed., *The North Will Rise Again: Manchester Music City 1976–1996* (London: Aurum, 2009), 193.
[15] Marr quoted in Robb, *North Will Rise*, 194.
[16] Morrissey quoted in Robb, *North Will Rise*, 195.

To 'turn back' in the way that Marr appears to have done with his 1950s getup is, however, not unusual, especially since most music, art and fashion is dialogic. Indeed, journalist Simon Reynolds highlights how for several musicians during the mid-1980s, 'the past started to seem alluring and intriguing, especially the sixties ... The re-issues industry, puny by today's standards, unleashed a torrent of sixties garage punk compilations and psychedelic anthologies.'[17] Reynolds lists The Smiths (alongside American rock group REM) as 'while not explicitly retro ... sixties-redolent because of their plangent guitar-chimes and folk-styled vocals'.[18] He continues,

> The Smiths were [an] eighties [band] only in the sense of being *against* the eighties. The Smiths shunned synths in favour of guitars and for a while adamantly refused to do videos. Their whole stance was predicated on their British audience being a lost generation, exiles in their own land.[19]

According to Reynolds, then, The Smiths' particular employment of 1960s musical gestures in their music was a response to the resurgence of right-wing politics at the beginning of the 1980s; they intended to invoke the 'very decade that Reagan and Thatcher were attempting to discredit'.[20]

While The Smiths' retrospection can perhaps be contextualised within the larger 1980s trend that Reynolds identifies, I propose that there is something specific in the tenor of The Smiths' backwards looking that can be read as queer. As scholar Scott Bravmann has noted, the world of ancient Greece served as a site of connection and inspiration for queer artists, especially writers such as Edward Carpenter, Havelock Ellis and John Addington Symonds. Bravmann demonstrates that while these writers did not unearth 'homosexual identities' per se, delving into Greek history 'opened up various new areas of imagination, dialogue, and organization' for them.[21] In the same sense, The Smiths' borrowings do not necessarily communicate an explicitly queer experience but they are all characterised by 'impossible love' or 'broken intimacies' and social exclusion, and thereby 'open up' possibilities for identification for social outsiders, those exiled 'in their own land', to reuse Reynolds's words.

---

[17] Simon Reynolds, *Rip It Up and Start Again: Postpunk 1978–1984* (New York: Penguin Books, 2006), 392. For more on Reynolds's ideas on falling in love with the past, see his *Retromania: Pop Culture's Addiction to its Own Past* (London: Faber and Faber, 2011).
[18] Reynolds, *Rip It Up*, 392.
[19] Reynolds, *Rip It Up*, 392.
[20] Reynolds, *Rip It Up*, 393.
[21] Scott Bravmann, *Queer Fictions of the Past: History, Culture and Difference* (Cambridge and New York: Cambridge University Press, 1997), 51.

'It Takes All Sorts, Dear': New Wave Drama's Failed Sociality

The Smiths' recurrent references to plays and films of the British new wave of the late 1950s and early 1960s (also known as 'kitchen-sink' repertoire) contribute to the project of retrospection, the communion with a 'lost generation'. For The Smiths and their audience, new wave drama may have aroused nostalgia for the 1960s of their childhood – be that nostalgia for the actual dramas themselves or for the general aura of what it was like to grow up in northern England at that time. Since Morrissey and Marr were both infants during the new wave heyday, however, it is likely that the structure of this nostalgia is characterised by fantasy and imagination, or an after-the-fact discovery, rather than personal recollection.[22]

One of the most memorable of The Smiths' uses of kitchen-sink repertoire appears in the title song from their 1986 album, *The Queen is Dead*. The song begins with a sample from the First World War song 'Take Me Back to Dear Old Blighty!' by A. J. Mills, Fred Godfrey and Bennett Scott from 1916. As a song designed to boost morale, 'Blighty' projects a longing for Britain, an idyllic place, far from the horror of war. Released in 1986, 'The Queen is Dead' could not have avoided alluding to Thatcher's new regime of flag-waving nationalism and xenophobia. On the one hand, therefore, by choosing to open *The Queen is Dead* (both the song and the album) with 'Take Me Back to Dear Old Blighty!' The Smiths reinforced the Conservative government's fetishisation of bygone Britain. On the other hand, and probably more accurately, the sample acts as an ironic negation of conservative values, since the jingoism aroused by the sample contrasts sharply with the anti-royalist title of the song-proper and Morrissey's plan for regicide, as the song begins: 'I don't bless them/Farewell to this land's cheerless marshes'. As film scholar Cecília Mello has noted, when Morrissey begins to sing he switches the direction of the song's sentiment from 'take me back' to farewell forever.[23]

It is Mello, furthermore, who has identified that The Smiths sampled 'Take Me Back to Dear Old Blighty!' from Bryan Forbes's 1962 film *The L-Shaped Room*, specifically from the scene in which 'aging lesbian' Mavis serenades a gathering of 'working class misfits' at a Christmas party.[24] Echoing Reynolds somewhat, Mello argues that Morrissey's 'nostalgic "looking back" has to be understood against the backdrop of the severe social and economic change that unfolded during the years of the Thatcher administration'.[25] For Mello the characters in *The L-Shaped Room*

---

[22] Historian David Lowenthal has remarked upon the early 1980s phenomenon of the '1960s party', suggesting that many who held them were either not old enough to remember the 1960s or in fact celebrating 'pre-natal times'. See David Lowenthall, 'Nostalgia Tells It Like It Wasn't', in *The Imagined Past: History and Nostalgia*, ed. Malcolm Chase and Christopher Shaw (Manchester: Manchester University Press, 1989).

[23] Cecília Mello, 'I Don't Owe You Anything: The Smiths and Kitchen-Sink Cinema', in Campbell and Coulter, *Why Pamper*, 144.

[24] Mello, 'Don't Owe You', 144.

[25] Mello, 'Don't Owe You', 135.

were themselves confronting the 'irreversible changes of the post-war period', characterised somewhat by the loss in the early 1960s of 'the idealized vision of the traditional and homely working-class community'. Mavis's performance of the song, therefore, hovers somewhere between irony and nostalgia; the gathered group of misfits are yearning for a place that they 'never quite had' (that is, an experience of 'Blighty' before the First World War, when most of the characters were either children or not yet born).[26] The inclusion of 'Blighty' in 'The Queen is Dead' adds yet another layer of complexity: Morrissey and The Smiths are nostalgic for someone else's nostalgia.

In addition to the political connotations of Morrissey's lyrical escapism into an idealised past, the sample's evocations of 'broken intimacies' and 'impossible love' cannot be overlooked. As Mello observes, the scene featuring the song in the film is marked by failed sociality and outsider-ness: Mavis is a middle-aged lesbian and her audience comprises 'her equally segregated housemates'.[27] It is not only Mavis's sexuality that connotes queer desire, her performance does so too. In the film, Mavis – a veteran of the boards herself – performs the song in semi-drag: she announces herself (and is dressed as) a military officer, refers to her comrades as 'chaps' and hails the assembled guests as a 'stag party'. In this regard, Mavis's performance evokes the rich history of women's drag acts in military costume in musical hall at the beginning of the twentieth century.[28] It also evokes the homosocial aspect of military camaraderie, perhaps more the case in the First World War than it is now.

Notably, in the song 'The Queen is Dead', the second half of the chorus to 'Blighty' fades as Morrissey's voice enters. But the lyrics should proceed: 'I should like to see my best girl, Cuddling up again we soon shall be', as Mavis sings in the film. The function of these lyrics in *The L-Shaped Room* adds to the mystique surrounding Mavis's sexuality, as do other scenes. For example, while writing Christmas cards with the young French mother-to-be, Jane, Mavis laments the 'disgraceful' fact that boys now play the male leads in Christmas pantomimes (whereas they were originally performed by young women). She also codedly admits to same-sex cohabitation when she tells Jane how she 'never went in' for marriage, but did have a 'friend', concluding coquettishly, 'it takes all sorts, dear'.

By deciding to use this particular sample in 'The Queen is Dead', The Smiths signify upon this complex of queer undercurrents. 'The Queen is Dead' therefore partakes in the practice of archiving, looking backwards to retrieve an artefact, Forbes's film, that expressed 'broken intimacies' and social exclusion via Mavis and the other 'misfits'. Furthermore, the sample itself is a song of longing and

---

[26] Mello, 'Don't Owe You', 144.
[27] Mello, 'Don't Owe You', 144.
[28] For more on the tradition of early twentieth-century male impersonators, see Gillian Rodger, '"He isn't a marrying man": Gender and Sexuality in the Repertoire of Male Impersonators, 1870–1920', in *Queer Episodes in Music and Modern Identity*, ed. Sophie Fuller and Lloyd Whitesell (Urbana: University of Illinois Press, 2002).

impossibility, and hopeless optimism in the face of horror, performed by characters who can only imagine, or project upon the song, the version of Britain it depicts. Finally, the tragedy and trauma of war – the millions of 'broken intimacies' – is figuratively resonant of the trauma of social exclusion.[29]

Despite the surface xenophobia and national supremacy projected by the 'Blighty' sample in 'The Queen is Dead', it is worth noting that one of the 'working class misfits' in the scene from *The L-Shaped Room* is Johnny, played by African-American actor Brock Peters (who had played Tom Robinson in Robert Mulligan's film adaptation of *To Kill a Mockingbird* earlier in 1962). The final section of this chapter provides a more substantial reading of The Smiths' engagement with issues of racial identity and how this, in turn, can be framed in terms of the archive of broken intimacies and social exclusion. Nonetheless, it is significant that The Smiths' use of new wave drama *also* tangentially touches upon issues of racial otherness. Morrissey's lyrics frequently invoke British playwright Shelagh Delaney's first play of 1958, *A Taste of Honey*, and Delaney herself also appeared on the album sleeve for the 1987 Sire Records release of The Smiths' compilation, *Louder Than Bombs*. By choosing lines from *A Taste of Honey*, Morrissey implies identification with the fraught lives of the three characters in Delaney's play, all of whom are social outcasts in their own way: the awkward working-class girl, Josephine, who ends up living with her gay best friend, Geoffrey, after falling pregnant to a black sailor ('The Boy') who abandons her.

References to *A Taste of Honey* appear in the lyrics of songs including 'Hand in Glove' ('I'll probably never see you again') and 'This Night has Opened My Eyes' ('The dream is gone but the baby is real').[30] The melancholy register of these lines combined with the way in which they depict failed connections are what lend them to a queer reading. In the line from 'Hand in Glove' the notion of 'impossible love' is explicitly evoked, and in 'This Night Has Opened My Eyes' the residue or remnants of a failed relationship take the form of an infant whose desirability is uncertain; it is not clear whether Josephine's child is burdensome or a joyous legacy of her fleeting but failed relationship with the sailor. At times Delaney depicts Josephine as violently resentful towards her pregnancy. To extend the exploration of queer signifiers in this web of artefacts, then, her unwilling motherhood might also be read as an example of Lee Edelman's anti-normative unproductivity.[31]

The Smiths' dialogue with the new wave genre thus fosters a sense of kinship with historical characters whose experience of social life is marked by exclusion or otherness: the coded queer sexuality of Mavis and Geoffrey, the racial otherness of Johnny and 'The Boy', and the two unmarried pregnant young mothers, Jane and Josephine.

---

[29] Cvetkovich, *Archive of Feelings*, 261–2.

[30] Shelagh Delaney, Act 1, Scene 2, *A Taste of Honey* (London: Theatre Workshop Press, 1959), 38, 75. For more of an idea about how Morrissey related to Delaney's work, see Morrissey, *Autobiography*, 92.

[31] Edelman, *No Future*.

'Wholesome, Warm, and Welcoming': Ugly Landscapes, Sites of Romance

In addition to Reynolds's observation regarding 1980s rock's retro-ism, several other writers have remarked that under the Thatcher administration British culture as a whole witnessed a turn towards nostalgia. Literature scholar Joseph Brooker notes the 1980s 'mood of English museology', reflected in the two Heritage Acts and the popularity of Merchant Ivory-produced period films, which he sees as a 'cultural corollary' to Thatcher's 'traditionalist and authoritarian dimension'.[32] Indeed, according to historian David Lowenthal, there appears to have been an inclination to depict even the abject parts of Britain's history as 'spuriously seemly and comfortable'.[33] Lowenthal quotes art critic Waldemar Januszczak's description of heritage centres' decision to present poverty as something 'wholesome, warm, and welcoming' and observes the ring-wing's 'sinister obfuscation' of the facts of poverty.[34] Similarly, The Smiths' 'archive' presents Britain's rotting landscape as whimsical and romantic. But rather than necessarily corresponding with conservative Britain's vision of poverty as cosy and character-building, I suggest that The Smiths' reconfiguration of the scars left by Britain's large-scale industrial practices are part of the backwards feelings of failed and ruined connections.

Almost all of the industrial locations and images that appear in The Smiths' lyrics are infused with failure and melancholy. This particular poetic approach can in many ways be related back to the kitchen-sink aesthetic discussed earlier. But one notices that many of these places are not only abject and depressing, but also sites of romance or sexual exploration.[35] In 'These Things Take Time' Morrissey sings, 'You took me behind/A disused railway line' and in 'Still Ill' he recalls, 'Under the iron bridge/We kissed'.

As much as the retro aspects of The Smiths' sound can be situated in the context of the 1980s fascination with the 1960s as Reynolds has suggested, the particular ways in which the band used folk-styled music can also be framed using both Love's and Cvetkovitch's ideas. As I suggested, The Smiths chronicle moments of love in 'impossible' places in such a way that their lyrics are odes to clandestine sexual exploration.

In one particular song, a whimsical musical setting reclaims ugly surroundings. The song 'Stretch Out and Wait' from the compilation *Louder Than Bombs* sings of adolescent sexual awakening amidst a high-rise council estate, but the musical setting's rustic simplicity suggests an unorthodox kind of romance. The Smiths

---

[32] Joseph Brooker, 'Has the World Changed or Have I Changed?', in Campbell and Coulter, *Why Pamper*, 25. I would also add that the worlds of camp and national heritage intersect in one of the UK's most well-known period adaptations of the era: Granada Television's 1981 screening of Evelyn Waugh's 1945 novel *Brideshead Revisited*, directed by Charles Sturridge and Michael Lindsay-Hogg.

[33] Lowenthal, 'Nostalgia', 25.

[34] Waldemar Januszczak, 'Romancing the Grime', *The Guardian*, 2 September, 1987.

[35] Mello, 'Don't Owe You', 138.

achieve this sense of rustic simplicity in the song via a number of characteristics: the song is in 6/8 metre; the mode is Ionian with lilting alternation between the 5th and 3rd scale degrees in the vocal part; the chord progression is, for the most part, simple and repetitive; and the band favour soft-timbre instrumentation on this particular track.

The song's harmony revolves predominantly around the chord progression I–V–IV–V. It is worth noting, however, that instances of more colourful harmony serve a narrative function. More adventurous-sounding chords enter as Morrissey deploys words with more sexual persuasion. At the very opening of the song, for example, when Morrissey delves into his partner's desires, an unexpected chord iii (G-sharp minor) substitutes the tonic (E major). The unexpected arrival of the iii chord, with its ambiguous inclusion of the leading tone (D-sharp), produces the musical equivalent of a raised eyebrow to aptly accompany Morrissey's leading question. Chord iii resolves, however, as though butter wouldn't melt, back to IV and into a IV–V–I progression.

Similarly, the moment Morrissey's seducee is invited to 'lose' him/herself, the bass part unexpectedly slides up a semi-tone to the flattened-submediant, supporting a C major-seven chord. The fresh, yet ambiguous or even timeless sound of this harmonic shift suggests that Morrissey is about to take his partner to the world of sexual knowledge, and it is then during the chorus, to the words 'Stretch out and wait' that the band turn on the coital *tristesse* with C-sharp minor. Example 10.1 shows part of the vocal melody and bass line, with the progression to the flattened-submediant at the lyrics 'let yourself lose yourself'.[36] The chorus begins in C-sharp minor after the C major-seven chord.

Acoustic guitar, bass, vocals and tambourine comprise the song's core instrumentation. Synthesisers are used sparingly. But when they do appear, as with the more adventurous-sounding harmony, they accompany the moment of sexual awakening and the flattened-submediant. The uncertainty or, indeed, portentousness of this sexual encounter is also highlighted by the distant sound of a thunderstorm.[37]

The wry juxtaposition of rustic musical simplicity and the urban narrative of sexual discovery of 'Stretch Out and Wait' can be interpreted in several equally valid ways, none of which are mutually exclusive. First, the folksy redolence of the music can be heard as a complement to the era's interest in older musical styles. Second, perhaps The Smiths were contributing to another symptom of the era's conservatism – that is, the romanticisation of poverty. A third way of framing this musical setting is to consider some of the band's musical influences. As both Mello and cultural historian Kari Kallioniemi have observed, Morrissey has expressed a fascination with old-time comedic singer-songwriter and ukulele

---

[36] All transcriptions are my own, The pitches and rhythms are intended as a guide rather than a precise depiction of the musical events.

[37] For a different interpretation and analysis of 'Stretch Out and Wait', see Jonathan Hiam, 'Toward a Musical Poetics of The Smiths', in Campbell and Coulter, *Why Pamper*, 129–33.

Example 10.1   Progression to the flattened-submediant at the lyrics 'let yourself lose yourself' in The Smiths, 'Stretch Out and Wait'

player George Formby.[38] The skiffle genre, too, with its particular appeal to British working-class youth, may also be an influence heard here.[39] In addition to these possible ways of contextualising 'Stretch Out and Wait', the song can also be read as an articulation of queer desire. Its musical setting beautifies or pastoralises the ugly scenery depicted in the text in an ironic and camp way. Even though the characters' circumstances are alienating and oppressive, their desire finds imaginative ways to negotiate and reclaim the romance-prohibiting world in which they find themselves: they find love in impossible places.

A 'Language of Despair': Unsung Voices in The Smiths

Morrissey is notorious for his dubious relationship to questions of nation and race. He famously denounced reggae as a 'glorification of black supremacy',[40] voiced his dislike for (implicitly black) 'dance music', appeared on stage in Finsbury Park in 1992 sporting a Union Jack and, most recently, has been part of the on-going 'kerfuffle over immigration' with UK music magazine *NME*.[41] Andrew

---

[38] Mello, 'Don't Owe You', 136; Kari Kallioniemi, '"Take Me Back to Dear Old Blighty": Englishness, Pop and The Smiths', in Campbell and Coulter, *Why Pamper*, 234.

[39] Mello, 'Don't Owe You', 139–40.

[40] Frank Owen, 'Home thoughts from Abroad', *Melody Maker*, 27 September, 1986, 14–16.

[41] Dave Simpson, 'Morrissey vs. NME: Mozgate Part I', The Guardian Music Blog, *The Guardian*, 28 November, 2007, accessed 27 August, 2013, http://www.theguardian.

Warnes has argued, furthermore, that the prevalence of white camp icons from the 1950s and 1960s on The Smiths' record sleeves created a 'smokescreen' or 'beard' that masked the band's African-American musical influences.[42] The influence of musicians such as Robert Johnson, Bessie Smith and Muddy Waters has been suppressed and the white icons served to create a 'pre-immigrant fantasy' of Britain.[43] Furthermore, Warnes argues that critics have found it easier to identify The Smiths' 'white heirs' than their black influences owing to the social, cultural and geographical gulf between 'white Lancashire' and the 'black South'.[44] The real taboo in The Smiths' music, Warnes argues, is not sexuality, but rather the fact that the theme of sexual ambiguity has disguised The Smiths' connection to questions of race.

Similarly, Julian Stringer has suggested that The Smiths cultivated an ideological English identity as a way to problematize attendant notions of whiteness and racism. He locates 'Englishness' in the music-hall-like quality of songs such as 'Frankly, Mr. Shankly' and their use of techniques from certain folk traditions.[45] Stringer has also argued that Morrissey 'studiously avoids the kind of "blue" or "dirty" notes associated with Afro-American vocal traditions' and instead emulates an 'English-gent style' of enunciation.[46] It is significant too, that Stringer connects The Smiths' white Englishness to their uncomfortable relationship to sexual expression, which may be read as a critique of what Paul Gilroy calls the 'pernicious metaphysical dualism' that associates whiteness with the mind and blackness with the body.[47]

Taken together, Morrissey's media comments, the white, homoerotic and gay-iconographic album art, and the fetish for bygone England in lyrics and performance persona certainly make the case for a carefully cultivated aestheticisation of whiteness in The Smiths' work. The musical influences of Formby and skiffle, furthermore, also contribute to this façade of a distinctly white, predominantly British heritage. As Warnes suggests, one is indeed *discouraged* from noticing the black Atlantic influences in The Smiths' music. It is worth reiterating, however, that one of Morrissey's most recurrent sources of inspiration is Delaney's *A Taste of Honey*, a play that challenged both racial essentialism and homophobia in England

---

com/music/musicblog/2007/nov/28/mozgate.

[42] Andrew Warnes, 'Black, White and Blue: Racial Antagonism in The Smiths' Record Sleeves', *Popular Music* 27 (2008), 147.

[43] Warnes, 'Black, White and Blue', 138.

[44] Warnes, 'Black, White and Blue', 142.

[45] Stringer, 'Repressed', 19.

[46] Stringer, 'Repressed', 20. To Stringer's list of 'English' vocal signifiers I would also add Morrissey's affectedly upper class rolled r's.

[47] Stringer, 'Repressed', 22. See also Paul Gilroy, *The Black Atlantic: Modernity and Double Consciousness* (Cambridge, MA: Harvard University Press, 1993), 97. For more on the sexualisation of the bodies of racial others, see Sander Gilman, *Difference and Pathology: Stereotypes of Sexuality, Race, and Madness* (Ithaca: Cornell University Press, 1985) and Frantz Fanon, *Black Skin, White Masks* (London: Pluto, 2008).

in the early 1960s. Furthermore, while Warnes and Stringer argue that influences such as the blues and African-American singing styles have been disguised by the white 'smokescreen' or erased altogether, I propose that other black-related genres are still audible in some of The Smiths' music.

Returning to Love's recommendation that the theme of 'impossible love' can serve as a model for queer historiography and that queer subjectivity extends to a general feeling of being a social outsider, the connotations of both the Brill Building and Motown – the history, music and lyrics – makes these genres apt archival material for queer backward glancing. While drawing inspiration from these genres affords retro cachet (in line with Reynolds's arguments), I think it is important to acknowledge the peculiarity of this instance of intertextuality. Motown and Brill Building songs often addressed the theme of 'impossible love', including abuse and violence, in their lyrics, and therefore codedly expressed histories and stories of failed attachments.

Given that both Morrissey and Marr would have been in the first decade of their lives during the rise of 1960s soul, this choice of genre can also be related to their fantasy nostalgia. The soundtrack to the moment that Morrissey met Marr was, apparently, the song 'Paper Boy' by mid-1960s all-girl group The Marvelettes.[48] Morrissey has also explicitly stated his affinity with the Brill Building and Motown groups:

> There seemed to be so much language of despair in those songs by the Marvelettes or Crystals or Supremes ... penalised for being in love, laughed at for being poor or unloved ... The Supremes are overlooked because they were so establishment-successful, but their output was apocalyptic – 'Remove this Doubt,' 'I Hear a Symphony,' 'I'm Livin' in Shame' are terrific bursts of emotion.[49]

The Smiths' 1987 single 'Last Night I Dreamt That Somebody Loved Me' projects a number of Motown's musical and lyrical signifiers. The song can be effectively compared to The Supremes' 1966 song 'Remove this Doubt', mentioned by Morrissey above. To begin with, both songs share a 12/8 time signature, a trademark of early soul music.[50] The Supremes' song stresses triplets in the piano

---

[48] Robb, *North Will Rise*, 195.

[49] Morrissey, quoted in Robb, *North Will Rise*, 195. There are some interesting resonances here between Morrissey and Ed Droste, the lead-singer from American indie band Grizzly Bear. Droste is gay and his group covered 'He Hit Me (and It Felt Like a Kiss)', originally recorded by The Crystals.

[50] In his research on Motown, musicologist Jonathan Andrew Flory has noted 'the use of compound duple or quadruple meters, with triple division of the beat frequently articulated in the piano, or the use of plain backbeat that stresses the second and fourth beats of each common time measure' as one of the musical characteristics of doowop, which was 'perhaps the most prevalent musical style in Motown's early years'. See Jonathan Andrew Flory, '"I Hear a Symphony": Making Music at Motown, 1959–79' (PhD Diss., University of North Carolina at Chapel Hill, 2006), 51.

(either in arpeggio form or as repeated chords) and the backbeat on beats two and four (counting four dotted crotchets per bar, as opposed to twelve quavers). The Smiths' song uses the same rhythmic punctuation (accented hits on two and four) and triplets passed between a very jangly sounding piano and Marr's lead guitar. The fact that 'Last Night' features a piano at all, and opens with a two-minute extemporisation on that instrument, is unusual in the context of the rest of The Smiths' oeuvre, but it was certainly a staple of early soul music.

The chromatic chord progression in 'Last Night' also strays outside the usual parameters of the rock genre. The opening verse moves through: i–i^9–vi–VI–v–V. The ascending chromatic movement as chords vi and v move to their major equivalents lends the song a similar kind of dramatic pathos to 'Remove this Doubt'. Indeed, since the opening chord progression of 'Remove this Doubt' begins with an ascending whole tone (from E to F-sharp in the bass), it appears as though The Smiths have tried to emulate this motion somewhat by adding the ninth (F-sharp) to the second iteration of their tonic chord (E minor).

To complement the aspirations towards sophistication alluded to in the harmony, 'Last Night' also has some string arrangements. Written in 1966, 'Remove this Doubt' was produced by Holland-Dozier-Holland (Eddie and Brian Holland, Lamont Dozier), the team responsible for The Supremes' songs and orchestration between 1963 and 1967.[51] For Andrew Flory the sound of the 'cartoonish tremolo' not only made Holland-Dozier-Holland productions distinct from other orchestral arrangements written for Motown songs but, combined with the complex harmonic progression, was also meant to signify 'classical music' in certain songs.[52] By employing a string arrangement to punctuate dramatic moments in 'Last Night', The Smiths seem to be aiming for not only the same kind of musical sophistication as these mid-1960s songs by Holland-Dozier-Holland and The Supremes, but also their 'apocalyptic' nature and 'terrific bursts of emotion'.

In her discussion of The Smiths' cover of 'I Want a Boy for My Birthday' by Brill Building girl group The Cookies, popular music scholar Sheila Whiteley identifies the connotations of same-sex desire that are engendered when the song is performed by an all-male group.[53] But the identification between The Smiths and the all-girl groups of the 1960s traverse the lines of race as well as those of gender. This would also connect The Smiths' music to the tradition of identification with the icon of the black diva in white gay male culture.[54] But Motown and the Brill Building's particular history also seem to be poignant sites for identifications with social outsiders. Not only were early doo wop recordings 'appropriated wholesale by white singers', but Motown boss Berry Gordy also exploited doo wop's 'upscale' image in order to present a 'middle-class' alternative to rock and roll's

---

[51] Flory, '"Hear a Symphony"', 17.
[52] Flory, '"Hear a Symphony"', 119.
[53] Whiteley, 'A Boy in the Bush', 108.
[54] For more on this, see Nadine Hubbs, 'I Will Survive: Musical Mappings of Queer Social Space in a Disco Anthem', *Popular Music* 26 (2007).

gruffness.[55] The exploitation of singers in the Brill Building (such as Little Eva and The Cookies) also makes the 'language of despair' audible in these recordings all the more moving. Indeed, Morrissey's allusion to the crossover appeal of The Supremes, by describing their 'establishment success', seems to suggest a sensitivity to the power asymmetries inherent in the 1960s girl group genre. At the same time, however, The Smith's decision to depict 1950s child star Billy Fury on the front of the cover for 'Last Night I Dreamt' is an ambiguous gesture: it is not clear whether this sleeve continues to disguise Motown and the Brill Building's unsung voices or whether it is an ironic acknowledgement of rock's history of appropriation.

Conclusions

The Smiths' incorporation of pre-existing material has been interpreted in a number of ways: from the photographs of white, gay icons that appear on their album sleeves as a way of masking their black Atlantic influences, to Morrissey's borrowing of kitchen-sink material as a reaction against the Thatcher government or as part of an overall fascination with the past, the 1960s or 'museology', to homoerotic significance in their covers of 1960s girl group tracks. Taken in conjunction with their fetishised depiction of England, projected primarily through Morrissey's performance persona but also present in media controversy and the references to new wave theatre/cinema, it may be possible to interpret some of this intertextuality as conservative or politically suspect.

I propose, however, that The Smiths' intertextuality also resonates with Love's vision of 'impossible love' and intersects with Cvetkovich's queer archive: it exemplifies 'looking backwards' to identify with and resuscitate 'social outsiders' from the past in order to articulate shared feelings of trauma and exclusion.[56] The contrariness of using the memory of traumatic experiences as sanctuaries is also well within the remit of queer knowledge and experience. As Whiteley writes about The Smiths' 'Reel Around the Fountain', the song 'causes us to reflect on how a seemingly perverse experience can, with hindsight, even evoke a nostalgic yearning'.[57]

The fact that the objects The Smiths have chosen for their archive are, and perhaps always were, 'beyond reach' (already gone, and also of a time before the band themselves reached maturity) is integral to their aesthetic and affective project. Play and imagination are central to The Smiths' output. As cultural critic Susan Sontag writes about camp, 'We are better able to enjoy a fantasy when it is not our own', and

---

[55] Flory, '"Hear a Symphony"', 53.
[56] Love, *Feeling Backwards*, 8.
[57] Whiteley, 'Boy in the Bush', 111.

> This is why so many of the objects prized by Camp taste are old-fashioned, out-of-date, démodé. It's not a love of the old as such. It's simply that the process of aging or deterioration provides the necessary detachment – or arouses a necessary sympathy.[58]

The Smiths reach backwards to archive the experiences and sentiments of characters from the past, empathising with those who have previously suffered through or negotiated oppressive social structures. Former sites of abjection, such as England's rotting industrial landscape, both as it has been depicted in new wave theatre/cinema and as it actually was during Thatcher's government, are magically transformed into sites of secret transgression, accompanied by acoustic, quasi-pastoral whimsy. In short, while intertextuality, borrowing and appropriation are by no means foreign concepts to the language of rock and pop, The Smiths' way of recycling deserves closer attention for its queer specificity. Importantly, hiding behind the white mask that Warnes has identified are those who have not only articulated or experienced feelings of 'impossible love', but were also cast as social pariahs owing to their sexual preferences or racial identities.

---

[58] Susan Sontag, 'Notes on Camp', *Against Interpretation and Other Essays* (New York: Picador, 2001), 113.

Chapter 11
'New Music' as Patriarchal Category

Lauren Redhead

Rebecca Saunders and Jennifer Walshe are both composers of what is often termed 'New Music'. As such, their work is received and assessed within the artistic and institutional structures which belong to New Music as a sub-category of contemporary music. In this discussion of their reception I will use the English term New Music to refer to what is most frequently described in German as *Neue Musik* – that is, a specifically European musical modernist tradition, believed to have originated from Schoenberg and the Second Viennese School, which now incorporates composers from North America, Australia and Asia who identify with this approach to music. In his essay 'New Music as Historical Category', Carl Dahlhaus begins by writing that the 'concept of "New Music" ... serves to pinpoint the difference between certain twentieth-century works and the mass of the remainder',[1] but goes on to acknowledge that the term is unhelpfully vague and defined individually by those who use it. He further writes that the 'concept of the "new" ... is, taken as an historical category, as unavoidable as it is precarious'.[2] What follows is a description of the relationship of the western classical music tradition with newness from around 1400 to around 1950, which defines newness and material or compositional attitudes as intrinsically linked. In this way, Dahlhaus notes that, 'what is seemingly most transient – the quality of incipient beginning, of "for the first time" – acquires a paradoxical permanence'.[3] So, for Dahlhaus, the concept of material is a grounding or integral concept for the New Music scene and its institutions, linked to both newness/innovation and tradition, and even from his short definition it is possible to see how New Music is also a social and ideological structure. Within this structure, as well as to musical elements, the term 'material' is used to refer to complexity and to the prioritising of certain cerebral concepts – usually in the pursuit of the new.

The term 'material' is, then, highly conceptualised and important within New Music discourse. Perhaps one reason for this is the discussion of 'material' in Adorno's work, and the continuing importance and influence of Adorno's writing

---

[1] Carl Dahlhaus, 'New Music as Historical Category', in *Schoenberg and the New Music*, trans. Derrick Puffett and Alfred Clayton (Cambridge: Cambridge University Press, 1988), 1.
[2] Dahlhaus, 'New Music', 2.
[3] Dahlhaus, 'New Music', 13.

on contemporary musical culture. Adorno defines 'material' early in his *Philosophy of Modern Music*, writing,

> material is traditionally defined – in terms of physics, or possibly in terms of the psychology of sound – as the sum of all sounds at the disposal of the composer. The actual compositional material, however, is different from this sum as is language from its total supply of sounds. It is not simply a matter of the increase and decrease of this supply in the course of history. All its specific characteristics are indications of the historical process.[4]

By this statement Adorno defines 'material' as an exclusive category, and one which is rooted in the history of music, stating further that 'the meaning of musical material is not absorbed into the genesis of music, and yet this meaning cannot be separated from it'.[5] Finally, Adorno goes on to claim that the creative (compositional) act is the 'demands made on the subject' by the material itself (and not, for example, by the composer's assessment of the material): 'an element socially determined by the consciousness of man'.[6] Max Paddison assesses this by stating that Adorno's materialist aesthetics 'makes the claim that judgements concerning the quality of a work, as consistency and progress (and ultimately as authenticity and "truth" to the material), can (and indeed must) be grounded in the technical structure of the work'.[7]

Thus, in Adorno's conception, composition, material and subjectivity are inseparable. These three interlinked concepts can also be found in a more popular or lay definition of material. When the word 'material' is used by composers and critics it is popularly taken to mean 'that which the composer works with', and, frequently, the use of the term 'material' indicates what might be described as conventional musical aspects such as rhythm, pitch and harmony.[8] When these elements are teamed with the consideration of material that arose from Dahlhaus's essay, this implies that only certain types of complexity, process and thinking are valued within a New Music conception of material. Specifically, this does not include the tactile or visual elements of works, or structural complexity that does not arise from within notation. Importantly, it describes material in words that are

---

[4] Theodor Adorno, *Philosophy of Modern Music*, trans. A. G. Mitchell and W. V. Blomster (London: Continuum, 2002), 32.

[5] Adorno, *Philosophy*, 32.

[6] Adorno, *Philosophy*, 33.

[7] Max Paddison, *Adorno's Aesthetics of Music* (Cambridge: Cambridge University Press, 1995), 89.

[8] Techniques for these are the focus of many composition programmes, and unsurprisingly there are many examples to support such teaching from the twentieth century. This, although not a negative thing in itself, might be a reason for the beginnings of a conception that those aspects are the most prominent parts of musical material (and since the majority of 'canonic' examples of composers from the early twentieth century are men, the beginnings of a conception that material is a male preserve).

familiarly gendered as male; these words are associated with what are considered to be behaviours, activities and thought processes traditionally undertaken by men.

However, the neutrality of material is not indisputable. As with any other term, it is subject to the social, political and ethical dimensions of language, cultural context and thought. That these discursive dimensions of music exist and are important is not an original insight. Jean-Jacques Nattiez's semiology of music considers them in some detail,[9] and many semiotic and poststucturalist investigations of music have since emphasised meanings that are conceived extra to compositional, material and subjective issues. Indeed, Kofi Agawu writes that when these are considered it can be possible to view analysis 'as a mode of performance, or a mode of composing, not as an unveiling of resident truths'.[10] Even further, feminist assessments of music have used consideration of the discursive and social elements of music to unveil symbolic violence within the conception of music and its materials. Susan McClary is one such author, and she writes,

> the structures graphed by the theorists, and the beauty celebrated by aestheticians are often stained with such things as violence, misogyny and racism. And perhaps more disturbing still, to those who would present music as autonomous and invulnerable [these] also frequently betray fear – fear of women, fear of the body.[11]

What both Agawu and McClary identify is the pressure of normative values within music which is exerted through the mechanisms by which music is engaged with. For Agawu, the analyst discovers not universal truths hidden in the beauty of the music but a familiar narrative of a dominance of certain ideas, individuals and characteristics, which are reaffirmed through this engagement with them. For McClary, this narrative is not only reaffirmed but reified as beauty itself in the denial of anything other than the neutral position of music, its institutions and its materials.

In such a context it is unsurprising that some composers might seek alternative 'materials' than those sanctioned by an historical narrative. And yet, the 'New Music' discourse itself is reluctant to accept these into a definition of material. I intend to argue that, rather than a neutral term, 'material' can be seen as an exclusive term within discourse about contemporary music – and specifically 'New Music' – and that this exclusivity is driven by an attempt to maintain institutional power. In order to investigate this, I employ a feminist poststructuralist critical

---

[9] Jean-Jacques Nattiez, *Music and Discourse: Towards a Semiology of Music*, trans. Carolyn Abbate (Princeton: Princeton University Press, 1990).

[10] Kofi Agawu, *Music as Discourse: Semiotic Adventures in Romantic Music* (Oxford: Oxford University Press, 2009), 4.

[11] Susan McClary, *Feminine Endings: Music, Gender, and Sexuality* (Minneapolis: University of Minnesota Press, 1991), 4.

discourse analysis methodology, and so as to achieve this with respect to music as well as the discussion of music, I accept the wide definition of discourse given by Foucault when he writes that discourse can be described 'sometimes as the general domain of all statements, sometimes as an individualisable group of statements, and sometimes as a regulated practice that accounts for a number of statements'.[12] Thus, I account for musical statements and the 'regulated practice' of contemporary music institutions as well as written and spoken statements in order to show that the system of the delineation and hierarchy of material serves to highlight which musical aspects are the thing(s) to be analysed, valued or considered when music is approached by critics, institutions and students. This therefore narrows 'what the composer works with' (as a taken definition of material) to a small group of considerations which have their origins within a particular conception of music history alone. More broadly, I will argue that this also limits the kinds of artists who can be described as composers since 'what the composer works with' indicates that composers are people who work with these elements. Therefore this discourse of material is central in delineating who composers are and what they can or may do.

One way in which material, composition and ideology meet is in the idea of transcendence: in particular the nineteenth-century aesthetic conception of transcendence, which stems from the thought of Kant and holds that there is knowledge beyond the possibility of human thinking or reasoning that can nevertheless be experienced by, for example, the contemplation of art or music. On this, Marcia J. Citron writes, '[a] central component of the metaphysical concerns the transcendence of the composer as subject. This situates attention on the ego, on a very strong, sometimes exaggerated notion of the self.'[13] In fact, she finds this narrative in the history of western music which both pre-dates and pre-supposes modernism, writing, 'the sonata aesthetic stands as a symbol and product of western patriarchal values ... The conventions and subtext of the sonata aesthetic have privileged the masculine and held lesser meaning for women.'[14] Citron goes on to explain the link between western music history, figures such as Beethoven and the cult of genius, and how this has no link to the figure of the composer as craftsperson as found in women's discourse, therefore concluding that western musical development both within musical forms and as an historical narrative has a male psychological profile.[15]

---

[12] Michel Foucault, *The Archaeology of Knowledge*, trans. A. M. Sheridan Smith (New York: Pantheon Books, 1972), 90.

[13] Marcia J. Citron, 'Feminist Approaches to Musicology', in *Cecilia Reclaimed: Feminist Perspectives on Gender and Music*, ed. Susan C. Cook and Judy S. Tsou (Urbana and Chicago: University of Illinois Press, 1994), 23.

[14] Citron, 'Feminist Approaches', 18.

[15] Anna Piotrowska makes similar claims about the cult of genius and the modernist understanding of the figure of the composer in Anna G. Piotrowska, 'Modernist Composers and the Concept of Genius', *International Review of the Aesthetics and Sociology of Music* 38 (2007).

Catherine Parsons Smith describes three patriarchal traditions at the beginning of the twentieth century – serialism, neoclassicism and futurism – claiming that all of these exclude women linguistically.[16] In fact, they all link to the New Music tradition in some way. Their convergence can be described broadly as 'Musical Modernism', which is also the best name I can give to the ideology of the new music scene in northern Europe and specifically Germany, as a set of ideas which owe their development to, and thus belong to, the mid-nineteenth to early twentieth century. As an obvious result of its historical nature, it might be said that women are not valued particularly highly within this construct. Parsons Smith later writes that 'Modernism in music, as in literature, may be understood as a reaction to the first wave of feminism.'[17]

Although materialism itself might be a cause of indirect subordination of women, this attitude is clearly reflected in Aaron Copland's statements about Nadia Boulanger. Copland writes: 'in so far as she composed at all she must of necessity be listed in that unenviable category of the woman composer'.[18] Despite popular recognition of Boulanger as a formative influence in Copland's compositional career, Copland prefers to focus on Boulanger's achievements as a teacher, although he does later speculate: 'Is it possible that there is a mysterious element in the nature of creativity that runs counter to the nature of the feminine mind? And yet there are more women composers than ever writing today. Writing, moreover, music worth playing.'[19] Copland, as Adorno, identifies an interaction of material and subjectivity which meet in the compositional act, but furthermore states that female subjectivity may not be able to enter into this relationship at all.

Copland's statement could easily pass for the attitude held in the European New Music scene today – while her male counterparts might already be automatically endowed with the title 'composer' a female musician in the same profession must first work to drop the gendered form of this title in favour of what is characterised as a neutral but is really a male term – 'composer'.[20] The ideology of materialism is, therefore, both a philosophical issue and a political one within music. Lacan writes that '[t]here is nothing more philosophical than materialism'.[21] Furthermore,

---

[16] Catherine Parsons Smith, '"A Distinguishing Virility": Feminism and Modernism in American Art Music', in Cook and Tsou, *Cecilia Reclaimed*, 92.

[17] Parsons Smith, '"A Distinguishing Virility"', 99.

[18] Aaron Copland, *Copland on Music* (New York: Doubleday, 1960), 84–5.

[19] Copland, *Copland on Music*, 85.

[20] This is linked to the perceived need for women to overperform at work, discussed in Luisa Martín and Concepción Gómez Esteban, 'The Gender of Power: The Female Style in Labor Organisations', in *Feminist Critical Discourse Analysis*, ed. Michelle M. Lazar (Basingstoke: Palgrave Macmillan, 2005), and Aino Saarinen, 'Feminist Research: In search of a New Paradigm?', *Acta Sociologica* 31 (1988). It is also different from the German distinction 'Komponist'/'Komponistin', which is linguistic but not ideological.

[21] Jacques Lacan, 'God and the Jouissance of Woman: A Love Letter', quoted in Diane Elam, *Feminism and Deconstruction* (London and New York: Routledge, 2003), 61.

Judith Butler writes that subjectivity itself, which in the context of the New Music conception of the composer stands in relation to material, is political:

> The subject is an accomplishment regulated and produced in advance. And is as such fully political; indeed perhaps *most* political at the point at which it is claimed to be prior to politics itself.[22]

Therefore, music composition – a meeting of the subjectivity of the composer and 'material' – is not a neutral activity but a social practice. And, as Michelle M. Lazar writes,

> social practices on the whole, far from being neutral, are gendered ... First, 'gender' functions as an interpretative category that enables participants in a community to make sense of and structure their social practices. Second, gender is a social relation that enters into and partially constitutes all other social relations and activities. Based on the specific, asymmetric meanings of 'male' and 'female', and the consequences being assigned to one or the other within concrete social practices, such an allocation becomes a constraint on further practices.[23]

I argue that the gendered nature of material leads to a preference for women composers whose music can be gendered as male and meets the terms of the discourse of materialism, rather than an outright preference for male over female composers. Rather than an explicit discrimination against women as a group this creates a more implicit discrimination of women who can only be spoken about in female terms (women who do not meet the materialistic and historical terms of the discourse). Aaron Copland's statement illustrates this problem: for him it is a statement about musical quality, but it is really a statement about the materiality of Boulanger's music. This has two consequences: those women composers who have not achieved acceptance by the New Music institution are not-yet-composers (not-yet-subjects), while those women composers who are accepted are presented as pillars of possibility, examples to other women; their difference is valued so they can stand as symbols of equality, but it is also diminished in order that they become subsumed into the male discourse of material.

In order to illustrate this I will briefly describe two examples of recent pieces by women composers. The two pieces are Jennifer Walshe's opera *XXX Live Nude Girls!!!* (2003) and Rebecca Saunders's *Caerulean* (2010). The instrumentation

---

[22] Judith Butler, 'Contingent Foundations: Feminism and the Question of Postmodernism', in *Feminists Theorize the Political*, ed. Judith Butler and Joan W. Scott (New York and London: Routledge, 1992), 13, quoted in Elam, *Feminism and Deconstruction*, 70.

[23] Michelle M. Lazar, 'Politicizing Gender in Discourse: Feminist Critical Discourse Analysis as Political Perspective and Praxis', in Lazar, *Feminist Critical Discourse Analysis*, 5.

and materials used in each work seem quite polarised, but there are also important similarities between them. Walshe's opera is scored for two female voices, two puppeteers, two camera operators, CD, a small chamber ensemble and Barbie dolls. The Barbie dolls take on the roles of the main characters, forming the visual material of the opera on stage and also projected onto a screen; parts of the Barbie dolls are also used to realise certain playing techniques within the ensemble and thus the dolls link the sonic and visual material throughout the work. Saunders's work is scored for solo bass clarinet. It is not a dramatic work but arises from a detailed study of bass clarinet multiphonics, made in collaboration with an established and accomplished contemporary music clarinet performer, Carl Rosman. Although very different on the surface, the linking actor between the two works is the issue of extended instrumental technique, which is, in some ways, central to both compositions as they offer the listener 'new', unexpected or extended approaches to sound in their instrumentation. In order to briefly compare the reception and discourse around these two works I have taken and examined statements which come from reviews of or discussion around the two pieces. It is also important to note that the final reviews and statements chosen as examples were all taken from positive interpretations of both works; this is not a case of a preference by any of the parties particularly for one composer and piece over the other, but only of the use of gendered statements in discourse.

The first statements concern Rebecca Saunders and the piece *Caerulean*. Before this piece was performed at the Huddersfield Contemporary Music Festival in 2010, Saunders was interviewed by Graham McKenzie, the artistic director of the festival. Addressing Saunders about her career, McKenzie says to her:

> you've developed a very particular relationship with some of arguably the best contemporary music ensembles in the world: Recherche, musikFabrik.[24]

Here, McKenzie emphasises the success of Saunders's work as a composer through her relationships with, and thus validation by, established (male) contemporary music institutions rather than through the materiality of her pieces. He regards her institutional relationships as a sign of a kind of achievement that is often synonymous with musical quality within New Music narratives: 'the best' ensembles would surely only perform 'the best' music. This agrees with Adorno's conception of 'New Music', when he writes, '[t]he concept of "new music" simply confirms the way it is institutionalized in studios, special societies and concerts'.[25]

---

[24] Rebecca Saunders with Graham McKenzie, 'Pre-Concert Talk (St Paul's Hall, Huddersfield: HCMF, 20 November 2011), transcript', 2. Audio archived at hcmf//, 'download free talks from hcmf// 2010', last modified 2010, http://www.hcmf.co.uk/Download-free-talks-from-hcmf-2010. Transcript archived at hcmf//, www.hcmf.co.uk/doc/download/51.

[25] Theodor Adorno, 'Music and New Music', in *Quasi una Fantasia: Essays on Modern Music*, trans. Rodney Livingstone (London: Verso, 2002), 250.

Adorno further claims that 'such organisations inadvertently negate [new music's] claims to truth and hence universal appeal, even though without them its cause would be hopelessly lost'.[26] So, the claim here is not that association with such ensembles is negative, but that materiality is assumed simply through association.

Rebecca Saunders then describes to McKenzie the work undertaken in the project to create her solo bass clarinet piece in collaboration with the performer. She states:

> we started discovering sounds in 2003.[27]

In this short statement, Saunders describes two facets of her work. By naming the process of composition as a process of 'discovering sounds' she identifies a process of engaging with the 'new' similar to that described by Dahlhaus. She infers that her music will present the innovative results of a collaboration and has arisen from an exploratory or experimental process. Her reference to the beginning of this process taking place in 2003 is significant as, speaking in 2010, she also draws attention to the time that has been taken on the composition.

The materiality of Saunders's work, and its link with her compositional and collaborative processes, is also described by her collaborator Carl Rosman. Writing for Huddersfield Contemporary Music Festival, where the premiere of the piece took place, Rosman says of her work:

> her music in general moves back and forth between almost impalpable delicacy and extreme violence.[28]

In this statement, Rosman emphasises Saunders's compositional control and technique. He places her music at the far reaches of what is achievable in contemporary music, and as such he also implies that there is connoisseurship in the appreciation of her music. Rosman has also spoken publicly at length about their collaboration. In a transcript from a podcast about his work and the piece, published on the website of musikFabrik (the New Music ensemble he regularly performs with), he states:

> I guess it's the way that Rebecca always works, I think, is that she establishes a particular – she focusses on a particular area of technique. It wouldn't normally be a classically essential area. It was basically one kind of multiphonic we worked on. And there's one particular kind of multiphonic with clarinets. Some multiphonics are quirky. Some multiphonics, it's a bit hard to pin down what

---

[26] Adorno, 'Music and New Music', 250.
[27] Saunders with McKenzie, 'Pre-Concert Talk', 3.
[28] Carl Rosman, 'Blurring Boundaries: Performing Rebecca Saunders', hcmf//, last modified 2011, accessed 1 February 2011, http://www.hcmf.co.uk/page/show/131. This page is no longer archived on the hcmf// site.

notes there are, how many notes there are. And then there is a certain kind of outcome where, in contrast to that, you hear two very pure notes quite clearly.[29]

In this statement, Rosman again emphasises the precision, focus and specificity of outcome in Saunders's music, and in this case in particular when she composes using extended instrumental techniques. These statements, taken as a whole, paint a picture of a composer who works in extreme detail with extended techniques and sound. In addition, the description of her collaboration with the performer as central in accessing this detail causes the New Music institution to become part of the materiality of the work itself. It is important that she collaborated not only with *a* performer, but with *this* performer. In this way the materiality of her work, assumed through her association with particular institutions, is validated by her inclusion of institutions in its materiality. This, then, affords her compositional technique and approach close attention as both accomplished and legitimate.

Reviews and assessments of Jennifer Walshe's opera also most frequently draw attention to her use of extended sound and techniques. Christopher Fox's review in *The Guardian* on the premiere of *XXX Live Nude Girls!!!* states that

> the musicians scratch at their instruments, exploring Walshe's trademark lo-fi white noise.[30]

The language used highlights some of the differences in the reception of the two composers. In Fox's description, the result of the use of technique in Walshe's music is imprecise and unrefined. While the assessment of Saunders's music made clear the effort made in finding the correct sounds, here the focus is on the sounds themselves as extraneous and alienating. As it is the musicians rather than the composer who are doing the 'exploring' in this case, this assessment of the work can also be understood as implying that the compositional work is done by the musicians and not by the composer. Fox further pinpoints this as a feature of her music as a whole. In an overview of Walshe's work, Michael Duggan of the Contemporary Music Centre Ireland writes that *XXX Live Nude Girls!!!* implies that

> the conventional definition of what opera is or who its audience should be will have to be abandoned.[31]

---

[29] Carl Rosman, 'Carl Rosman-Clarinet', *musikFabrik blog*, last modified 2 March 2011, http://musikfabrik-blog.eu/2011/03/02/carl-rosman-clarinet/.

[30] Christopher Fox, 'Barbie: The Opera', *The Guardian*, 24 October 2003, accessed 26 September 2012, http://www.guardian.co.uk/music/2003/oct/24/classicalmusicandopera1.

[31] Michael Duggan, 'Opera: Just Another Art Form?', *The Contemporary Music Centre Ireland*, last modified 2003, accessed 26 September 2012, http://www.cmc.ie/articles/article652.html.

Despite being a positive assessment of Walshe's work – a post intended to promote the work of an Irish composer – this statement places her opera outside of operatic or contemporary music tradition and the contemporary music audiences who might watch it; this is particularly pertinent when it could be considered that the opera does have a direct relationship with the Mozartian tradition of marionette operas. Again, the focus is on the alienating rather than the compositional.

Finally, the entry for *XXX Live Nude Girls!!!* in *The Multimedia Encyclopedia of Women in Today's World* also brings out these same features. Courtney Cauthon writes:

> The score is unmelodic and harsh. The vocalists sing, shout, whisper, and speak. The musicians play instruments, but also make sounds using objects such as telephones and toy cars. The marionettes are not traditional puppets, but instead are Barbie dolls ... In the performance, there is little done to make the production seem realistic.[32]

Although the author gives this description as evidence of the notability and uniqueness of the work, she also makes the same claims for the work that arise from its materiality and use of technique: the work is outside of a tradition, the techniques employed by the performers are outside of a musical approach to performance, the sound is alienating.

The conclusions that can be drawn about the differing reception of these two composers, as demonstrated by these statements, are summarised in Table 11.1.

Table 11.1   Comparison of Saunders's and Walshe's works arising from discourse analysis

Rebecca Saunders, *Caerulean*	**Jennifer Walshe,** *XXX Live Nude Girls!!!*
The piece is 'internal', arising from thought	The piece is external, arising from action
Her use of extended technique is complex, and exploratory	Her use of extended technique is noisy and unrefined
The piece is an extension of the clarinet within the 'New Music' tradition	The piece is outside of the 'New Music' tradition
Her compositional approach is complex and conceptual	Her compositional approach is social, visual and tactile

The major difference here is the perception of the material used by the composers, particularly where extended uses of sound and instrumental technique

---

[32]   Courtney Cauthon, 'XXX Live Nude Girls!!!', in *The Multimedia Encyclopedia of Women in Today's World*, 2nd edn, ed. Mary Zeiss Stange, Carol K. Oyster and Jane E. Sloan (Thousand Oaks, CA: Sage, 2013).

are concerned, and the perception of the relationship of the composers with their own material. The link of the compositional act, material and subjectivity is therefore evident within the reception of these works. A gendered difference is constructed between the music of the two women not only because of the difference in reception but because of the specific details of the music: one piece belongs to thought, to tradition, to complexity and to sustained investigation; the other belongs to 'unthinking' action, to the senses and is outside of the accepted norms. They fall into a male:female structuralist binary.

This discussion in no way speaks to the quality or value of the music at hand, or the accomplishment of either composer. Both were selected, in part, because their works are increasingly but perhaps equally well known and celebrated. The conclusion is not that the quality of the music is less in the case of either composer, or that either composer is more genuinely a 'female composer' than the other, or that the experience of either composer causes them to be less of a subject than the other. I hope to emphasise that the system of values by which both composers are judged in the context of 'New Music' prefers the music that holds most in common with a male, patriarchal, discourse of material. Therefore, the label 'female composer' is, in the terms of this discourse, reserved as a derogatory term which might be excused should one's music appear to negate the 'female' part of this label; and the notion of a New Music subject is only credible when conceived of as one who accepts the terms of the discourse and its restrictions and limitations on behalf of the composer. In this respect, then, Jennifer Walshe is not a 'composer' (subject) nor is what she creates 'music' since its materiality is one which is against the dominant discourse.

Aino Saarinen describes similar issues within scientific research as colouring research institutions as 'cultural and ideological institutions of domination',[33] and this is the role that the New Music institution takes on in my reading. In such an environment, Margit Eichler perceives that 'women's goals and activities are seen as functions of the goals and activities of men'.[34] This is subtle since it allows the institution to claim inclusivity by denying that there is any other state of affairs to be included in. It is linked with the erroneous conceptualisation that men are neutral, meaning that any struggle for women's equal representation within the institution becomes what Diane Elam describes as 'the struggle for women's rights to be men'.[35]

One conclusion that can be drawn from this, then, is that the discourse of material is a form of social closure, described by Luisa Martín and Concepción Gómez Esteban as 'a process through which social groups attempt to maintain exclusive control over resources ... by restricting access to them'.[36] The resources

---

[33] Saarinen, 'Feminist Research', 37.
[34] Margrit Eichler, *The Double Standard: A Feminist Critique of Feminist Social Sciences* (London: Croon Helm, 1980), 118–19, in Saarinen, 'Feminist Research', 38.
[35] Elam, *Feminism and Deconstruction*, 60.
[36] Martín and Esteban, 'The Gender of Power', 75.

in question here, such as restricted arts funding, are not themselves gendered, but the process of maintaining them for the limited groups who already control them infers the need for patriochialism.[37] But also worth considering is Nancy Harstock's statement that 'power and community are closely linked';[38] in order to maintain the idea of a structured New Music community, it may seem that gendered power relationships need to be preserved. Harstock writes that '[m]en's power to structure social relations in their own image means that women too must participate in social relations that manifest and express abstract masculinity'.[39]

However, the link between the perceived relationship of the composer with their material and the notion of a New Music subjectivity is a key concept in which this social closure is enacted. Elizabeth Grosz addresses subjectivity and women's activities when she writes:

> The question of freedom for women, or for any oppressed social group, is never simply a question of expanding the range of available options so much as it is about transforming the quality and activity of subjects who choose and made themselves through how and what they do.[40]

And further that

> The problem, rather, is how to expand the variety of activities and knowledge production so that women and men may be able to act differently and open up activities to new interests, perspectives, and frameworks hitherto not adequately explored or invented.[41]

In order to enact this within New Music a move not just from a particular definition of material but from a materialist conception of the work to a more open definition is required.

Consideration of materialism in Derrida's writing leads Pheng Cheah to say that 'the force of materiality is nothing other than the constitutive exposure of

---

[37] '"patriochialism": the assumption that women are a subgroup, that "man's world" is the "real" world, that patriarchy is equivalent to culture and culture to patriarchy, that the "great" or "liberalizing" periods of history have been the same for women as for men.' Adrienne Rich, *Of Woman Born: Motherhood as Experience and Institution* (New York: Norton, 1976), 16.

[38] Nancy C. M. Harstock, *Money, Sex, and Power: Towards a Feminist Historical Materialism* (New York and London: Longman, 1983), 31.

[39] Harstock, *Money, Sex, and Power*, 245.

[40] Elizabeth Grosz, 'Feminism, Materialism and Freedom', in *New Materialism: Ontology, Agency and Politics*, ed. Diana Coole and Samantha Frost (Durham, NC and London: Duke University Press, 2010), 151.

[41] Grosz, 'Feminism, Materialism and Freedom', 154.

(the subject of) power to the other'.[42] The link between power, materialism and subjectivity is at the heart of the critical relationship with Walshe's and Saunders's work that influences their reception. Sonia Kinks writes that materialist theories traditionally, 'emphasize the ways in which subjectivity arises as the reflex of expression of social practices, or as the effect of discourses',[43] which has been the case here. I have emphasised that within the New Music discourse materialism functions to create composers as subjects only in their interaction with specific materials and the interaction of these materials with each other. Thus, 'composer' presented as a neutral term is really a male term, while 'female composers' must work to drop the preface and become neutral but therefore male. Equally, the use of material composers must aspire to is not neutral but a male exclusionary construct, and quality in this context is the ability to execute the discourse of material to an acceptable degree within one's compositions. This, then, prevents female (and male) composers who wish to produce something outside of this discourse from entering into the social practice and excludes composers and music which do not fit into it. As a result, the possibility for social change through integration of 'othered' elements is slim. Patriochialism in new music is, therefore, not merely a preference and perseverance of male-dominated institutions but a consequence of the materialism of New Music itself.

---

[42] Pheng Cheah, 'Non-Dialectical Materialism', in Coole and Frost, *New Materialism*, 81.

[43] Sonia Kinks, 'Simone de Beauvoir: Engaging Discrepant Materialisms', in Coole and Frost, *New Materialism*, 259.

Chapter 12

multiple/radical/forms/comma/*traces/ creativity/of/constraint*: A piece for solo voice and various accompaniment

Caroline Lucas

> I was in a queer mood, thinking myself very old: but now I am a woman again – as I always am when I write.[1]

multiple/radical/forms (2012) maps the course of my doctoral study in music practice, which used the methodologies of practice-as-research to enable an exploration of theory and creative practice, presenting a multimodal analysis of the critical implications of artistic invention. My PhD examined experimental composition practices, collective (national) identity and music as a means of resistance to hegemonic power, resulting in seven examples of practice and accompanying exegesis.[2] Combining theory, reflexive writing, sound and image, this work utilises the reciprocity of practice and theory as methods *and* subjects of research. It explores discourse constructed using the disciplinary language of praxis and posits the potentiality of *meaning* democratised through the ambivalent traces of experience.

multiple/radical/forms traces the development of my artistic and scholarly practices, which have changed from me 'thinking myself very [young]' and exterior to my work, to finding ways of asserting that:

> *I am ... artist ...*
> *I am ... scholar ...*
> *I am ... feminist ...*
> *I am ... a woman again.*

Furthermore, it charts the relationship between a shift in my theoretical and personal concern for what Elin Diamond has labelled the 'imperialistic and

---

[1] Virginia Woolf, 'Diary entry for 31 May 1929', in *The Diary of Virginia Woolf, Vol. 3, 1925–1930*, ed. Anne Olivier Bell, assisted by Andrew McNeillie (London: Hogarth, 1980), 231.

[2] Caroline Lucas, 'Portfolio of Original Musical Compositions with Written Commentary' (PhD diss., University of Leeds, 2012).

narcissistic' violence of the 'authoritative "we"' to the individualised transgressive act of identification.[3]

Reflecting my experimental approach to composition, this chapter combines the multifaceted approaches to practice-as-research: scholarly discourse, traces of subjectivities, sounds and images. As such, you are invited to read/imagine/hear/view the piece as you wish; however, there are markers in the text to guide you through the layers of discussion. A reflexive exploration of my identity as an artist is indicated by the use of this font; this discussion is contextualised within the more traditional academic discourse found in the standard font. The text presented in *italics* relates directly to the artworks and provides traces of the sounds and images to be found in them, marking the boundaries of the scholarly and reflexive narratives through its creative realisation.[4] Subjectivity and the privileging of individual meaning-making are positioned throughout my study and this chapter as a means of resisting frameworks of power and disrupting dominant discourses. This approach also enabled me to negotiate the authorised 'we' of academia, constructing multiple forms of 'self' as artistic production until finally able to confidently assert:

||: *I am ... I am ...* :||

The Masked Composer

The need for reflexivity within practice-as-research and the responsibility of the artist-intellectual in navigating culture as a battleground for power calls for a consideration of the location of the composer and associated relationships. Within the ideology of western art music, the composer has been privileged as an autonomous author, and hence owner of a 'work' in a hierarchical imagining of creative production. This positions the score as text (static representation of the 'work'), the performer as reader (with some recognition of the interpretive work involved) and audience as receiver (passive). Not only has this delineation been entangled with notions of the transcendental power of creation possessed by composers, fitting with the archetypal 'composer as genius' model, but it has also led to a separation from the wider context (and material reality) of production leading to absolutism. A reimagining of the processes, spaces, participants and relationships involved in creative enterprise resists and reframes these traditional roles, creating a democratised and fluid space for meaning-making.

---

[3] Elin Diamond, 'The Violence of "We": Politicizing Identification', in *Critical Theory and Performance*, ed. Janelle G. Reinelt and Joseph R. Roach (Ann Arbor: University of Michigan Press, 2007).

[4] I am grateful to my PhD examiners, James Saunders and Martin Iddon, for challenging me to develop my writing in this way.

Even as an undergraduate student I found the game of 'academic tennis' a loathsomely masculinised and competitive exchange of, what appeared to me, pointless 'facts' – something that had more to do with the assertion of cultural capital than the dissemination of knowledge. As a postgraduate student my peers were critical of it, yet the forwards-backwards ping-pong of information occurred even in informal settings.

I have never been able to remember names and dates and titles; perhaps if I tried really hard then I could retain some of this information. It has never felt like the most useful information to retain; what's more, the fear of exposing inexperience and lack of knowledge by exchanging erroneous information made it an easy decision to watch from the sidelines.

My dread of the academic point-scoring exchange followed me throughout my studies. I have concluded that, in the pursuit of academic debate, I do not care *what* my peers know, what interests me is *how* they apply that knowledge to provoke and agitate. Fortunately, my closest academic friends provided encouragement and were motivated, to varying degrees, by thoughts of rebellious progress. However, as I approached the deadline for submission of my thesis, thoughts turned to the impending doom of my *grand finale* – the viva voce exam; I became nervous at the absence of names and dates and titles in my thesis.

||: *I am not ... John Cage.*
I am not ... Earle Brown.
I am not ... Wolff or Walshe. :||

This absence of traditional references was not because I was doing something *so* unique that it did not warrant comparison, or because my creative capabilities were *so* original as to be removed from any form of influence. In fact, it was a recognition of the very unquantifiable nature of influences that shape the minutiae of process and practice involved in the creation of a piece. More than this though, the identity of the artist (see Figure 12.1) and how she locates herself in relation to other creators is wholly political; it has the ability to reify authorised narratives and ultimately seeks to manipulate reception. It also tends, often rather arrogantly, to overlook the location of the audience, their respective individual histories, traditions and experiences.

188   Gender, Age and Musical Creativity

Figure 12.1   Example of composer biography

A distorted fanfare sounds. You sh/could stand ... you sh/could raise your hand to your breast ... Triumphant chords strike, snare drums roll into cadences marching on and on and on ...

In negotiating the politics of 'influence' and 'location' appropriation is utilised as a method of subverting the power of dominant cultural frameworks. Abrogation and appropriation are strategies used in post-colonial practice, to reject what is privileged and normative by re-inventing and re-coding existing modes of production, making critical and critiquing existing forms of creative practice privileged as normative. Homi K. Bhabha's focus on the ambivalent nature of culture (at once complicit and resistant) highlights an inherent tension (at once settling and disruptive) that is a necessary condition for cultural dominance.[5] My collection of electronic miniatures *...and them* (2011) does not completely separate its samples of national anthems from their original source. There are moments where the timbral qualities of the instruments are clearly discernible, melodic fragments and harmonic movement occasionally become perceptible. The appropriation of the familiar (yet ambiguous) sounds of national anthems, reinvented as unfamiliar fragments, makes use of a fluctuation between the 'attractive' and the 'abject'. Moments of familiarity are interrupted through alteration, by the return of unfamiliar sounds or, being miniatures of short duration, by the sonic break that disrupts at the end of each track.

```
    I knew that my examiners would want to ask me about
my work in relation to other composers; they would
want names and dates and titles. I retrospectively (and
slightly begrudgingly) shoe-horned some composer names
into my commentary and hoped my examiners would not
```

---

[5]   Homi K. Bhabha, *The Location of Culture* (London: Routledge, 2004).

ask me directly about dates and titles, exposing my
ignorance. As it was they noted the absence of comparison
and when pushed to discuss I provided a couple of names
from my sphere of influence, to which they added names
from their sphere of influence. More constructively
though, the expectation that comparative location would
be negotiated within this type of academic study meant
that my examiners requested I outline my position in a
footnote early on in the thesis, which resulted in the
following statement:

> [M]y concern with the reproduction of power structures
> required the avoidance of defining (or legitimising) my
> work within the boundaries of privileged narratives
> of the 'composer' in Western musical discourses – the
> model of the composer as '(dead) white male'.[6]

My music has reimagined the role of the composer in a variety of ways, all of which attempted to destabilise the positioning of the composer as gatekeeper to a definitive understanding of a work's meaning. Roland Barthes's essay 'The Death of the Author' recognises the problematic nature of discussing authorial intention and calls for the separation of the author from interpretation of the work, placing greater emphasis on the role of the reader in constructing meaning(s).[7] This destabilises the interpretive strategy as an attempt at deciphering the 'truth' of a work and enables the possibility for multiple readings. Michel Foucault suggests that the author provides a restrictive and classificatory function. He describes a contradictory presentation of the author 'as a perpetual surging of invention', who is then actually made to function as a limit to meaning, impeding 'free manipulation ... free composition'.[8] Rather than viewing the author's name as indicating the individual producer, exterior to the work, Foucault suggests that the author is located within the interior of a discourse, 'marking off the edges of the text, revealing ... its mode of being' and indicating the status of the discourse in society.[9] In order to negotiate the interior location of the author, as well as its potential limiting interpretive function, different modes/masks of self-presentation were explored throughout my study. Not only did this facilitate a negotiation of the composer's presence within a piece, but it enabled a reimagining of the relationships involved in creative production.

---

[6] Lucas, 'Portfolio of Original Musical Compositions', 3.
[7] Roland Barthes, 'The Death of the Author', in *Image, Music, Text*, trans. Stephen Heath (London: Fontana, 1977).
[8] Michel Foucault, *Essential Works of Foucault 1954–1984*, vol. 2: *Aesthetics* (London: Penguin, 2000), 221.
[9] Foucault, *Essential Works*, 211.

Different framings of anonymity were explored as a way of attempting to resist the hegemonic authorial control granted to the author-composer. Modes of anonymity were not intended to suggest that there is no person behind a work, but the act of obscuring, through the masking of the composer, consciously becomes part of the construction of the work. Positioning the composer as one of the material forces in the facilitation of a piece is not intended to negate the initial creative intentions of the composer, but instead recognises their limitations in shaping the individual's experience of a piece. In creating open works the composer as 'facilitator' becomes someone who contributes towards the creation of the conditions for a particular experience, without having the power to define what that experience actually is. The aim of this is to recognise the intrinsic loss of control (and I would go so far as to say ownership) involved in the process of transferring ideas from the private realm of the creative mind to the multiple public sites of creative expression (sketches, scores, performances and so on). While early on in my studies this was a useful mechanism for hiding myself – a comfort blanket protecting my exposure in having to be recognised as the composer/author/creator of the work – it later became much more about negotiating this position of power and exploring the processes of construction.

```
I nearly gave up learning the violin as a young
teenager; I disliked the exams, didn't practise my
scales and found the syllabus very restrictive. Most of
all - having been raised around folk music and having
had a life changing moment when, as a young child,
I realised I could play and adapt the theme tune to
a popular cartoon on the recorder without needing a
score - I didn't like being told exactly how I should
be playing each and every dot on the page. Fortunately,
my parents found a wonderful teacher who shared my
rebellious streak and encouraged me to play jazz and
folk music alongside continuing my 'formal' studies.
The creative role of performer and listener has always
been central in my understanding of sonic production.
More than this, though, the potential for continuous
transformation inreproduction has always seemed the
much more exciting option.
```

> *After that,*
> *quite simply,*
> *After that,*
> *quite calmly,*
> driving forward
> *make your own stones*
> driving forward
> *your own floor plan*

building
your own sound[10]

I attempted to explore this idea in the first piece that I wrote for my doctoral study: *stick, sand, stones*. The score, written for a set ensemble of seven performers, moves between conventional notation and modular graphic notation attempting to examine perceptions of shifting levels of control. However, in rehearsals I was regularly asked for explicit directions and explanations. While, at first, I was disappointed at the performers' reticence in approaching the more open sections of the piece, my unease during the process made me realise that I had not gone far enough and had conservatively underestimated my intentions. My presence at rehearsals contradicted my desire to challenge the traditional role of the composer as author and democratise the creative process. Looking back, I felt like I had raided my mother's wardrobe and was playing dress-up in the part of PhD student. I was out of my depth and had tried to write music that sounded and looked like the names and dates and titles I thought I should be referencing as a postgraduate composer. It was experimental to a point, but it did not do what I wanted my music to do; it did not sound as I wanted my music to sound.

The radio is on in the next room: white noise waves crash, crackle, swell. Malin, Hebrides, Bailey ... slow moving ... easterly, north-easterly ... Wight, Plymouth ... increasing, six at times ... Thames ... declining ... Sole ... veering north ... Forth, Tyne ... Fair Isle ... losing its identity ...

The *[Unnamed Maps Series]* (2009–11) is an example of pieces that were intended to form continuous movement and transformation, with 'completeness' reliant on the quality of openness and ownership available to whoever engages with the work. The maps utilise cartographic imagery, text and graphic scoring, and are accompanied by sample-based fixed-media parts to serve as part of an improvisatory performance. The piece is designed to privilege the interpretive autonomy of the performer, with the composer taking a radically 'hands-off' role beyond the basic presentation of materials. This has been described by Lauren Redhead as a 'focussed indeterminacy', recognising the 'extreme freedom' and 'extreme complexity' present in the work due to the multiplicity of potential outcomes.[11] Attempting to limit the composer's influence (and hence control) to the symbolic material and creative context constructed within the maps, suggestions and fixed-media part is further emphasised by the adoption of a pseudonym 'The Cartographer'. Not only does this avoid the self-identification of the composer, but it also denies the act of composing itself, acknowledging the constructive role the

---

[10] Performance notes from *stick, sand, stones* (2008). The text in italics is from Anne Sexton's poem 'A Little Uncomplicated Hymn'. Anne Sexton, *Live or Die* (London: Oxford University Press, 1967).

[11] Lauren Redhead, 'Young British Women: New Directions in Sound Art', *Terz Magazin* (2012), accessed 24 June 2012, http://terz.cc/magazin.php?z=44&id=205.

performer plays in interpreting and shaping the piece. The performer is furthermore invited to create a title for 'their' piece, giving them additional authorial control.

In a similar vein, the identification of self within my composer biography is often masked in similar ways. My biography was written to pastiche a newspaper dating advert and uses my initials to form a pseudonym. The decision to present biographical information in this way was, in part, a reaction against the formulaic model that many composer/academic biographies follow. It was partly a desire to continue to construct a persona as an artist, and not limit my creativity solely to the music, but also to set the tone for playful interaction as opposed to the reverential *seriousness* demanded by the narratives of one's successes that most commonly feature in this kind of autobiographical writing.

> **Culture Lover:** Originally Worcester, now Leeds. Composer, fiddler, flashmob convenor. Interests: Englishness, morris dancing and composting. WLTM like minded individuals to share in long walks and cartography. Must have own wheelbarrow.

Paul Hegarty suggests that sound art 'often reflects on its own production ... as a questioning of listening and the position of the listener'.[12] Just as my use of portable tape machines in performance or the invitation to 'cut-up' and 're-mix' my music draw attention to the means of (re)production of the sonic, so the 'lonely hearts' style biography draws attention to the means of (re)production of the self. The constructed ambiguity and limited specificity in my biographical narrative is part of a wider strategy to democratise meaning-making and draw attention to processes of production. Accompanying this, there is also a desire for the piece to be judged on its own merits, rather than on the privileging narratives of reputation or association. This negotiation of the role of author also facilitates an avoidance of the historically engendered gendering of the author/composer as masculine. However, anonymity is not about wishing to negate my gender identity, rather it is about not wanting this aspect of my personhood, or the expectation of implicit femininity, to become imposed on an experience of the work. However, this is countered by moments where my gender is used as an explicit political statement within the music, moments where my radical specificity is called upon to frame and illustrate a particular lived experience.

Women (Re)producing/(Re)producing Women

To be accompanied by an assemblage of female screams: high-pitched shrieks; swelling moans and groans; crying; growling; breathy labouring, pain or pleasure/ pleasure or pain?

---

[12] Paul Hegarty, *Noise/Music: A History* (London: Continuum, 2008), 171.

A central concern running throughout my work is the reproduction of frameworks of power and privileged discourses, the role of women as symbolic and biological reproducers, as well as the reproduction of 'women' as a collective category. The hegemonic gendered construction of the nation relies on the discursive production of women as the reproducers of the nation and men as its defenders. The language of nation and gender situates motherhood as the normative role for women, binding them to the biological myth of the common origin and collective destiny of the community.

I am ... ||: mother/daughter/whore/
mother/daughter/whore :||[13]

The positioning of women as reproducers of the nation relates to both biological and symbolic concerns. Nira Yuval-Davis suggests that the assertion of *woman-as-mother* burdens women with the role of symbolically representing the collective's identity and 'honour', while they often face exclusion from the collective body politic and are positioned as object rather than subject.[14] Despite the nation being constructed as a male project, women often have agency in constructing and maintaining (as well as resisting) the boundaries of 'acceptable' femininity (see Figure 12.2), which symbolically and culturally reproduces (and negotiates) the nation and national cultural traditions through notions of sexual morality, appropriate behaviour and normative constructions of familial arrangements. A recognition of women's agency, however, acknowledges the fluidity of gender relations and the possibility for resistance to the hierarchies of power encoded within the nation, which presents the potential for reimagining the position of women as constructors, rather than reproducers, of nation.

The process of reproduction has been a critical consideration in my exploration of sound practices, informing both the use of technologies and, more generally, relational interactions between performers, the sonic, the visual, the composer and the audience. The process of reproduction is essential to an understanding of sound technologies and their creative use in electronic musics and, as Tara Rodgers suggests, the privileging of music as a domain of masculinity. Her account of *'Pink Noises'* attempts to uncover the multiplicitous nature of reproductive sounds, challenging the 'patrilineal lines of descent' and the totalising male claims to creation which characterise dominant discourses of electronic music and music-making more generally.[15] The basis for this reimagining of narratives of electronic music practices is founded on the recognition that 'reproductive sounds are variously *produced ... reproduced* in multiple reflections ... *reproducible*

---

[13] Looped text taken from *There was an Englishman, an Irishman and a Scotsman* (2010–11).

[14] Nira Yuval-Davis, *Gender and Nation* (London: Sage, 1997), 45, 47.

[15] Tara Rodgers, *Pink Noises* (Durham, NC and London: Duke University Press, 2010), 15.

Figure 12.2 Photograph of a section of the 'life-sized' score for *multiple/radical/forms...*

within spaces of memory ... and *productive*, by generating multiple meanings in various contexts'.[16]

Pierre Bourdieu's concept of 'symbolic violence' has poetic, as well as theoretical, significance; it describes the strategies which maintain domination through the implicit and everyday exercise of symbolic capital, which establishes relations of dependence and hierarchical classifications disguised, or 'misrecognised', as natural. Bourdieu's description of how this mode of domination is 'not so much undergone as chosen' resonates with Gramsci's depiction of hegemonic power through consensus.[17] The dominant gendered construction of the nation relies on the symbolic violence of the discursive production of women as reproducers of the nation and men as its defenders. The language of nation and gender situates motherhood as the normative role for women, binding them to the biological myth of the common origin and collective destiny of the nation. The symbolic violence of this discourse implicitly relates to the control of female bodies, as well as the assertion of sexual ethics and normative sexuality. The moralistic construction of

---

[16] Rodgers, *Pink Noises*, 15; emphasis in original.

[17] Pierre Bourdieu, *Outline of a Theory of Practice* (Cambridge: Cambridge University Press, 1977), 192.

motherhood discourses marks the boundaries of normative gender and sexuality, as well as delineating a space of abjection when these limits are crossed.

I spent some time volunteering at a charity that worked with women involved in prostitution. Every week I would go out with a team of volunteers into the darkest corners of the city to offer food and friendship to women who were often driven to the streets by the most desperate of circumstances. During this time, in the next city along, there was a breaking news story which involved the discovery of a number of women who had been brutally murdered. It was reported that all of the women had at some point worked as prostitutes, and from this point forward the media stopped referring to these victims as murdered women, murdered mothers or daughters, but as murdered prostitutes. In my experience of building relationships with individuals involved in prostitution, they were first and foremost women, mothers and daughters. A couple of years after this, two women were violently murdered about a mile from where I was living, while they were carrying out their duties as police officers. This time the discourse in the media focused on rejecting calls to discuss the specific safety of *female* officers, while constructing an infantilisation of the victims through repeated use of the term 'girl', heightening the sense of vulnerability to the limit. The symbolic violence of differentiation through language both marks and *re*-marks on the gender of women working within spaces imagined to be masculine.

> *woman; she, her female petticoat. feminality; muliebrity; womanhood, womankind; the fair sex, softer sex. dame madam mistress ...*
> *good woman, good wife; squaw; wife; bachelor girl; new woman; feminist; suffragette; suffragist; nymph; wench; grisette;*
> *girl; effeminacy; sissy; betty; cotquean; henhussy; molly coddle; muff;*
> *female; she; feminine; womanly ladylike; matronly maidenly; wifely womanish; effeminate unmanly; gynecic; gynaecic.*
> *Antonyms; man*
> *Antonyms; man*
> *Antonyms; man*[18]

The text that is sampled and looped during the performance paper *There was an Englishman...* explores the symbolic violence of various gender terms applied

---

[18] Text taken from *There was an Englishman, an Irishman and a Scotsman*.

to women, with an online voice generator producing a quality of anonymised mechanical precision, negating the affective experience of human verbalisation. The application of these terms within the piece was based on Joanna Herbert's assertion that 'individuals are located within power hierarchies and interlocking inequalities in which class, gender and race are not autonomous spheres but enmesh to create a matrix of domination'.[19] The looping of these samples within the performance creates a layering of terms, which, by the end of the piece, becomes so concentrated as to be indistinct and obscured. This looping then not only becomes an exploration of the semantic power of words, but also reduces the audible expression of language to the sonic conditions of the piece, resulting in noise.

The samples featured in *There was an Englishman...* utilise a practice of 'glitching' to distort and disrupt the quoted source material with the erroneous properties of noise. Various interpretations of *Rule, Britannia!* are time stretched and interjected with micro-silences, repetitive skipping fragments and shifts in pitch, which disrupt the flow of the sample. The fixed-media part from *That Snayped The Wylde* (2009–10) also employs techniques of glitching to interrupt the domestic soundscape. The intersections of the piece are marked by a presentation of the 'rough edges' of the samples, utilising the noise created from switching the field recorder on and off. This makes use of sonic content which is normally deleted or faded out to create a polished extract of audio; instead, these fragments are employed to connect the four sections of the piece while drawing attention to the means of production.

Caleb Kelly describes the 'noising-up' of experimental music as a combination of 'the "clean" world of the digital with a "dirty", detritus-driven sound'.[20] This identifies the binary nature of these electronic practices, which are reliant on the production possibilities of recording technologies while exhibiting a destruction of this potential and associated aesthetics. The recognition of failure and the intentionality of destruction in the practice of glitching embraces the fundamental potential of experimentation – reimaging the boundaries of 'successful' invention. However, electronic music and performance art group Le Tigre acknowledge a disparity in the reception of failure, suggesting that 'when men make mistakes, it's fetishized as a glitch … [and] when women do it, it's like … a hideous mistake'.[21] Glitching, then, provides an interesting commentary on the control and rejection of the perfectionism of 'maximum performance' technology and the gendering of skills and expertise, and, further, the perception of intentionality in creative acts based on processes of destruction.[22]

---

[19] Joanna Herbert, *Negotiating Boundaries in the City: Migration, Ethnicity, and Gender in Britain* (Aldershot: Ashgate, 2008), 6.

[20] Caleb Kelly, *Cracked Media: The Sound of Malfunction* (Cambridge, MA: MIT Press, 2009), 8.

[21] Rodgers, *Pink Noises*, 249.

[22] Mark Nunes, ed., *ERROR: Glitch, Noise, and Jam in New Media Cultures* (London: Continuum, 2011), 5.

To be accompanied by the ubiquitous drone of domestic noise: the whirring tick of the central heating timer; the swirling throb of the washing machine; the bass moan of pipes echoing within the creaking chambers of expanding and contracting floorboards.

During the final two years of my doctoral study, I moved out of my shared postgraduate house in Yorkshire to my partner's house in Cheshire. Previously, my days were varied through working from home and at the university; in both environments there was space for individual study and interaction with those also experiencing postgraduate life. Suddenly, in leaving Yorkshire, there was no longer the welcome distraction of my peers with their spontaneous sharing of ideas, their boosting reassurances and caffeine hits. In Cheshire, a singular space had become my place of work; it was also my leisure and living space; it was also a space that demanded work. Domestic responsibilities while my partner worked the 9-5 infused into the routine of my everyday practices. The privilege of being able to stay at home to complete my studies cost the price of maintaining the order of that work/living/working space, which produced a tension in my perception of self and my relationship to this space. The irony in moving from independence to dependence (with the end of temporary lecturing contracts and scholarship payments) and the adoption of an archetypal housewife role in order to complete a thesis about practices which challenge hegemonic power structures was difficult to shrug off. Yet my melodramatic sense of domestic imprisonment became productively subverted into a freedom to create utilising the noise of the everyday.

Everyday practices are used by Michel de Certeau to conceive of new ways for researching the creative workings of culture. He suggests that these discussions are made possible 'if everyday practices, "ways of operating" ... no longer appear as merely the obscure background of social activity, and if a body of theoretical questions, methods, categories, and perspectives, by penetrating this obscurity, make it possible to articulate them'.[23]

These ideas resonate with the Gramscian concept of resisting hegemony through a critical engagement with appropriation and the reimagining of existing practices. Yet, the temporal limits of this process are explored in Kelly's application of de Certeau to 'cracked' media practices; with the concept of 'making do' creating a

---

[23] Michel de Certeau, *The Practice of Everyday Life* (Berkeley: University of California Press, 1984), xi.

temporality which is depicted as a momentary freedom to *recreate*.[24] The use of the 'everyday' in my practice is located in an engagement with a *lo-fi/DIY* sound world, which is based on a rejection of the hi-fidelity standards of beauty, expertise and cultivation. In addition, reimagining creativity within everyday practices democratises invention and, to an extent, liberates it from the standardisation of institutional control.

Underlying these theorisations is the conception of noise as negativity, destruction, disruption and, as Hegarty suggests, something destined only for constant failure – 'failing to stay noise, as it becomes familiar, or acceptable practice'.[25] This concept of failure recognises the 'incessant' crossing and re-crossing of transgression, as described by Foucault, in which the line 'closes up behind it in a wave of extremely short duration ... return[ing] once more right to the horizon of the uncrossable'.[26] The transgressive power of noise imagined as opposition and resistance can then be located in the transient experience of unfamiliarity. Therefore, noise offers a means of resisting the control of information, as well as an acceptance and creative utilisation of the unpredictable. Most significantly, however, it creates a space *beyond* meaning, containing the potential for unbounded meaning and avoiding the futile endeavour of *clear* communication. Noise creates a disruptive fissure in which meaning becomes wholly democratised.

The fixed-media part of *That Snayped The Wylde* is constructed from recordings of 'noise' found within my home. The ambient sonic space of the domestic setting – captured from the bathroom extractor fan, the heating timer and the combined sound of appliances in the kitchen – forms the foundational sound of the piece, creating a drone-like continuity of noise. This base-level is interrupted by samples of domestic appliances – such as the sound of a vacuum cleaner, of the washing machine and dishwasher – which delineate the boundaries of a space and labour explicitly marked as feminine. This sonic exploration of space works alongside the imagery of the fixed-media part, which visually depicts the control of environmental and domestic space, the everyday materiality of *man*-made boundary maintenance. Mavis Bayton's article 'Women Making Music' identifies subcultural theory's failure to conceptualise the implications of gender on leisure time, suggesting a matrix of material, spatial and regulatory constraints which limit female access to music outside of the domestic setting.[27] Alongside economic restrictions, she describes exclusionary practices which limit female participation in music, protecting it as masculine. The use of domestic noise as a continuous drone in *That Snayped The Wylde* marks the boundaries of the piece with the

---

[24] Kelly, *Cracked Media*.
[25] Hegarty, *Noise/Music*, ix.
[26] Foucault, *Essential Works*, 73.
[27] Mavis Bayton, 'Women Making Music: Some Material Constraints', in *The Popular Music Studies Reader*, ed. Andy Bennett, Barry Shank and Jason Toynbee (Abingdon: Routledge, 2006).

imposing restriction of domesticity, while the electronic experimentation within the study mostly occurred within the confines of this private space.

The use of noise in artistic production and its associated technological practices identify spaces which are implicitly gendered male. This ties in not only with historically defined notions of practices gendered as masculine, but also with a wider domination of the discourses that shape those practices and afford visibility to particular practitioners. Further, this is combined with the control of knowledge forms, which Rodgers's study *Pink Noises* describes as a privileging and protectionism of technical knowledge, as well as a general denial of women's participation in electronic music.[28] Her book attempts to re-balance the historical accounts of electronic musical cultures, to include the wide range of practices and negotiations of gender explored by female musicians, as well as to reimagine the relationships between sound, modes of production and gender.

	: *I am not ... silenced.* :	
	: *I am not ... Cage's silence.* :	
	: *I am ... caged by silence.* :	

Key to exploring processes of (re)production within my practice has been the concept of 'do-it-yourself', which has been a significant strategy employed within music and art cultures attempting to resist and counter the hegemonic power structures of the 'mainstream' and capitalism, gaining independence from the mass mediation of cultural production. This rejection of the authorised institution's control of creative goods and labour appropriates the power to create and disseminate for the *everyday* individual rather than the 'expert' or 'elite', which democratises the opportunity for creation and reimagines the aesthetic of the artistic object.

The subversive practice of radical embroidery (along with other crafts such as knitting and crochet) has, since the suffragettes and later feminist art movements, appropriated and reimagined craft practices which have been historically marked as feminine. This gendered activity has been associated with both the division of labour and the restrictive control of feminine leisure pursuits. Needlework as 'appropriate' leisure activity has been historically constructed as feminine (and hence marginal) through its limited location in the private sphere of the home; it connotes a silenced, still space of restricted physicality and the pursuit of innocuous *beauty* delineated as 'craft' rather than artistic production. The use of embroidery within my graphic scores draws on the subversive appropriation of *feminine* practices to critique the gendered control of modes of cultural production, as well as a reimagining of the media through which musical scores can be constructed. The process of sewing through paper and card makes tangible the material reality of the action in its enactment of resistance (see Figure 12.3).

---

[28] Rodgers, *Pink Noises*, 3.

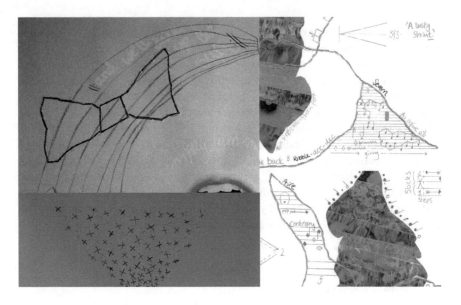

Figure 12.3   Examples of embroidery in graphic scores for (L–R) *multiple/radical/forms...* and *[Unnamed Maps Series]*

It wasn't until my Grandma was being described as 'quiet and unassuming' by a family friend at her funeral that I really reflected on the kind of woman my maternal grandmother had been. My Grandma's humble modesty, her 'quiet and unassuming' nature masked a wide range of talents. My Grandma was a skilled craftswoman. My Grandma was an artist. Not that she would have ever said or thought so. I developed my interest in needlework within the familial setting, in time spent making things with my Grandma and Mum. At the same time, my brothers learnt model making from our paternal Grandfather and Dad. While my brothers mastered the technical skills of building model planes, I developed the craft of needlework. This delineation sits with Bourdieu's depiction of cultural capital as being, in part, acquired within the familial setting. Further, its acquisition as gendered knowledge suggests the way in which cultural capital organises the social in hierarchical gender relations, legitimising inequality. The use of embroidery in my practice seeks to appropriate existing gendered modes of creation, often dismissed as 'craft', and reposition it as critical artistic production, as art in and of itself.

The 'handmade' process involved in *do-it-yourself* practices has particular implications for concepts of reproduction and repetition. The concept of reproduction is key to a discussion of graphic scoring versus ideas about the interpretation of conventional western notation. While the aim of traditional notation may be the accurate replication of similar sounds and effects, repetition of the sonic is rejected by the indeterminacy of graphic scores. This resistance is embodied in the specific mode of production employed in creating the map scores for the *[Unnamed Maps Series]*, where the accuracy of reproduction is negotiated in the handmade quality of the scores, as much as in the realisation and performance of that work. All copies of the maps are handcrafted, rather than being digitally copied, recognising that 'accurate' mechanical reproductions of the scores would, in fact, transform the material qualities of the works, reducing it to the condition of ink and paper. The handmade production also, therefore, involves the notion of difference as a central quality in the work, creating the context for variance, which challenges the authority of the notion of the singular 'original' work, acknowledging that each copy possesses the quality of originality.

***

Practice-as-research is ideally placed to examine the workings of cultural power, with innovation and invention as central methodologies for the practical pursuit of critical understanding; it does, by its very nature, resist and reimagine dominant forms of knowledge. Further, the reflexive necessity of practice facilitates a 'dialectical movement' between self and the wider frameworks of power, which utilises the *radical specificity* of lived experience to construct an embodied negotiation of practices which essentialise and fix identity.

The ambiguity of graphic scoring, of fragmentation and *glitched* (mis)communication, creates a context in which the very process of individualised meaning-making (rather than the content) is privileged. The subversion of gendered practices and the distortion of differentiating language confronts the symbolic violence of the [re]presentation of women working in spaces imagined to be masculine. The inherent noise of communicative failure and the assertion of interpretive ambivalence creates an open space in which meaning becomes democratised. As such, the music in my doctoral study, as a social practice, presents a process of resisting the hegemonic organisation of location and identification within the multidimensional space of the dominant collective, utilising indeterminate *glitches* of the individualised *I am* to disrupt the unity of the authorised *we*.

Bibliography

Abramov-van Rijk, Elena. *Parlar Cantando: The Practice of Reciting Verses in Italy from 1300 to 1600*. Bern: Peter Lang, 2009.
Adorno, Theodor. 'Music and New Music'. In *Quasi una Fantasia: Essays on Modern Music*. Translated by Rodney Livingstone, 249–68. 1963. Reprint, London: Verso, 2002.
——. *Philosophy of Modern Music*. Translated by A. G. Mitchell and W. V. Blomster. London: Continuum, 2002.
Agacinski, Sylviane. *Time Passing: Modernity and Nostalgia*. Translated by Jody Gladding. New York: Columbia University Press, 2003.
Agawu, Kofi. *Music as Discourse: Semiotic Adventures in Romantic Music*. Oxford: Oxford University Press, 2009.
Allott, Robert. *Englands Parnassus*. London, 1600.
Althusser, Louis. *Lenin and Philosophy, and Other Essays*. Translated by Ben Brewster. New York: Monthly Review Press, 2001.
Améry, Jean. *On Aging: Revolt and Resignation*. Translated by John D. Barlow. Bloomington: Indiana University Press, 1994.
Anon. *The Art of Courtship*. London, 1686.
Ascham, Roger. *Toxophilus the Schole of Shootinge*. London, 1545.
Auerbach, Nina. 'Alice and Wonderland: A Curious Child'. *Victorian Studies* 17 (1973): 31–47.
Austern, Linda Phyllis. '"Alluring the Auditorie to Effeminacie": Music and the Idea of the Feminine in Early Modern England'. *Music and Letters* 74 (1993): 343–54.
——. 'Domestic Song and the Circulation of Masculine Social Energy in Early Modern England'. In *Gender and Song in Early Modern England*, edited by Leslie Dunn and Katherine Larson, 123–38. Farnham: Ashgate, 2014.
——. '"For, Love's a Good Musician": Performance, Audition and Erotic Disorders in Early Modern Europe'. *Musical Quarterly* 82 (1998): 614–53.
——. '"Lo Here I Burn": Musical Figurations and Fantasies of Male Desire in Early Modern England'. In *Eros and Euterpe: Eroticism in Early Modern Music*, edited by Bonnie Blackburn and Laurie Stras. Farnham: Ashgate, forthcoming.
——. 'Music and Manly Wit in Seventeenth-Century England: The Case of the Catch'. In *Concepts of Creativity in Seventeenth-Century England*, edited by Rebecca Herissone and Alan Howard, 281–308. Woodbridge: Boydell, 2013.
Bailey, Peter. *Leisure and Class in Victorian England: Rational Recreation and the Contest for Control, 1830–1885*. London: Routledge & Kegan Paul, 1978.

―――. 'The Victorian Middle Class and the Problem of Leisure'. In *Popular Culture and Performance in the Victorian City*, 13–29. Cambridge: Cambridge University Press, 1998.

Barbaro, Francesco. *De re uxorial*. Edited by Attilio Gnesotto. Padua: Tipografia Giov. Batt. Randi, 1915.

Barker, Emma. 'Reading the Greuze Girl: The Daughter's Seduction'. *Representations* 117 (2012): 86–119.

Barthes, Roland. 'The Death of the Author'. In *Image, Music, Text*. Translated by Stephen Heath, 142–8. London: Fontana, 1977.

Battersby, Christine. *Gender and Genius: Towards a Feminist Aesthetics*. Bloomington: Indiana University Press, 1989.

Bayton, Mavis. 'Women Making Music: Some Material Constraints'. In *The Popular Music Studies Reader*, edited by Andy Bennett, Barry Shank and Jason Toynbee, 347–54. Abingdon: Routledge, 2006.

Bembo, Pietro. *Gli Asolani*. Translated by Rudolf B. Gottfried. Bloomington: Indiana University Press, 1954.

―――. *Prose e rime*. Edited by Carlo Dionisotti, 2nd edn. Turin: Unione Tipografico-Editrice, 1966.

Ben-Amos, Ilana Krausman. *Adolescence and Youth in Early Modern England*. New Haven and London: Yale University Press, 1994.

Benjamin, Walter. 'On Some Motifs in Baudelaire'. In *Illuminations*. Translated by Harry Zohn. Edited by Hannah Arendt, 155–200. New York: Schocken, 2007.

Bertoni, Giulio. *La Biblioteca Estense e la coltura Ferrarese ai tempi del duca Ercole primo (1471–1505)*. Turin: Loescher, 1903.

Bernstein, Robin. *Racial Innocence: Performing American Childhood from Slavery to Civil Rights*. New York: New York University Press, 2011.

Bhabha, Homi K. *The Location of Culture*. London: Routledge, 2004.

Blackburn, Bonnie J. 'Anna Inglese and Other Women Singers in the Fifteenth Century: Gleanings from the Sforza Archives'. In *Sleuthing the Muse: Essays in Honour of William Prizer*, edited by Kristine K. Forney and Jeremy L. Smith, 237–52. Hillsdale, NY: Pendragon, 2012.

Blaikie, Andrew. *Ageing and Popular Culture*. Cambridge: Cambridge University Press, 1999.

Bloom, Harold. *The Anxiety of Influence: A Theory of Poetry*, 2nd edn. New York and London: Oxford University Press, 1997.

Bobbio, Norberto. *Old Age and Other Essays*. Translated and edited by Allan Cameron. Cambridge: Polity, 2001.

Bourdieu, Pierre. *Outline of a Theory of Practice*. Cambridge: Cambridge University Press, 1977.

Boyd, Malcolm. *Grace Williams*. Cardiff: University of Wales Press, 1996.

Bracciolini, Poggius. *Opera Omnia*. 4 vols. Turin: Bottega d'Erasmo, 1964.

Braham, Humphrey. *The Institucion of a Gentleman*. 1555. Reprint, London, 1568.

Brandt, Stefan. '"…um die Oper der Aufmerksamkeit des Publikums noch würdiger zu machen". Zum Einfluß des sängerischen Personals auf Arienkompositionen bei Porpora und Händel'. In *Barocktheater heute. Wiederentdeckungen zwischen Wissenschaft und Bühne*, edited by Nicola Gess, Tina Hartmann and Robert Sollich, 105–19. Bielefeld: Transcript, 2008.
Brathwaite, Richard. *The English Gentleman*. London, 1630.
Brocken, Michael. *The British Folk Revival 1944–2002*. Aldershot: Ashgate, 2003.
Brown, Howard Mayer. 'Women Singers and Women's Songs in Fifteenth-Century Italy'. In *Women Making Music: the Western Art Tradition, 1150-1950*, edited by Jane Bowers and Judith Tick, 62-89. Urbana: University of Illinois Press, 1986.
Bravmann, Scott. *Queer Fictions of the Past: History, Culture and Difference*. Cambridge and New York: Cambridge University Press, 1997.
Bray, Alan. 'To be a Man in Early Modern Society: The Case of Michael Wigglesworth'. *History Workshop Journal* 41 (1996), 155–65.
Breitenberg, Mark. *Anxious Masculinity in Early Modern England*. Cambridge: Cambridge University Press, 1996.
Breton, Nicholas. *The Good and the Badde, or Descriptions of the Worthies, and Vnworthies of this Age*. London, 1616.
Brooker, Joseph. 'Has the World Changed or Have I Changed?' In *Why Pamper Life's Complexities? Essays on The Smiths*, edited by Sean Campbell and Colin Coulter, 22–42. Manchester: Manchester University Press, 2010.
Brosses, Charles de. *Lettres historiques et critiques sur l'Italie*, vol. 3. Paris: Ponthieu, 1799.
Brown, Lennox, and Emil Behnke. *The Child's Voice: Its Treatment with Regard to After Development*. London: Sampson Low, Marston, Searle, and Rivington, 1885.
Bryce, Judith. 'Performing for Strangers: Women, Dance, and Music in Quattrocento Florence'. *Renaissance Quarterly* 54 (2001): 1074–107.
Burney, Charles. *A General History of Music*, vol. 4. London: Burney, 1776.
Burton, Robert. *The Anatomy of Melancholy*. Oxford, 1621.
Butler, H. E. *The Institutio Oratoria of Quintilian*. London: Heinemann, 1920.
Butler, Judith. 'Contingent Foundations: Feminism and the Question of Postmodernism'. In *Feminists Theorize the Political*, edited by Judith Butler and Joan W. Scott, 3–21. New York and London: Routledge, 1992.
Byrd, William. *Psalmes, Sonets, & Songs of Sadnes and Pietie*. London, 1588.
Calasanti, Toni M., and Kathleen F. Slevin, eds. *Age Matters: Realigning Feminist Thinking*. New York: Routledge, 2006.
Calmeta. *Prose e lettere edite e inedited*. Translated by H. E. Butler. Edited by Cecil Grayson. Bologna: Commissione per i testi di lingua, 1959.
——. *Triumphi*. Edited by Rossella Guberti. Bologna: Commissione per i Testi di Lingua, 2004.
Campbell, Sean, and Colin Coulter, eds. *Why Pamper Life's Complexities? Essays on The Smiths*. Manchester: Manchester University Press, 2010.

Castiglione, Baldassare. *Il cortegiano, con una scelta delle opere minore*. Edited by Bruno Maier. Torino: UTET, 1955.
——. *The Book of the Courtier*. Translated by George Bull. London: Penguin, 1967.
——. *The Courtyer of Count Baldessar Castilio*. Translated by Thomas Hoby. London, 1561.
Cauthon, Courtney. 'XXX Live Nude Girls!!!' In *The Multimedia Encyclopedia of Women in Today's World*, edited by Mary Zeiss Stange, Carol K. Oyster and Jane E. Sloan, 2nd edn, 2207–10. Thousand Oaks, CA: Sage, 2013.
Cavarero, Adriana. *Relating Narratives: Storytelling and Selfhood*. Translated by Paul A. Kottman. London and New York: Routledge, 2000.
Cheah, Pheng. 'Non-Dialectical Materialism'. In *New Materialism: Ontology, Agency and Politics*, edited by Diana Coole and Samantha Frost, 70–91. Durham, NC and London: Duke University Press, 2010.
Chesler, Phyllis. *Letters to a Young Feminist*. New York: Four Walls Eight Windows, 1997.
Chiappini, Luciano. *Eleonora d'Aragona, prima duchessa di Ferrara*. Rovigo: S.T.E.R., 1956.
Childs, Martin. *Labour's Apprentices: Working-Class Lads in Late Victorian and Edwardian England*. McGill: Queen's University Press, 1992.
Cibber, Colley. *An Apology for the Life of Colley Cibber*, 3rd edn. London: Dodsley, 1750.
Cicali, Giani. *Attori e ruoli nell'opera buffa italiana del Settecento*. Firenze: Le Lettere, 2005.
Ciliberti, Galliano. 'Ferri, Baldassare'. *Grove Music Online*. Oxford Music Online. Oxford University Press. Accessed 13 December 2013, http://www.oxfordmusiconline.com/subscriber/article/grove/music/09539.
Citron, Marcia J. 'Feminist Approaches to Musicology'. In *Cecilia Reclaimed: Feminist Perspectives on Gender and Music*, edited by Susan C. Cook and Judy S. Tsou, 15–34. Urbana and Chicago: University of Illinois Press, 1994.
——. *Gender and the Musical Canon*. Urbana: University of Illinois Press, 2000.
Clark, Ira. *Comedy, Youth, Manhood in Early Modern England*. Newark and London: University of Delaware Press and Associated University Presses, 2003.
Clay, John H. *Black Dyke: An Inside Story*. Stockport: Jargen's, 2005.
Code, Lorraine. 'Age'. In *Encyclopedia of Feminist Theories*, edited by Lorraine Code, 12–14. London: Routledge, 2000.
Cohodas, Nadine. *Princess Noire: The Tumultuous Reign of Nina Simone*. New York: Pantheon, 2010.
Collins, Judy. *Sweet Judy Blue Eyes: My Life in Music*. New York: Three Rivers Press, 2011.
Collis, Louise. *Impetuous Heart: The Story of Ethel Smyth*. London: William Kimber, 1984.
Conti, Antonio. *Lettere da Venezia à madame la comtesse de Caylus, 1727–1729*, edited by Sylvie Mami. Florence: Olschki, 2003.
Copland, Aaron. *Copland on Music*. New York: Doubleday, 1960.

Cuffe, Henry. *The Differences of the Ages of Mans Life*. London, 1607.
Cullington, Donald J. ed. and trans., with Reinhard Strohm. *'That liberal and virtuous art': Three Humanist Treatises on Music*. Newtownabbey: University of Ulster, 2001.
Cvetkovich, Ann. *An Archive of Feelings: Trauma, Sexuality, and Lesbian Public Cultures*. Durham, NC: Duke University Press, 2003.
Dahlhaus, Carl. 'New Music as Historical Category'. In *Schoenberg and the New Music*. Translated by Derrick Puffett and Alfred Clayton, 1–13. Cambridge: Cambridge University Press, 1988.
Dale, Kathleen. 'Memories of Marion Scott'. *Music and Letters* 35 (1954): 236–40.
Davis, George. *Saint Monday; or Scenes from a Low Life*. Birmingham: The Author, 1790.
Day, John. *Tenor of the Whole Psalmes in Foure Partes*. London, 1563.
De Certeau, Michel. *The Practice of Everyday Life*. Berkeley: University of California Press, 1984.
D'Cruze, Shani. 'Sex, Violence and Local Courts: Working-Class Respectability in a Mid-Nineteenth-Century Lancashire Town'. *British Journal of Criminology* 39 (1999): 39–55.
Dennis, Flora. 'Unlocking the Gates of Chastity: Music and the Erotic in the Domestic Sphere in Fifteenth and Sixteenth-Century Italy'. In *Erotic Cultures of Renaissance Italy*, edited by Sara F. Matthews-Grieco, 223–46. Farnham: Ashgate, 2010.
Delaney, Sheila. *A Taste of Honey*. London: Theatre Workshop Press, 1959.
Diamond, Elin. 'The Violence of "We": Politicizing Identification'. In *Critical Theory and Performance*, edited by Janelle G. Reinelt and Joseph R. Roach, 403–12. Ann Arbor: University of Michigan Press, 2007.
Dowland, John. *A Pilgrimes Solace*. London, 1612.
——. *The Second Booke of Songs or Ayres*. London, 1600.
——. *Varietie of Lute-Lessons*. London, 1610.
Duncan-Jones, Katherine. '"Melancholie Times": Musical Recollections of Sidney by William Byrd and Thomas Watson'. In *The Well Enchanting Skill: Music, Poetry, and Drama in the Culture of the Renaissance: Essays in Honour of F. Sternfield*, edited by John Caldwell, E. Olleson and S. Wollenburg, 171–80. Oxford: Clarendon Press, 1990.
Earle, John. *Micro-cosmographie*. London, 1628.
Edelman, Lee. *No Future: Queer Theory and the Death Drive*. Durham, NC: Duke University Press, 2004.
Edwards, Jeanette. 'Ordinary People: A Study of Factors Affecting Communication in the Provision of Services'. PhD diss., University of Manchester, 1990.
Eichler, Margrit. *The Double Standard: A Feminist Critique of Feminist Social Sciences*. London: Croon Helm, 1980.
Elam, Diane. *Feminism and Deconstruction*. London and New York: Routledge, 2003.

Elliott, Richard. *Fado and the Place of Longing: Loss, Memory and the City*. Farnham: Ashgate, 2010.
——. *Nina Simone*. Sheffield: Equinox, 2013.
Elyot, Thomas. *The Boke Named the Gouernour*. London, 1537.
——. *The Castel of Helth*. London, 1561.
Fahy, Conor. 'Three Early Renaissance Treatises on Women'. *Italian Studies* 2 (1956): 30–55.
Fanon, Frantz. *Black Skin, White Masks*. London: Pluto, 2008.
Finnegan, Ruth. *The Hidden Musicians: Music-Making in An English Town*. Cambridge: Cambridge University Press, 1989.
Fisher, Will. *Materializing Gender in Early Modern English Literature and Culture*. Cambridge: Cambridge University Press, 2006.
Fletcher, Anthony. 'Manhood, the Male Body, Courtship and the Household in Early Modern England'. *History* 84 (1999): 419–36.
Flory, Jonathan Andrew. '"I Hear a Symphony": Making Music at Motown, 1959–79'. PhD diss., University of North Carolina, Chapel Hill, 2006.
Foucault, Michel. *Essential Works of Foucault 1954–1984*, vol. 2: *Aesthetics*. London: Penguin, 2000.
——. *The Archaeology of Knowledge*. Translated by A. M. Sheridan Smith. New York: Pantheon Books. 1972.
Foyster, Elizabeth, *Manhood in Early Modern England: Honour, Sex and Marriage*. New York: Longman, 1999.
Francis, Martin. 'The Domestication of the Male? Recent Research on Nineteenth- and Twentieth-Century British Masculinity'. *Historical Journal* 45 (2002): 637–52.
Franzen, Trisha. *Spinsters and Lesbians: Independent Womanhood in the United States*. New York: New York University Press, 1996.
Freud, Sigmund. 'On Transience'. *The Standard Edition of the Complete Psychological Works of Sigmund Freud*, vol. 14. Translated and edited by James Strachey, 303–7. London: Hogarth Press, 1957.
——. *The Interpretation of Dreams*. Translated by James Strachey. Edited by James Strachey, Alan Tyson and Angela Richards. Harmondsworth: Penguin, 1991.
Gackle, Lynn. *Finding Ophelia's Voice, Opening Ophelia's Heart: Nurturing the Female Adolescent Voice*. Dayton, OH: Heritage Music Press, 2011.
Galliard, J. E. trans. *Observations on the Florid Song*. London: Wilcox, 1743.
Gannon, Linda R. *Women and Aging: Transcending the Myths*. London and New York: Routledge, 1999.
Ghirardo, Diane Yvonne. 'Lucrezia Borgia's Palace in Renaissance Ferrara'. *Journal of the Society of Architectural Historians* 64 (2005): 474–97.
Gibson, Kirsten. 'Music, Melancholy and Masculinity in Early Modern England'. In *Masculinity and Western Musical Practice*, edited by Ian Biddle and Kirsten Gibson, 41–66. Farnham: Ashgate, 2009.
Gilman, Sander. *Difference and Pathology: Stereotypes of Sexuality, Race, and Madness*. Ithaca: Cornell University Press, 1985.

Gilroy, Paul. *The Black Atlantic: Modernity and Double-Consciousness.* Cambridge, MA: Harvard University Press, 1993.
Goeurot, Jehan. *The Regiment of Life.* Translated by Thomas Phayer. London, 1546.
Graaf, Melissa J. de. '"Never Call Us Lady Composers": Gendered Receptions in the New York Composers' Forum, 1935–1940'. *American Music* 26 (2008): 277–308.
Greer, Germaine. 'Serenity and Power'. In *The Other Within Us: Feminist Explorations of Women and Aging*, edited by Marilyn Pearsall, 253–73. Boulder, CO: Westview Press, 1997.
——. *The Change: Women, Aging and the Menopause.* New York: Alfred A. Knopf, 1992.
——. *The Whole Woman.* London: Anchor Books, 2000.
Gross, Olga. 'Gender and the Harp. I'. *American Harp Journal* 13 (1992): 30–33.
——. 'Gender and the Harp. II'. *American Harp Journal* 14 (1993): 28–35.
Grosz, Elizabeth. 'Feminism, Materialism and Freedom'. In *New Materialism: Ontology, Agency and Politics*, edited by Diana Coole and Samantha Frost, 139–57. Durham, NC and London: Duke University Press, 2010.
Gubar, Marah. 'Peter Pan as Children's Theatre: The Issue of Audience'. In *The Oxford Handbook of Children's Literature*, edited by Julia L. Mickenburg and Lynne Vallone, 475–95. Oxford: Oxford University Press, 2011.
Gundersheimer, Werner L. 'Women, Learning and Power: Eleonora of Aragon and the Court of Ferrara'. In *Beyond their Sex: Learned Women of the European Past*, edited by Patricia Labalme, 43–65. New York: New York University Press, 1984.
Halberstam, Jack (Judith). *The Queer Art of Failure.* Durham, NC: Duke University Press, 2011.
Hapke, Laura. *Daughters of the Great Depression: Women, Work and Fiction in the American 1930s.* Athens: University of Georgia Press, 1995.
Harris, Jose. *Private Lives, Public Spirit: Britain 1870–1914.* Oxford: Oxford University Press; London: Penguin, 1994.
Harstock, Nancy C. M. *Money, Sex, and Power: Towards a Feminist Historical Materialism.* New York and London: Longman, 1983.
Harvey, Karen, and Alexander Shepard. 'What Have Historians Done with Masculinity? Reflections on Five Centuries of British History, circa 1500–1950'. *Journal of British Studies* 44 (2005): 274–80.
Heartz, Daniel. 'From Garrick to Gluck: The Reform of Theatre and Opera in the Mid-Eighteenth Century'. *Proceedings of the Royal Musical Association* 94 (1967–68): 111–27.
Hegarty, Paul. *Noise/Music: A History.* London: Continuum, 2008.
Heller, Wendy, 'Reforming Achilles: Gender, "opera seria" and the Rhetoric of the Enlightened Hero'. *Early Music* 26 (1998): 562–81.
Henry, Astrid. *Not My Mother's Sister: Generational Conflict and Third-Wave Feminism.* Bloomington: Indiana University Press, 2004.

Herbert, Joanna. *Negotiating Boundaries in the City: Migration, Ethnicity, and Gender in Britain*. Aldershot: Ashgate, 2008.

Herbert, Trevor, ed. *The British Brass Band: A Musical and Social History*. Oxford: Oxford University Press, 2000.

Herbert, Trevor, and John Wallace. 'Aspects of Performance Practices: The Brass Band and its Influence on Other Brass Playing Styles'. In *The British Brass Band: A Musical and Social History*, edited by Trevor Herbert, 278–306. Oxford: Oxford University Press, 2000.

Heylin, Clinton. *No More Sad Refrains: The Life and Times of Sandy Denny*. London: Omnibus, 2011.

Hiam, Jonathan. 'Toward a Musical Poetics of The Smiths'. In *Why Pamper Life's Complexities? Essays on The Smiths*, edited by Sean Campbell and Colin Coulter, 121–34. Manchester: Manchester University Press, 2010.

Hichens, Robert. *The Garden of Allah*. London: Methuen, 1904.

——. *The Woman with the Fan*. New York: Frederick A. Stokes, 1904.

Higford, William. *Institution of a Gentleman*. London, 1660.

Hill, George Francis. *A Corpus of Italian Medals of the Renaissance Before Cellini*. 2 vols. London: British Museum, 1930. Reprint, Florence: Studio per edizioni scelte, 1984.

Hisama, Ellie. *Gendering Musical Modernism: The Music of Ruth Crawford, Marion Bauer, and Miriam Gideon*. Cambridge: Cambridge University Press, 2001.

Hobsbawm, Eric. 'The Making of the Working Class, 1870–1914'. In *Uncommon People: Resistance, Rebellion and Jazz*, 78–99. London: Abacus, 1999.

Hoffman, Eva. *Time*. London: Profile, 2011.

Hollybande, Claudius. *The French Schoolmaister*, London, 1573.

Holmen Mohr, Lillian. *Frances Perkins: 'That Woman in FDR's Cabinet!'* Croton-on-Hudson, NY: North River Press, 1979.

Holmes, William C. *Opera Observed*. London and Chicago: University of Chicago Press, 1993.

Hubbs, Nadine. 'I Will Survive: Musical Mappings of Queer Social Space in a Disco Anthem'. *Popular Music* 26 (2007): 231–44.

——. 'Music of the Fourth Gender: Morrissey and the Sexual Politics of Melodic Contour'. In *Bodies of Writing, Bodies in Performance*, edited by Thomas Foster, Carol Siegel and Ellen E. Berry, 266–96. New York: New York University Press, 1996.

Huyssen, Andreas. *After the Great Divide: Modernism, Mass Culture, Postmodernism*. Bloomington: Indiana University Press, 1986.

Johnstone, Nick. *Patti Smith*. London: Omnibus, 1997, revised edn, 2012.

Joncus, Berta, 'Producing Stars in *Dramma per musica*'. In *Music as Social and Cultural Practice: Essays in Honour of Reinhard Strohm*, edited by B. Joncus and M. Bucciarelli, 275–93. Woodbridge: Boydell, 2007.

Joyce, Patrick. *Work, Society and Politics: The Culture of the Factory in Later Victorian England*. London: Methuen, 1982.

Kallberg, Jeffrey. 'Gender'. In *New Grove Dictionary of Music and Musicians, 2nd Edition*, edited by Stanley Sadie and John Tyrrell, vol. 8, 645–7. London: Macmillan, 2001.

Kallendorf, Craig W., ed. and trans. *Humanist Educational Treatises*. Cambridge, MA: Harvard University Press, 2002.

Kallioniemi, Kari. '"Take Me Back to Dear Old Blighty": Englishness, Pop and The Smiths'. In *Why Pamper Life's Complexities? Essays on The Smiths*, edited by Sean Campbell and Colin Coulter, 225–40. Manchester: Manchester University Press, 2010.

Kelly, Caleb. *Cracked Media: The Sound of Malfunction*. Cambridge, MA: MIT Press, 2009.

Kennedy, Kirsten. 'Protecting the Body, Portraying the Soul'. In *Medieval and Renaissance Art: People and Possessions*, edited by Glyn Davies and Kirsten Kennedy, 299–355. London: V&A Publishing, 2009.

King, Catherine E. *Renaissance Women Patrons: Wives and Widows in Italy c. 1300–1550*. Manchester: Manchester University Press, 1998.

Kinks, Sonia. 'Simone de Beauvoir: Engaging Discrepant Materialisms'. In *New Materialism: Ontology, Agency and Politics*, edited by Diana Coole and Samantha Frost, 258–80. Durham, NC and London: Duke University Press, 2010.

Kohl, Benjamin G., and Ronald G. Witt, eds and trans. *The Earthly Republic: Italian Humanists on Government and Society*. Philadelphia: University of Pennsylvania Press, 1978.

Kramer, Lawrence. *Franz Schubert: Sexuality, Subjectivity, Song*. Cambridge: Cambridge University Press, 1998.

Kristeva, Julia. 'Women's Time'. Translated by Alice Jardine and Harry Blake. *Signs* 7 (1981): 13–35.

Kunkel, Benjamin. 'Still Ill. The Smiths, *The Queen is Dead*'. In *Heavy Rotation: Twenty Writers on the Albums that Changed their Lives*, edited by Peter Terzian, 1–15. New York: Harper Perennial, 2009.

Laing, Dave, Karl Dallas, Robin Denselow and Robert Shelton. *The Electric Muse: The Story of Folk into Rock*. London: Methuen, 1975.

Laqueur, Thomas. *Making Sex: Body and Gender from the Greeks to Freud*. Cambridge, MA: Harvard University Press, 1990.

Lawe, Kari. 'La medaglia dell'Amorino bendato: uno studio su una delle medaglie di Lucrezia Borgia'. In *The Court of Ferrara and its Patronage, 1441–1598*, edited by Marianne Pade, Lene Wange Petersen and Daniela Quarta. Copenhagen: Copenhagen University, 1990.

Lazar, Michelle M. 'Politicizing Gender in Discourse: Feminist Critical Discourse Analysis as Political Perspective and Praxis'. In *Feminist Critical Discourse Analysis*, edited by Michelle M. Lazar, 1–30. Basingstoke: Palgrave Macmillan, 2005.

Leech, Isaac. *Reminisces of The Bacup Old Band, Which Appeared in the Columns of the Bacup Times in 1893*. Bacup: L. J. Priestley, 1893.

LeFanu, Nicola. 'Master Musician: An Impregnable Taboo?' *Contact: A Journal of Contemporary Music* (1987): 4–8.

Lemnius, Levinus. *The Touchstone of Complexions ... Englished by Thomas Newton*. London, 1576.

Leppert, Richard, and George Lipsitz. '"Everybody's Lonesome for Somebody": Age, the Body and Experience in the Music of Hank Williams'. *Popular Music* 9 (1990): 259–74.

Lhamon, W. T. *Raising Cain: Blackface Performance from Jim Crow to Hip Hop*. Cambridge, MA: Harvard University Press, 1998.

Libby, Dennis. 'The Singers of Pergolesi's Salustia'. *Studi Pergolesiani* 3 (1999): 173–81.

[Ling, Nicholas] N. L. *Politeuphuia VVits common wealth*. [London], 1598.

Lockwood, Lewis. *Music in Renaissance Ferrara 1400–1505: The Creation of a Musical Centre in the Fifteenth Century*. Oxford: Oxford University Press, 1984.

Lorenzetti, Stefano. '"Quel celeste cantar che mi disface": Immagine della donna ed educazione alla musica nell'ideale pedagogico del rinascimento italiano'. *Studi musicali* 23 (1994): 241–61.

Love, Heather. *Feeling Backwards: Loss and Politics of Queer History*. Cambridge, MA: Harvard University Press, 2007.

Lowenthall, David. 'Nostalgia Tells It Like It Wasn't'. In *The Imagined Past: History and Nostalgia*, edited by Malcolm Chase and Christopher Shaw, 18–32. Manchester: Manchester University Press, 1989.

Lucas, Caroline. 'Portfolio of Original Musical Compositions with Written Commentary'. PhD diss., University of Leeds, 2012.

McClary, Susan. *Feminine Endings: Music, Gender, and Sexuality*. Minneapolis: University of Minnesota Press, 1991.

McClelland, Keith. 'Masculinity and the Representative Artisan in Britain, 1850–80'. In *Manful Assertions: Masculinities in Britain since 1800*, edited by Michael Roper and John Tosh, 74–91. London and New York: Routledge, 1991.

Macey, Patrick. 'Filippo Salviati, Caterina de' Ricci, and Serafino Razzi: Patronage Practices for the Lauda and Madrigal at the Convent of S. Vincenzo in Prato'. In *Cappelle musicali fra corte, stato e chiesa nell'Italia del Rinascimentoi*, edited by Franco Piperno, Gabriella Biagi Ravenni and Andrea Chegai, 349–71. Florence: Leo S. Olschki, 2007.

——. '"Infiamma il mio cor": Savonarolan *Laude* by and for Dominican Nuns in Tuscany'. In *The Crannied Wall: Women, Religion, and the Arts in Early Modern Europe*, edited by Craig A. Monson, 161–89. Ann Arbor: University of Michigan Press, 1992.

McGeary, Thomas. 'Verse Epistles on Italian Opera Singers, 1724–1736'. *Royal Musical Association Research Chronicle* 33 (2000): 29–88.

McKinnon, James, ed. *Music in Early Christian Literature*. Cambridge: Cambridge University Press, 1987.

Maddison, Sarah, and Rosemary Grey. 'New Feminist Generations: The Intergenerational Conversation Continues'. *Australian Feminist Studies* 25 (2010): 485–92.
Madonna. *The English Roses*. London: Puffin, 2003.
Mancini, Giambattista. *Riflessioni pratiche sul canto figurato*. 1777. Facsimile edn, Bologna: Forni, 1996.
Mangan, J. A., and James Walvin, eds. *Manliness and Morality: Middle-Class Masculinity in Britain and America, 1800–1940*. Manchester: Manchester University Press, 1987.
Marsh, Christopher. *Music and Society in Early Modern England*. Cambridge: Cambridge University Press, 2010.
Martín, Luisa, and Concepción Gómez Esteban. 'The Gender of Power: The Female Style in Labor Organisations'. In *Feminist Critical Discourse Analysis*, edited by Michelle M. Lazar, 61–89. Basingstoke: Palgrave Macmillan, 2005.
Mathias, Rhiannon. *Lutyens, Maconchy, Williams and Twentieth-Century British Music: A Blest Trio of Sirens*. Farnham: Ashgate, 2012.
Mello, Cecília. 'I Don't Owe You Anything: The Smiths and Kitchen-Sink Cinema'. In *Why Pamper Life's Complexities? Essays on The Smiths*, edited by Sean Campbell and Colin Coulter, 135–55. Manchester: Manchester University Press, 2010.
Merkley, Paul A., and Lora L. M. Merkley. *Music and Patronage in the Sforza Court*. Turnhout: Brepols, 1999.
Mitchell, Elizabeth. 'An Odd Break with the Human Heart'. In *To Be Real: Telling the Truth and Changing the Face of Feminism*, edited by Rebecca Walker, 49–60. London: Anchor Books, 1995.
Moore, Mary Carr. 'Is American Citizenship a Handicap to a Composer?' *Musician* 40 (1935): 5, 8.
Moore, Wendy. *How to Create the Perfect Wife: Britain's Most Ineligible Bachelor and his Enlightened Quest to Train the Ideal Mate*. New York: Basic Books, 2013.
Morley, Thomas. *A Plaine and Easie Introduction to Practicall Musicke*. London, 1597.
Morrissey. *Autobiography*. London: Penguin Classics, 2013.
Mulcaster, Richard. *Positions ... which are Necessarie for the Training vp of Children*. London, 1581.
Nachman, Gerald. *Raised on Radio*. Los Angeles: University of California Press, 1998.
Nattiez, Jean-Jacques. *Music and Discourse: Towards a Semiology of Music*. Translated by Carolyn Abbate. Princeton: Princeton University Press, 1990.
Nunes, Mark, ed. *ERROR: Glitch, Noise, and Jam in New Media Cultures*. London: Continuum, 2011.
O'Brien, Karen. *Joni Mitchell: Shadows and Light*. London: Virgin, 2001.

O'Brien, Lucy. 'Madonna: Like a Crone'. In *'Rock On': Women, Ageing and Popular Music*, edited by Ros Jennings and Abigail Gardner, 19–34. Farnham: Ashgate, 2012.
——. *Madonna: Like An Icon*. London: Bantam, 2007.
——. *She Bop: The Definitive History of Women in Rock, Pop and Soul*. London: Penguin, 1996.
O'Connor, Jane. *The Cultural Significance of the Child Star*. Abingdon: Routledge, 2008.
Pachmuss, Temira, ed. and trans. *Between Paris and St Petersburg: Selected Diaries of Zinaida Hippius*. Urbana: University of Illinois Press, 1975.
Paddison, Max. *Adorno's Aesthetics of Music*. Cambridge: Cambridge University Press, 1995.
Peacham, Henry. *Minerua Britanna*. London, 1612.
——. *The Compleat Gentleman*. London, 1622.
Peele, George. *Polyhymnia*. London, 1590.
Phillips, Edward. *The Mysteries of Love and Eloquence*. London, 1685.
[Pickering, Richard]. *Reflections Upon Theatrical Expression in Tragedy*. London: Johnston, 1755.
Piotrowska, Anna G. 'Modernist Composers and the Concept of Genius'. *International Review of the Aesthetics and Sociology of Music* 38 (2007): 229–42.
Pirrotta, Nino. 'Music and Cultural Tendencies in 15th-Century Italy'. *Journal of the American Musicological Society* 19 (1966): 127–61.
Plato. *The Republic*. Translated by Paul Shorey. London: Heinemann, 1930.
Potter, John, and Neil Sorrell. *A History of Singing*. Cambridge: Cambridge University Press, 2012.
Prizer, William F. 'Games of Venus: Secular Music in the Late Quattrocento and Early Cinquecento'. *Journal of Musicology* 9 (1991): 3–56.
——. 'Isabella d'Este and Lucrezia Borgia as Patrons of Music: The Frottola at Mantua and Ferrara'. *Journal of the American Musicological Society* 38 (1985): 1–33.
——. 'Laude di popolo, laude di corte: Some Thoughts on the Style and Function of the Renaissance Lauda'. In *La Musica a Firenze al Tempo di Lorenzo il Magnifico*, edited by Piero Gargiulo, 167–94. Florence: Leo S. Olschki, 1993.
——. 'Music at the Court of the Sforza: The Birth and Death of a Musical Centre'. *Musica Disciplina* 43 (1989): 141–93.
——. 'Una "Virtù Molto Conveniente a Madonne": Isabella d'Este as a Musician'. *Journal of Musicology* 17 (1999): 10–49.
Proust, Marcel. *Swann's Way, In Search of Lost Time*. Translated by C. K. Scott Moncrieff and Terence Kilmartin. Revised by D. J. Enright. London: Vintage, 2002.
Prynne, William. *Histrio-mastix*. London, 1633.

Purvis, Jennifer. 'Grrrls and Women Together in the Third Wave: Embracing the Challenges of Intergenerational Feminism(s)'. *NWSA Journal* 16 (2004): 93–123.
Ralegh, Walter. *The History of the World.* London, 1617.
Reid, Douglas A. 'The Decline of Saint Monday 1766–1866'. *Past and Present* 71 (1976): 76–101.
Reynolds, Simon. *Retromania: Pop Culture's Addiction to its Own Past.* London: Faber and Faber, 2011.
——. *Rip It Up and Start Again: Postpunk 1978–1984.* New York: Penguin Books, 2006.
Reynolds, Simon, and Joy Press. *The Sex Revolts: Gender, Rebellion and Rock 'n' Roll.* London: Serpent's Tail, 1995.
Rich, Adrienne. *Of Woman Born: Motherhood as Experience and Institution.* New York: Norton, 1976.
Roach, Joseph R. 'Cavaliere Nicolini: London's First Opera Star'. *Educational Theatre Journal* 28 (1976): 189–205.
——. *The Player's Passion: Studies in the Science of Acting.* Ann Arbor: University of Michigan Press, 1993.
Robb, John. *The North Will Rise Again: Manchester Music City 1976–1996.* London: Aurum, 2009.
Rodger, Gillian. '"He isn't a marrying man": Gender and Sexuality in the Repertoire of Male Impersonators, 1870–1920'. In *Queer Episodes in Music and Modern Identity*, edited by Sophie Fuller and Lloyd Whitesell, 105–33. Urbana and Chicago: University of Illinois Press, 2002.
Rodgers, Tara. *Pink Noises.* Durham, NC and London: Duke University Press, 2010.
Rogan, Johnny. Liner notes to Judy Collins, *Judy Collins #3 & The Judy Collins Concert*, CD, Elektra/WSM 8122 76505-2, 2004.
Roper, Michael, and John Tosh, eds. *Manful Assertions: Masculinities in Britain Since 1800.* New York and London: Routledge, 1991.
Rose, Jacqueline. *The Case of Peter Pan, or, the Impossibility of Children's Fiction.* London: Macmillan, 1984.
Russell, Dave. 'Music in Huddersfield, c. 1820–1914'. In *Huddersfield: A Most Handsome Town: Aspects of the History and Culture of a West Yorkshire Town*, edited by E. A. Hilary Haigh, 653–79. Huddersfield: Kirklees Metropolitan Council, 1992.
——. *Popular Music in England 1840–1914: A Social History*, 2nd edn. Manchester: Manchester University Press, 2004.
——. 'The Popular Music Societies of the Yorkshire Textile District: A Study of the Relationship between Music and Society'. PhD diss., University of York, 1979.
Saarinen, Aino. 'Feminist Research: In Search of a New Paradigm?' *Acta Sociologica* 31 (1988): 35–51.
Said, Edward. *On Late Style.* London: Bloomsbury, 2006.
Sartori, Claudio. *I libretti italiani a stampa dalle origini al 1800. Catalogo analitico con 16 indici.* Cuneo: Bertola & Locatelli, 1990–94.

Savage, Roger. 'Staging an Opera: Letters from the Cesarian Poet'. *Early Music* 26 (1998): 583–95.
Schilt, Kristen, and Danielle Giffort. '"Strong Riot Women" and the Continuity of Feminist Subcultural Participation'. In *Ageing and Youth Cultures: Music, Style and Identity*, edited by Andy Bennett and Paul Hodkinson, 146–58. London and New York: Berg, 2012.
Scott, J. L. 'The Evolution of the Brass Band and its Repertoire in Northern England'. PhD diss., University of Sheffield, 1970.
Seddon, Laura. *British Women Composers and Instrumental Chamber Music in the Early Twentieth Century*. Farnham: Ashgate, 2013.
Seehofer, Thomas. '"Wie ein gutgemachts kleid [sic]". Überlegungen zu einer mehrdeutigen Metapher (nebst einigen Randbemerkungen zu Mozart)'. In *'Per ben vestir la virtuosa'. Die Oper des 18. und frühen 19. Jahrhunderts im Spannungsfeld zwischen Komponisten und Sängern*, edited by D. Brandenburg and T. Seedorf, 11–21. Schliengen: Edition Argus, 2011.
Selfridge-Field, Eleanor. *A New Chronology of Venetian Opera and Related Genres, 1660–1760*. Stanford, CA: Stanford University Press, 2007.
Sexton, Anne. *Live or Die*. London: Oxford University Press, 1967.
Seymour, Clare. *The Operas of Benjamin Britten: Expression and Evasion*. Woodbridge: Boydell, 2007.
Shakespeare, William. *As You Like It*. In *William Shakespeare The Complete Works*, edited by W. J. Craig. London: Magpie Books, 1993.
Shepard, Alexandra. *Meanings of Manhood in Early Modern England*. Oxford: Oxford University Press, 2003.
Shephard, Tim. 'Constructing Isabella d'Este's Musical Decorum in the Visual Sphere'. *Renaissance Studies* 25 (2011): 684–706.
Simone, Nina, and Stephen Cleary. *I Put a Spell On You: The Autobiography of Nina Simone*. New York: Da Capo Press, 2003.
Smith, Catherine Parsons. '"A Distinguishing Virility": Feminism and Modernism in American Art Music'. In *Cecilia Reclaimed: Feminist Perspectives on Gender and Music*, edited by Susan C. Cook and Judy S. Tsou, 90–106. Urbana: University of Illinois Press, 1994.
Smith, Catherine Parsons, and Cynthia S. Richardson. *Mary Carr Moore, American Composer*. Ann Arbor: University of Michigan Press, 1987.
Smith, Bruce. *The History of Little Orphan Annie*. New York: Ballantine Books, 1982.
Smith, Bruce R. *Shakespeare and Masculinity*. Oxford: Oxford University Press, 2000.
Smith, Patti. *Just Kids*. London: Bloomsbury, 2010.
Sneider, Beth E. 'Political Generations and the Contemporary Women's Movement'. *Sociological Inquiry* 58 (1998): 4–21.
Sontag, Susan. 'Notes on Camp'. In *Against Interpretation and Other Essays*, 275–92. 1964. Reprint, New York: Picador, 2009.

Southern, Eileen. 'A Prima Ballerina of the Fifteenth Century'. In *Music and Context: Essays for John M. Ward*, edited by Anne Dhu Shapiro, 183–97. Cambridge, MA: Harvard University, 1985.

Spáčilova, Jana. 'Libretto as a Source of Baroque Scenography in the Czech Lands'. In *Theatralia/Yorick 2011/1*, edited by Christian M. Billing and Pavel Drábek, 87–92. Brno: Masaryk University, 2011.

Steadman Jones, Gareth. *Outcast London*. Oxford: Oxford University Press, 1971.

Steedman, Carolyn. *Strange Dislocations: Childhood and the Idea of Human Interiority, 1780–1930*. Cambridge, MA: Harvard University Press, 1995.

Steele, Richard. *A Discourse Concerning Old-Age*. London, 1688.

Stewart, Susan. *On Longing: Narratives of the Miniature, the Gigantic, the Souvenir, the Collection*. Durham, NC and London: Duke University Press, 1993.

Stone, George Winchester Jr., and George M. Kahl. *David Garrick: A Critical Biography*. London: Feffer & Simons, 1979.

Stringer, Julian. 'Repressed (But Remarkably Dressed)'. *Popular Music* 11 (1992): 15–26.

Strohm, Reinhard. 'Zenobia: Voices and Authorship in Opera Seria'. In *Johann Adolf Hasse in seiner Zeit*, edited by Szymon Paczkowski and Alina Żórawska-Witkowska, 53–68. Warsaw: Instytut Muzykologii Uniwersytetu Warszawskiego, 2002.

Strunk, Oliver, and Leo Treitler, eds. *Source Readings in Music History*. New York: Norton, 1998.

Stubbes, Philip. *The Anatomie of Abuses*. London, 1583.

Sweers, Britta. *Electric Folk: The Changing Face of English Traditional Music*. Oxford: Oxford University Press, 2005.

Syson, Luke, and Dora Thornton. *Objects of Virtue: Art in Renaissance Italy*. London: British Museum Press, 2001.

Talbott, Susan Lubowsky, and Erin Monroe. *Patti Smith: Camera Solo*. New Haven: Yale University Press, 2012.

Taylor, Arthur. *Notes and Tones: Musician-to-Musician Interviews*. New York: Da Capo Press, 1993.

Taylor, Arthur R. *Brass Bands*. London: Hart-Davis MacGibbon, 1979.

Taylor, Deems. 'Music'. In *Civilization in the United States*, edited by Harold Stearns, 199–214. New York: Harcourt, Brace, 1922.

Tick, Judith. 'Charles Ives and Gender Ideology'. In *Musicology and Difference: Gender and Sexuality in Music Scholarship*, edited by Ruth A. Solie, 83–106. Berkeley: University of California Press, 1993.

Tinctoris, Johannes. *Concerning the Nature and Propriety of Tones*. Translated by Albert Seay, 2nd edn. Colorado Springs: Colorado College Music Press, 1976.

———. *Dictionary of Musical Terms*. Translated and edited by Carl Parrish. London: Free Press of Glencoe, 1963.

———. *Opera Theoretica*. Edited by Albert Seay. 2 vols. Rome: American Institute of Musicology, 1975.

Tosh, John. *A Man's Place: Masculinity and the Middle-Class Home in Victorian England*. New Haven: Yale University Press, 2007.
Unterberger, Richie. *Turn! Turn! Turn! The 60s Folk-Rock Revolution*. Milwaukee: Backbeat Books, 2002.
Vaughan, William. *Approved Directions for Health*. London, 1612.
Visconti, Gasparo. *I Canzonieri per Beatrice d'Este e per Bianca Maria Sforza*. Edited by Paolo Bongrani. Milan: Il saggiatore, 1979.
Walkerdine, Valerie. *Daddy's Girl: Young Girls and Popular Culture*. Cambridge, MA: Harvard University Press, 1997.
Wallach Scott, Joan. *The Fantasy of Feminist History*. Durham, NC and London: Duke University Press, 2011.
Ward, Philip. *Sandy Denny: Reflections on Her Music*. Kibworth Beauchamp: Matador, 2011.
Warnes, Andrew. 'Black, White and Blue: Racial Antagonism in The Smiths' Record Sleeves'. *Popular Music* 27 (2008): 135–49.
Warwick, Jacqueline. *Girl Groups, Girl Culture: Popular Music and Identity in the 1960s*. New York: Routledge, 2007.
——. *Musical Prodigies and the Performance of Childhood*. New York: Routledge, forthcoming.
Waters, Chris. *British Socialists and the Politics of Popular Culture, 1884–1914*. Stanford, CA: Stanford University Press, 1990.
Watson, Paul, and Diane Railton. 'Rebel without a Pause: The Continuing Controversy in Madonna's Contemporary Music Videos'. In *'Rock On': Women, Ageing and Popular Music*, edited by Ros Jennings and Abigail Gardner, 139–54. Farnham: Ashgate, 2012.
Wearing, Sadie. 'Subjects of Rejuvenation: Aging in Postfeminist Culture'. In *Interrogating Postfeminism: Gender and Politics of Popular Culture*, edited by Yvonne Tasker and Diane Negra, 277–310. Durham, NC and London: Duke University Press, 2007.
Welch, Evelyn. 'The Art of Expenditure: The Court of Paola Malatesta Gonzaga in Fifteenth-Century Mantua'. *Renaissance Studies* 16 (2002): 306–17.
White, Maude Valérie. *Friends and Memories*. London: Edward Arnold, 1914.
——. *My Indian Summer*. London: Grayson & Grayson, 1932.
Whiteley, Sheila. 'A Boy in the Bush: Childhood, Sexuality and The Smiths'. In *Why Pamper Life's Complexities? Essays on The Smiths*, edited by Sean Campbell and Colin Coulter, 104–20. Manchester: Manchester University Press, 2010.
Whitesell, Lloyd. *The Music of Joni Mitchell*. New York: Oxford University Press, 2008.
Whittier, Nancy. *Feminist Generations: The Persistence of the Radical Women's Movement*. Philadelphia: Temple University Press, 1995.
Whythorne, Thomas. *The Autobiography of Thomas Whythorne*, Modern-Spelling Edition. Edited by James M. Osborn. London: Oxford University Press, 1962.
Winters, Pam. Liner notes to Sandy Denny, *Gold Dust*, CD, Island 524493-2, 1998.

Wistreich, Richard. 'Music Books and Sociability'. *Il saggiatore musicale* 18 (2011): 230–44.
Woloch, Nancy. *Women and the American Experience*. New York: McGraw-Hill, 1984.
Woodward, Kathleen. *Aging and Its Discontents: Freud and Other Fictions*. Bloomington and Indianapolis: Indiana University Press, 1991.
—. 'Inventing Generational Models: Psychoanalysis, Feminism, Literature'. In *Figuring Age: Women, Bodies, Generations*, edited by Kathleen Woodward, 149–70. Bloomington: Indiana University Press, 1999.
—. 'Performing Age, Performing Gender'. *NWSA Journal* 18 (2006): 162–89.
Woolf, Virginia. *The Diary of Virginia Woolf, vol. 3, 1925–1930*. Edited by Anne Olivier Bell, assisted by Andrew McNeillie. London: Hogarth, 1980.
Wright, Thomas, The Journeyman Engineer. 'Willie Tyson's Turkey'. *Leisure Hour* 991 (1870): 824–9.
Young, Rob. *Electric Eden: Unearthing Britain's Visionary Music*. London: Faber and Faber, 2010.
Yuval-Davis, Nira. *Gender and Nation*. London: Sage, 1997.
Zambrini, Francesco. *La Defensione delle Donne d'Autore Anonimo*. Bologna: Commissione per i testi di lingua, 1876.
Zerbinati, Giovanni Maria. *Croniche di Ferrara: quali comenzano del anno 1500 sino al 1527*. Edited by Maria Giuseppina Muzzarelli. Ferrara: Deputazione Provinciale Ferrarese di Storia Patria, 1989.
Zita, Jacqueline N. 'Heresy in the Female Body'. In *The Other Within Us: Feminist Explorations of Women and Aging*, edited by Marilyn Pearsall. Boulder, CO: Westview Press, 1997.
Zornado, Joseph. *Inventing the Child: Culture, Ideology and the Story of the Child*. London: Routledge, 2004.

Index

Addison, Joseph 61, 63
Adorno, Theodor 171–2, 175, 177–8
age 41–59, 129–39
    'ages of man' 43–59
    childhood 43, 44, 45–8, 59, 129, 130, 131, 134, 138, 158
    manhood 41, 43, 44, 46, 48, 51, 53–6, 57, 58, 59
    maturity 3, 4, 43, 53, 70, 100, 142, 169
    menopause 8–10, 18
    middle age 14–15, 17, 20–21, 44, 48, 53, 68, 77, 161
    old age 11, 43, 44, 51, 56–8, 59, 83, 112, 117, 151, 152
    youth 4, 43, 44, 45, 48–53, 54, 56, 57–8
Améry, Jean 150–51, 152
Annie 129–39
    film 129, 130, 133, 136
    musical 129, 133, 134, 135–8
    radio series 132–3
    songs
        'Hard Knock Life' 129, 135, 137
        'Hard Knock Life (Ghetto Anthem)' 137–8
        Little Orphan Annie 4, 132–3, 134–5, 139
        'Maybe' 129, 135, 136, 138
        'Tomorrow' 129, 134, 135
        'You're Never Fully Dressed without a Smile' 135
d'Aragona, Beatrice 29, 36
d'Aragona, Eleanora 34, 35
Aristotle 35, 37, 41, 43
Armatrading, Joan 2, 13, 16, 19
A Taste of Honey 162, 166

Barthes, Roland 189
Bauer, Marion 115, 116, 118, 120, 124
Bayton, Mavis 198
Bembo, Pietro 33, 39–40
Beyer, Johanna 116, 121–3
Bobbio, Norberto 150, 151, 152
Borgia, Lucrezia 27, 30, 34, 38, 39
Boulanger, Nadia 102, 175, 176
Bourdieu, Pierre 194, 200
Boyd, Malcolm 10, 11
Braham, Humphrey 47, 53
brass bands 3, 83–100
    band room 3, 89–90, 92, 99
    Black Dyke Mills Band 87, 98, 99, 100
    Brass Band News 87, 94
    British Bandsman 95, 96, 100
    contests 85, 87, 92, 95–8
    homosocial environment 90, 96, 99
    and Methodism 86
    National Brass Band Festival 83
    role of women 93–6, 97, 99
    Slaithwaite brass bands 85
    social interaction 89–90
    social network 85–7, 88, 95, 96, 99
    training 87–8
Brill Building 167–9
Britten, Benjamin 1, 11, 22
Burton, Robert 49–50, 52, 56
Butler, Judith 176
Byrd, William 48, 51, 54

Calasanti, Toni 116–17
Calmeta, Vincenzo 27–8, 29, 30, 32
camp 156, 163, 165, 166, 169–70
Castiglione, Baldassare 28, 29, 30–31, 35, 42, 47, 57
castrati 3, 61–2, 65–72, 77
Cavarero, Adriana 149
Certeau, Michel de 197
Charnin, Martin 133, 134, 136
Citron, Marcia J. 108, 174
Collins, Judy 1, 11, 141–2, 145, 147–9, 152–3
Conti, Antonio 61, 62, 63
Cooper, Yvette 8

Copland, Aaron 115, 175, 176
Crawford, Ruth 115, 116, 118, 121, 122–3
creativity 175, 185–93, 196–9
Cuffe, Henry 43–5, 48–9, 53, 56
Cvetkovich, Ann 155, 157, 162, 163, 169

Dahlhaus, Carl 171, 172, 178
Delaney, Shelagh 162, 166
Denny, Sandy 4, 142–53
Dowland, John 57–8
dramma per musica 62, 65–7, 69, 75–8
    aria and recitative 67, 72–3
    costumes 65, 75–6
    operatic roles 65–70, 72, 75–80

Early Modern England 41–59
    Ages of Man, the 43–59
    masculinity 41–2, 45, 46, 49, 51, 52, 53, 56, 59
    music and education 46–8, 59
    singing 47–8, 51–2, 54, 57, 58
Eaton, Gertrude 102, 107
effeminacy 28–30, 42, 48–52, 53, 59, 195
Eggar, Katherine 102, 106, 107, 108, 109, 112
Elyot, Thomas 44, 46, 53
d'Este, Isabella 3, 27, 30, 31, 39

Farinelli, Carlo Broschi ('Farinelli') 62–3, 75
female composers 4, 11–13, 109, 110, 113, 115–16, 117, 118–21, 123–5, 175–6, 183
femininity 2, 8, 18–19, 39, 42, 45, 119–21, 192, 193, 195, 198, 199
feminism and feminists 5, 7, 8, 9, 88, 101, 103–8, 109, 111–13, 116–18, 173–6, 181–2, 195, 199
Finnegan, Ruth 85
Foucault, Michel 174, 189, 198
Fox, Christopher 179
Freud, Sigmund 149–50

Galen 41, 43
Garrick, David 63, 64, 77
gender stereotypes 10, 22, 120, 130
glitching 196, 201
Greer, Germaine 8, 9, 10, 101, 113

Grimaldi, Nicolò ('Nicolini')
Grosz, Elizabeth 182

Hegarty, Paul 192, 198
Higford, William 47, 52
humoral theory 41, 43–4, 49, 50, 53

Jay-Z 137–8, 139
Joplin, Janis 152

Kallberg, Jeffrey 1
Keal, Minna 2, 12–13

Lazar, Michelle M.
LeFanu, Nicola 1, 6
lesbianism 107, 120, 123, 155, 160–61
Love, Heather 156–7
Lowenthal, David 160, 163
Lutyens, Elisabeth 10, 11, 12

McArdle, Andrea 135–7
McClary, Susan 173
McClelland, Keith 84, 90–91, 97
McKenzie, Graham 177–8
Maconchy, Elizabeth 2, 10, 11–12, 102, 108, 109
Madonna 2, 7, 8, 15, 17–19, 22
    Material Girl 8, 17
    MDNA 7, 17
Mannheim, Karl 104
man-tone 121
Marr, Johnny 158–9, 160, 167, 168
marriage 30, 38, 39, 41, 52, 53, 59, 84, 97
Marvelettes, The 167
masculinity 8–84, 88, 90–91, 97–8, 117–18, 120, 182, 193
materiality 5, 172, 175–8, 180, 181, 182–3
Meehan, Tom 133, 134
Mello, Cecilia 160–61, 163, 165
Minogue, Kylie 19
Mitchell, Joni 2, 13, 19–20, 21, 23, 141
    'Both Sides Now' 141, 145
modernism 117–18, 121, 125, 174–5
Morley, Thomas 46, 50, 54
Morrissey 5, 155, 156, 158, 160–62, 163, 164–5, 166–7, 169
motherhood 22, 38, 162, 193, 194–5
Mulcaster, Richard 46–8

music in education 28, 33, 35–6, 45–8, 59, 113

New Music 5, 171–83
New York City Composers' Forum 116–25

O'Brien, Lucy 17, 19
outsiders 5, 167–9

Parsons Smith, Catherine 117, 121, 175
patriarchy 5, 41, 45, 46, 53, 55–9, 174–83
Perkins, Frances 117
Pettis, Ashley 115, 117, 118–19, 122, 124
Plato 35–6, 45, 52
Poston, Elizabeth 102, 108, 112

queer culture 155–69
Quintilian 28, 30, 356

Rainier, Priaulx 11, 12
Ralegh, Walter 43
Renaissance Italy 27–40
   music and education 35–7
   noblewomen
      as audience 27–30
      and chastity 29–31
      and marriage 30, 38
      as performers 31–4
Reynolds, Simon 143, 144, 159, 160, 163, 167
Rodgers, Tara 193, 199
Roper, Michael 88
Rosman, Carl 177, 178–9
Royal Academy of Music 12, 13
Royal College of Music 101, 102, 143

Saunders, Rebecca 5, 171, 176–80, 183
   Caerulean 5, 176–7, 180
Scott, Marion 102, 104, 106, 107, 109
Schuman, William 117
Senesino, Francesco Bernardi 62, 63, 64
Simone, Nina 142, 145, 146–8, 149, 150, 153
sisterhood 101, 103, 111
Slevin, Kathleen 117
Society of Women Musicians, The 101–14
Smith, Patti 2, 13, 21–2, 23, 156, 158

Smiths, The 4, 5, 155–70
   'Hand in Glove' 162
   'I Want a Boy for My Birthday' 168
   'Stretch Out and Wait' 163–5
   'The Queen is Dead' 160–62
   'This Night has Opened My Eyes' 162
Smyth, Ethel 13, 14, 15, 22, 109
Steedman, Carolyn 129, 131
Strouse, Charles 134–5
suffragettes 15, 102, 106, 107, 111, 199

'Take Me Back to Dear Old Blighty' 160–62
Tate, Phyllis 11, 109
Temple, Shirley 131, 134, 135
Thatcher, Margaret 159, 160, 163, 169, 170
Tinctoris, Johannes 29, 36–7
Tosh, John 88, 90
transcendence 70, 151, 174, 186

Uncle Tom's Cabin 130

Vaughan Williams, Ursula 12, 110, 111
Victorian society 3, 86, 91, 92, 121, 131
   ideology 121, 131
   leisure and recreation 86, 91, 92
Vigard, Kristen 135–6
viol 36, 47, 52, 54
violence 173, 178, 186, 194–5, 201
Visconti, Gasparo 32, 33

Walshe, Jennifer 5, 176–7, 179–80, 181, 183
   XXX Live Nude Girls!!! 5, 176, 179–80
Warnes, Andrew 166–7, 170
White, Maude Valérie 2, 13, 14–15
Whittier, Nancy 107, 108
'Who Knows Where the Time Goes' 4, 141, 142, 144–7, 148, 149, 151–2
Whythorne, Thomas 47, 52
Williams, Grace 2–3, 10–11, 12, 13, 15, 23
Willie Tyson's Turkey 91–2
Wood-Hill, Mabel 119, 124
working class culture 83–100, 132, 162
Wright, Thomas 84, 87, 91–2

Yuval-Davis, Nira 193

Zita, Jacqueline 8, 9, 22